The**Good**Book
FOR KIDS

D1004437

LISA T. BERGREN

The **Good** Book
FOR KIDS

How the Bible's Big Ideas
Relate to YOU

David C Cook®
transforming lives together

THE GOOD BOOK FOR KIDS
Published by David C Cook
4050 Lee Vance Drive
Colorado Springs, CO 80918 U.S.A.

David C Cook U.K., Kingsway Communications
Eastbourne, East Sussex BN23 6NT, England

The graphic circle C logo is a registered trademark of David C Cook.

The website addresses recommended throughout this book are offered as a
resource to you. These websites are not intended in any way to be or imply an
endorsement on the part of David C Cook, nor do we vouch for their content.

Details in some stories have been changed to protect
the identities of the persons involved.

Unless otherwise noted, all Scripture quotations are taken from the Christian
Standard Bible®, Copyright © 2017 by Holman Bible Publishers. Used by
permission. Christian Standard Bible® and CSB® are federally registered
trademarks of Holman Bible Publishers. The Ten Commandments listed in
chapter 8 are taken from the King James Version of the Bible. (Public Domain.)
The author has added italics to Scripture quotations for emphasis.

LCCN 2016958398
ISBN 978-1-4347-1024-6
eISBN 978-1-4347-1104-5

© 2017 Lisa T. Bergren
Published in association with the literary agency of Ann Spangler &
Company, 1415 Laurel Avenue Southeast, Grand Rapids, Michigan 49506.

The Team: Catherine DeVries, Beth Leuders, Nick Lee, Jennifer
Lonas, Andrew Sloan, Helen Macdonald, Susan Murdock
Interior Illustrations: Luke Flowers Creative
Cover Design: Amy Konyndyk
Cover Photo: Kirk DouPonce, DogEared Design

Printed in the United States of America
First Edition 2017

1 2 3 4 5 6 7 8 9 10

011217

*For my Jack, with prayers that you might
someday know how much God loves you and
what it means to fully love him in return.*
—Mama

Contents

Note to the Reader

Hi! There are several ways you can slice and dice this book …

1. Read the Bible chapter referenced at the beginning
    of each chapter (we made it easy by putting the
    associated CSB text in the back of this book!), and
    then read what I wrote. All on your own, think
    about the questions at the end.
2. Read the Bible chapter with your parent(s), and
    then, on your own, read what I wrote. Discuss the
    questions at the end with your parent(s).
3. Read it all / discuss it all with your parent(s) or a
    friend.

If you have questions or feel an urge to talk through some of
what you read, be sure to seek out a parent or youth leader. This is big
stuff—stuff that God wants you to understand as much as you can.
So it's important.

Most of what you're about to read is my own, but I was inspired
by Pastor Deron Spoo's book, *The Good Book*, which your parent(s)
might be reading too. Some facts are direct quotes from his book, and
some thoughts are originally his; I just presented them in a different
way so that you might better understand. He gave me permission to
do that.

My prayer for you is that when you finish reading this book, you'll know how much God loves you and wants the very best for you. He totally does. You'll see …

Love,

Lisa

Acknowledgments

I'm grateful to Ann Spangler, Linda Kenney, and Deron Spoo for bringing me into this project; it pushed me beyond my comfort zone, and God grew me through the process. I'm extremely grateful for the expertise of Catherine DeVries, Andrew Sloan, and Jennifer Lonas in editing this book. Thank you for your insights, questions, and pushes—I count them all as coming from the Spirit, helping make this the best book possible! I'm also so grateful for the entire David C Cook team, from other editors involved to the designers to marketing to sales. Thank you for all you have done, and will do, on my behalf.

IN THE BEGINNING

1

God Rocks ... the World
Genesis 1

If you've ever opened the Bible and started reading at the beginning, you've likely read this chapter! Many don't read farther than Genesis, but you and I are going to make it all the way to Revelation (the very last book of the Bible) by the time you're finished with *The Good Book for Kids*. And while reading about creation is amazing—*Hello, very first platypus! Hello, very first pelican!*—the biggest idea in Genesis is this: *Hello, very first people, Adam and Eve! That's pretty cool that you were made in God's own image.*

Whoa. *What?*

Yeah. Adam and Eve were made in God's image.

Just like you and me. We all were.

Whether you grow up to be a model in a magazine—or not—you were made in God's image. The Bible tells us, "God created man in his own image; he created him in the image of God; he created them male and female" (Genesis 1:27).

> Don't get hung up on LOOKS. We resemble God in SPIRIT, and that's what makes us all beautiful! Out of all of creation, we're the only creatures who have a spirit, or soul, that connects us forever with God.

We also resemble God in how we connect to others. Even if you're an introvert (someone who is pretty happy being alone), you probably want to be close to your family and have at least a few good friends.

Our hearts encourage us to be nice to the shy new kid at school or the lab partner who cracks us up or the guy on our team who seems a little sad, because we were designed to connect with one another rather than to be lonely. That built-in need is 100 percent from God. In you! In me!

So God knew us even when we were still in our mothers' bellies. He wanted us in this big, beautiful world he created so we could build relationships with him and others. Because he loves us and knows what's good for us.

Imagine This ...
A Front-Row Seat to Creation

I didn't run and hide when I saw that gigantor of a dude filling the front doorway of my house. Not even when I noticed his weird glow and saw wings curving over his huge NFL-sized shoulders. It would've freaked me out more if he hadn't looked at me with kind eyes that made me instantly feel known, understood, connected. "I am Gabriel," he said, "an angel of the Most High."

I won't lie—this Gabe guy was kind of scary. I'd always thought of angels as soft and sweet, protective. Gabe was fierce, all business. "The Lord God has chosen you, Jack," he announced, eyes sparkling with anticipation. "You're about to witness the beginning ... of everything."

I tried to swallow, but all the spit had dried up in my mouth. It was as though I'd forgotten to drink water all day. Or all week. *You have been chosen.* His words seemed to echo in my head and in my chest too. "I ... I know," I managed to say. Somehow I did know already. As if I'd been in on this plan all along.

Gabe straightened and looked at me. I let out a breath that I didn't realize I was holding in. I was freaking out on the inside, my stomach almost in knots. Yet I was also squirming with excitement.

"What do you think you've been called to, Jack?" Gabe asked as if he sensed my fear.

"I don't know. But it feels like the first time I ever got on a plane to go someplace cool," I said with a shrug.

Gabe smiled with a mysterious twinkle in his eyes. A carved wooden staff with a curved top suddenly appeared in his hand. His huge wings lifted and partially flared, big enough for a massive wrestler and yet delicate and shimmery like my little sister's fairy costume. That was Gabe in a nutshell. He was almost too much one second and almost nothing the next. He could either dominate or disappear in the time it took to take half a breath.

"Oh, we're going somewhere cool, all right," he said, his gaze steady. "You're about to witness the beginning … of everything."

With that, he tapped his staff on my porch, and we were zapped into … *Nothing.*

Totally black nothing. I had to tell myself to breathe and not panic.

It was weird. My brain was telling me I should panic. If there was ever a good time to panic, this was it. I felt as if I were floating, suspended like an astronaut in a space shuttle and yet surrounded by a warm presence that made me feel totally safe. Peaceful.

"Uh … Gabe?" I said, concentrating hard to form the words.

"Wait," he said gently. "Watch."

I knew from his tone that something big was about to—

"Let there be light."

I wasn't sure if I'd actually heard the words. But somehow I recognized the voice, as if I'd always known it.

His voice. God's voice. Here. *With us.*

As though he'd always been nearby.

Distant arcs of light began to rise and fall and swirl together, racing toward us, above us, building, building, building in intensity. I squeezed my eyes shut against the flashes, scared the brightness might blind me. Then I felt warmth wash over me.

I sensed God's pleasure surround me. In a way it was like Grandpa beginning to laugh before uttering a sound. Total joy seemed to pour through me, around me.

"SKY," God called out, "and land." This time I was sure I'd heard the words.

I dared to peek, and I noticed then that I wasn't alone. Surrounding me were kids from all around the world, each with an angel beside them. We slowly floated downward from our suspended state to the sand beneath our bare toes. I didn't know when I'd lost my shoes, but I was glad I had. The toasty sand felt silky soft, and the sky beamed bluer than the best summer day.

I grinned and looked at the other kids. They were all grinning too. Some were spinning, arms outstretched as they stared upward. Others were hugging themselves. Some had tears streaming down their faces.

Night came and then morning right after, all within a breath.

God commanded the land to produce. Trees and bushes sprouted all around us and instantly climbed and spread like some sort of whacked-out Jurassic Park taking shape in time-lapse video. The plants shimmered with a deep green, and the flowers and fruit were like gems among the leaves.

Oh, the *smell* of it. I inhaled as deeply as I could. It was like black, perfect soil turned up in a garden and water from a mountain spring and tropical flowers and yeasty bread right out of the oven and piles of fragrant spices in the breeze. (I know. It sounds weird. But I swear, I didn't even want to exhale. I'd give you my brand-new gaming system if I could go back and smell it all again.)

Another breath ... another night ... another morning.

I stared in disbelief, mouth hanging open, to watch Insta-earth-Garden grow and the sun and moon pop into sight and then fade.

"Let the water swarm with living creatures," God's voice rumbled.

I froze in amazement as fish and sharks and dolphins and stingrays and whales whirled in a cauldron of bubbling blue-green water. Hundreds—no, *thousands*—of them all hurtled into the air and back into the sea.

"It's like they're celebrating!" I shouted.

"Indeed!" said Gabe.

Birds soared into view next. Geese and swallows and swans and hummingbirds and blue jays and a thousand other species I'd never seen before.

Another night. Another morning.

Zoo-rama burst forth next. Every imaginable sort of creature zipped by us into the forest, where they lazed around or meandered away. I blinked, wondering if my imagination was tricking me, but the animals were real. One more inhale proved these less-than-sweet-smelling critters were alive, if you know what I mean. *Whew!* They were all *smelly*! But it was still good, *so* good.

Then the action slowed. I got the sense that God was looking at and speaking to his heavenly court of angels as he made this amazing announcement: "Let us make man in our own image, according to our likeness."

God went on, "They will rule the fish of the sea, the birds of the sky, the livestock, the whole earth."

At that moment a man rose before us. And then a woman. I sensed God's immense pleasure and pride in creating these humans, and started laughing and crying all at once. I wasn't even embarrassed about my emotions because I was too wrapped up in that incredible moment. It was all so new! Everything fresh! Perfect!

In total awe I fell to my knees next to Gabe and watched as the first man and woman on earth hugged and then walked into the forest, hand in hand. I was so wrapped up in the joy and wonder of seeing God's new creations that it took me a while to realize that Adam and Eve were totally naked.

I know. Weird, right?

Just trust me. If you'd been there, you would've responded exactly the same. Witnessing the beginning of this world and the first humans was sheer … glory.

The Skinny on Genesis 1

- Our creative God has done things we could only dream about. He created a hummingbird with a heart that weighs less than an ounce and beats eight hundred times a minute. He also created a whale with a heart that can weigh a thousand pounds.

  > A thousand pounds! That's about what a grand piano weighs!

- God's creation is vast. The Amazon jungle teems with more than a thousand species of birds, forty thousand plant species, and thousands upon thousands of insect species!

  > Forty thousand plant species? How many different plants can you count in your backyard?

- What was God's response to all he created? "[He] saw that it was good" (Genesis 1:10, 12, 18, 21, 25).

- But God seemed most pumped about making the man and woman on day 6: "God saw all that he had made, and it was very good indeed" (v. 31).

  > It's kind of like God was giving himself a high five, huh?

- We're not expected to handle life on our own; we're God's responsibility. It's a little like being our parents' responsibility. God willingly took on that responsibility when he knit you together in your mother's womb (Psalm 139:13), because he wants to "do life" with you.

WHAT STRUCK YOU IN THIS CHAPTER?

What do you think would have been the coolest thing to watch being "born" into creation? Light? Land and sea? Animals? The sun and stars? Humans? Why?

How do you think it affects your life to be made in God's image? Think of what it would be like if you wore a uniform that identified you as God's child. Would it change the choices you make or how you act? How so?

YOUR FUTURE STORY

God is right *here*. With us. Ready to live life with us all day long (and through the night too). Think about how you build relationships with friends. How do you get closer to them over time?

Now consider how you could build a closer relationship with God. Do you need to learn more about him? How can you "do life" more with him all through the day rather than turning to him only when you're stressed out or when your parents encourage you to pray?

God saw all that he had made, and it was very good indeed.
—Genesis 1:31

2

When Everything Broke— Including You
Genesis 3

Even if you weren't a little kid who went to Sunday school or kids' club at church, you've probably heard of Adam and Eve. Most of us have wondered about being in that garden ourselves, when life wasn't marked by pain and sickness and hunger, before death became part of our world. Sometimes we'd like to blame Adam and Eve for destroying that crazy-cool perfection with their very first sins, but the fact is, we'd likely have done the same thing. While God made us with the possibility of perfection—like him—he also gave us the power of choice. Instead of *making* us choose him over everything and anything else, he wanted us to choose him *freely*.

> God didn't want his kids to be like robots! Robots don't make very good companions.

Notice how God kept his instructions simple for Adam and Eve. He basically said, "Live. Take care of things. Have babies. But you know that one tree in the middle of the garden? That one in a thousand? Don't eat from it." Jesus gives us simple commands too: love God with everything in us and love our neighbors as we love ourselves.

> These two commands are like the "prime directives" of the faith!

In giving us freedom of choice, God allowed evil to exist as the counterpart to his great goodness. So even in that perfect first garden, the serpent wriggled his way in. And he knew exactly how to get to Eve. First, he planted a question in her head: "Did God really say …?" (Genesis 3:1). Second, he denied the truth: "You will not die" (v. 4). Third, he planted the idea that maybe Eve shouldn't entirely trust God's motives (v. 5)—that maybe God's command was all about control or power rather than love.

Think of it this way. You spot a plate of fresh-baked cookies on the kitchen counter. Your mom says you can have only one cookie, but later on, you're tempted to grab a second. You might ask yourself, *Did she really say I could have only one? Why'd she say that? It won't hurt me to eat just one more cookie.*

Sound familiar?

We're all drawn toward sin because we want it all. *We* want to be first in everything rather than giving *God* first place. We will all sin and fall short of what God intended for us until the day we die, just like Adam and Eve did (Romans 3:23). But thankfully Jesus died to save us from those sins and helped restore us to a right relationship with God.

Now just because Jesus covered our sins—and therefore, God always forgives us—doesn't mean that we shouldn't *try* to make choices every day that please God! To honor him, we must try. Today. Tomorrow. And the next day …

Imagine This …
Adam and Eve Taking That First Terrible Bite

It's me again. Jack. The dude who got to see creation unfold firsthand.

If you're thinking the garden of Eden was awesome, you're wrong; it was the most fantastic place EVER. And while the other kids were into exploring the jungle of a garden or swimming with the brand-new seals, Gabe let me hang with Adam and Eve for a while, watching as they explored their beautiful new world.

They were just ahead of me, talking with some guy. At one point I could hear them chuckling. Adam eventually veered off among the ferns with the guy, and I could see only Eve now. She slowed down, looking distracted.

The closer I got, the more I felt a strange chill. Goosebumps covered my arms, but as I rubbed them, it felt more like a deep chill than just cooler air.

I followed Eve into a clearing and realized that we'd reached the middle of the garden. All around us monkeys chattered and birds sang. But Eve wasn't looking at any of them. She walked toward an impossibly long snake winding down a branch toward her and then slithering along the ground.

Now I'm no Bible expert, but I had a pretty good idea about how this was going to go down. For the first time I knew—really knew—what was at stake. This perfect place God made for the first humans was about to be totally ruined.

I rushed toward the woman. "Don't do it, Eve! Look away from him!" I pleaded. "Don't listen to him!"

But Eve couldn't hear me.

The serpent was slithering up a new tree now, and Eve looked confused, as if she wanted to walk away but couldn't quite make herself do it. The serpent looked back at her and then up into the tree branches, where juicy purple plums hung heavy on their stems.

I swallowed hard. The sight of that fruit made me feel as if I hadn't eaten all morning. I wanted one of those plums in the worst way. I could almost feel its sweet juice on my tongue. My stomach rumbled. I wondered why I couldn't just swipe a plum and bite into it right now. Why was that fruit off-limits? I wanted it *so* bad.

Just like Eve.

Eve shook her head, eyes wide as if she was frightened. What had the serpent said to her? He looked upward again, his triangular head swooping right below the best plum on the branch. The crafty snake hovered there a moment and then moved on, turning to squint at Eve again.

I felt more than heard his question: "Did God *really* say, 'You can't eat from any tree in the garden'?"

Eve lifted her chin and straightened her shoulders. "We may eat fruit from the trees in the garden. But God said we couldn't from this tree, the one in the middle." She looked around again, as if wondering if this was really the forbidden tree. But she knew. And so did I.

"No! You will not die," the serpent assured the woman, as if he thought she was an idiot. "In fact, God knows that when you eat it your eyes will be opened and you will be like God, knowing good and evil." The serpent's tone grew soothing, reasonable, wise. As if God should actually *want* Eve to enjoy the sweet fruit rather than *warn* her against it.

The creature raised his head again, and his odd nostrils flared right below another glistening ripe plum. My tongue could almost taste the sweet purple fruit already.

"No," I whispered, trying to summon some inner strength. I coughed. "No," I repeated, a bit stronger this time. "Eve, try and say no!"

I knew Eve still couldn't hear me. But I felt like I had to try.

This was it. When pure goodness came crashing down.

When perfection failed.

Because of Eve. Because of Adam.

Because of me too, had I been in their place.

Eve's hand hovered under that plum. She was thinking twice; for a second I hoped that somehow, some way the story would change. But then Eve clamped her lips into a determined line and plucked the fruit from the tree. When she took a bite, her eyes immediately widened with wonder. She eagerly devoured more, the juice trickling down her chin.

I had to clench my fists to avoid picking a plum myself.

"Eve?" Adam called out, parting huge palm fronds to enter the clearing. "What have you found?"

Eve handed him a plum. "Taste it, Adam," she encouraged, refusing to meet his gaze. "It's the best in all the garden."

"But isn't this the …" he began, looking up at the tree that spread above us, full of that glorious purple fruit.

"Just taste it, and you'll see," Eve confidently replied.

I could only stand there watching in mute horror.

Then Adam took a bite.

But as he chewed, at first quickly and then slowing, I felt as if I was going to throw up. Choosing to eat from *this* tree was so clearly wrong. It was like slapping God in the face.

My heart sank. I knew why Adam and Eve had done it. How many times had I done the same thing? Taken a cookie I knew was off-limits. Watched a TV show on my computer when I was supposed to be asleep. But at that moment I felt the tragedy of their decision like it was my own. What they did way back then—turning their backs on God—was what I did, what my friends did, whenever we chose our own way.

Adam and Eve had disappeared into the palm fronds and were madly plucking fig leaves, trying to cover themselves. They'd discovered that they were naked, and I was embarrassed too. For a while I'd forgotten about it. It hadn't mattered. But now it did.

Moments later I could hear someone whistling, coming closer, talking to the birds and animals as he approached.

Adam and Eve froze and then slowly crouched behind the palm fronds.

"Where are you?" God called.

It wasn't as if he didn't know precisely where Adam and Eve were among the thick leaves. I sensed God's heart breaking over the sudden separation between his people and himself. I wanted to cry.

Slowly Adam stood, and after him, Eve. They looked scared. And ashamed.

Then God entered the clearing. I wasn't brave enough to look at him. Not in the face. Not ... now. After ... *this* had happened.

"I heard you in the garden, and I was afraid because I was naked, so I hid," Adam said, timidly stepping out from between the palms, a fig leaf now hanging from his waist.

"Who told you that you were naked? Did you eat from the tree that I commanded you not to eat from?"

"The woman you gave to be with me," Adam began, glancing back at Eve, who was just stepping into view, "she gave me some fruit from the tree, and I ate."

Sheesh, I thought. *Man up, dude. You made that decision too. Own it!*

It struck me then that God was sad about Eve's separation from Adam too. Moments ago they'd felt so *together*, so warm and loving, and now there was a cold distance between them. I couldn't help but think about how I always wanted to shift blame for my own bad choices to my sisters, my friends, and even my parents. Doing that always made me feel alone in the end.

God gazed at Adam and Eve for a very long time.

I fought the urge to cry. All God had wanted was a great relationship with the people he lovingly created. He longed to be close to them. Yet he had also wanted them to freely choose to obey him.

It reminded me of that horrible day when I'd disappointed my own dad. He'd looked at me as if he wanted to cry. And now I got the feeling that God felt the same way.

Times infinity.

The Skinny on Genesis 3

- God hates sin—because it draws us away from him rather than toward him! Sin leads to shame and blame, fear and separation, none of which help build a good relationship.

  > Shame? Blame? Fear? Satan loves those things! It's how he tries to drive a wedge between us and God!

- We tend to think of sins as big or small. Killing someone is a big sin, and telling a fib is a small one. But no matter how big or small our sins may be, all sin harms our relationships

  > God is like the ultimate BFF, wanting to connect with every one of us any way he can. He loves us like crazy!

with God and others. Even the smallest sin is big in God's eyes, because it means we've broken his perfect law of love.

- Genesis 3 is kind of like seeing a row of dominoes topple over. God wanted nothing more than for humans to have a strong, loving, and obedient relationship with him. But the sins Adam and Eve committed set in motion a tendency for all of us to turn away from God's best for us. Eating from the tree God told them to avoid affected all of creation, forever. From then on, everything about life became harder from birth to death.

- In the beginning, there was no death! God's original intention was for us to live forever with him in the perfect world he created. If Adam and Eve hadn't

Don't get too bummed over this. God knew what was going to happen and had a plan to restore us. Hint: his name begins with a J. (More on this to come.)

broken God's rules, we'd never have known what it's like to get sick or become old and die! The fall—what happened when Adam and Eve sinned—interrupted God's hope of unending life together.

WHAT STRUCK YOU IN THIS CHAPTER?

Would you have been more likely to listen to the doubts ("Did God really say…?") that the serpent planted in Eve's mind? Or would you have been more like Adam, who was tempted when Eve offered him the fruit? Would you have eaten the fruit right away or thought about it for a few hours … or a few days? If you really, really wanted that fruit, like Jack did, how long do you think you could have held out?

YOUR FUTURE STORY

Are you more tempted to break the rules or do something wrong because it feels good, or because you think it *shouldn't* be off-limits? Have you ever had a moment when you stopped to think about doing something a parent told you not to but then did it anyway? How did that feel to you after?

Most of us find that even if a sin or a bad choice feels good for a moment, we experience shame and pain afterward—or others do. What might help you avoid sin from the start?

God never leaves us alone, and the Holy Spirit helps us avoid sin. How can we tell when God's encouraging us to do good rather than bad?

Did God really say …?

—Genesis 3:1

3

WWND? (What Would Noah Do?)

Genesis 6

Even if you haven't read the Bible much, you might be familiar with the story of Noah and the ark. Maybe you had a cute pastel-colored storybook when you were little, with adorable animals peering over the edge of a boat. Or maybe you had a picture of the ark on your wall or even a little ark night-light! Many of us feel all warm and fuzzy when we think about Noah and the ark.

But you know what's crazy? It's probably the worst subject ever for a cutesy storybook. Why? Because Noah lived in a time of total chaos and sadness, when people had wandered far—very far—from the heart of God and his intentions. With all the bad things people were doing, God wanted to protect and save only Noah and his family. Everyone else? Well, it made him really sad, but he'd decided they all had to go.

What happened in the story of Noah is like your computer. It works well for a while, and then something goes drastically wrong. It's so broken that the only answer is to wipe the hard drive clean and reinstall the software. People started off okay but then began to get more and more sinful. When things were so dark, God had to send the flood to wipe them all out and begin anew.

God had given people free choice, wanting nothing more than for his sons and daughters to choose to follow him and be in a relationship with him. But they didn't. In fact, the rebellious people of Noah's day were as far from God as they could get. Genesis 6 tells us that "the LORD regretted that he had made man on the earth, and he was deeply grieved" (v. 6).

Thankfully Noah was there in the midst of that mess. And Scripture tells us in verse 9 that he was "righteous," which means he was living in a right way. Noah was also "blameless among his contemporaries," meaning that his neighbors didn't have any complaints about him. And the best part—Noah "walked with God."

> There's a difference between just living with God and walking with him. It's like Noah and God were besties!

Noah stood out for sure, but don't think he was perfect or sinless. We won't be sinless either, but we can have a close relationship with God. He wants us to have a growing relationship with him. So when we're called to do something small (or BIG!) for God, we can follow Noah's example. Noah wasn't a superhero; he was just obedient to the Lord. If Noah built an ark longer than a football field because he trusted what God asked him to do and was committed to being obedient, we can do anything God asks of us too.

Imagine This ...
Fire Ants in a Flood

After school, Aiden followed Dr. Jacobs down the long line of aquariums. Some contained snakes—from the garden variety to a huge boa—and others held lizards like geckos or bearded dragons. Dr. J also had a wall of preserved spiders that Aiden liked to study from time to time and see if he remembered their names. Like the disgustingly awesome wasp spider,

Argiope bruennichi, with her huge yellow, black, and white body, or the ghostly crab spider, *Misumena vatia*, with her wide white legs. Aiden loved that crab spiders could change their body color over time. Someday, as a grown-up entomologist trapping spiders in the United Kingdom, Africa, and Asia, he hoped to see those spiders in the wild. And, you know, *alive*.

But Dr. Jacobs was all about the fire ants that day, and he'd set up a huge aquarium extension to find out one thing: What do ants do to survive a flood?

"Now fire ants have a unique ability to survive floods," Dr. J said, peering over the rim of his glasses to observe the colony of skittering creatures.

"How?" Aiden asked. "It seems like they'd just swim until they were exhausted and then drown."

"That's what you'd think. But watch and learn."

Dr. Jacobs moved to the end of his modified aquarium and opened up a gate that sent water flooding through the structure. Ants scurried madly, climbing out of their tunnels and up to the tops of small hills of dirt until even the protective mounds caved in. As the tsunami swallowed their tiny island, the biggest ant group clung together and floated with the water down the miniature riverway that Dr. Jacobs had constructed. Aiden and Dr. J followed along, watching them.

"They grab hold of one another by the jaw or the leg," Dr. Jacobs explained, holding a magnifying glass over the largest ant pack as the water inched along. "They pull others in, creating a living raft of bodies. Some researchers say they can live for weeks this way, afloat."

"What happens if one of them abandons ship?" Aiden asked.

"They make him stay," Dr. Jacobs calmly replied. "It's a matter of their mutual survival. Watch," he said, handing the boy the magnifier. "As they pass others, they'll collect them too, creating their own island."

"Cool!" Aiden said, watching it happen just as Dr. Jacobs described. More and more of the tiny insects joined the ant island as it floated along, some ants even climbing on top of the others. "I wish we could do that."

"We can, in certain measure," Dr. J responded. "If your neighborhood was flooding and you had something to float on, wouldn't you reach for others who were drowning beside you?"

"Yeah," Aiden said as the ant island bumped into a corner and rounded it into the next flume.

"We all need one another," Dr. Jacobs pointed out. "More than we know. Whether it be a flood or drought. Together we're stronger. That's what separates us now from those in Noah's day."

"What do you mean?"

Dr. Jacobs straightened and moved toward the far end of the aquarium. "Well, in Noah's day, God wanted to start over. Today God wants to rescue everyone."

Aiden bent and observed the ants, half of them holding on to one another, half of them crawling over the rest. And for a moment he could almost see the people in his own neighborhood.

The Skinny on Genesis 6

- Want to be considered "righteous" in the eyes of God? It's not as hard as it sounds. Just work at *right living*! You can do this by following Jesus, loving God with everything in you, and loving everyone as much as you love yourself (Deuteronomy 6:4–5; Leviticus 19:18; Mark 12:30–31).

- We need community on our "little arks" to help us make it through modern-day floods that threaten to destroy us. God promised not to send another flood to destroy the earth. Because Jesus loved us and died for us, we'll never be separated from God again. Other people who truly love Jesus can help keep us strong and growing closer to him.

- Can you imagine building something the size of that ark—450 feet long (longer than a football field), 75 feet wide, and 45 feet high (higher than a four-story building)? People built a replica of the ark in Kentucky that you can tour. That'd be something to see!

- God is in the business of coming to the rescue of his children—us. Back in Noah's day, he wanted to "wipe the hard drive" on all he had created; now he urges us to "redirect" when we get off track and seek a lifesaving and *life-giving* relationship with him as we face the evils and sadness of our own era.

> God can send help in a variety of ways, such as your best friend, a stranger on the street, or something you hear on the radio, right when you need it!

- Find it hard to believe that Noah could put a pair of every animal on that big ark? Well, think of the space as the equivalent of 569 railroad stock cars. Each car can carry 120 animals the size of a sheep. And many species that can live in water wouldn't have needed rescue.

> The worst part would have been *cleaning up* after all those animals. Ever mucked out a horse stall? *Pee-ew!*

WHAT STRUCK YOU IN THIS CHAPTER?

Think about a time you or someone you loved was in danger and needed rescue. Did God send an "ant raft" to help? What happened? Did he send protection in the moment? Or perhaps a friend or family member to help?

YOUR FUTURE STORY

We don't want to be like the people of Noah's day and live far from the way God wants us to. Like Noah, we want to learn how to walk with God, realizing he is with us all the time, even though we can't see him. But how do we walk with God?

Could it mean setting time aside to literally go for a walk and take time to talk with him in prayer? Or weaving God into your day, thinking about him in the morning, at lunch, and at dinnertime and asking him what he wants you to do or think about?

> *Noah was a righteous man, blameless among his*
> *contemporaries; Noah walked with God.*
> —Genesis 6:9

4

Faith Means Taking Risks
Genesis 12

Do you have a hard time believing things will turn out right when they seem scary or impossible or overwhelming? I do. But God routinely asks us to believe he can do miraculous, big things and not just help us with little things. Old Abe—or Abram, whose name was later changed to Abraham—was a hero, earning an A-plus on the faith front because he believed that God could both promise and deliver BIG. Later the apostle Paul would call Abraham the "father of all who believe" (Romans 4:11).

From the start, here in Genesis 12, when God called Abram to join him in what he was doing on earth, Abram showed off his mad faith skills. Abram was pretty set, liking life just as it was, when—*boom!*—God commanded the young man to go to a country he hadn't seen before.

Now what I love about Abram is that he wasn't perfect. We see him act like a monumental coward when he advised his pretty wife Sarai (later called Sarah) to tell the pharaoh of Egypt that she was Abe's sister rather than his wife. Yep, Abram asked Sarai to lie so Pharaoh wouldn't kill Abram so he could take Saria as his own girlfriend or wife.

> Weird, huh? God can use even cowards and liars for his good purposes!

Later we see God promising all kinds of land (we're talking hundreds of square miles) to the A-man and his descendants (his children's children). And as a dude who didn't even have a son or daughter yet, Abram believed God's promise of property and lots of kids.

In Genesis 15, the Lord took Abram outside and said, "'Look at the sky and count the stars, if you are able to count them.... Your offspring will be that numerous.' [And] Abram believed the LORD, and [God] credited it to him as righteousness" (vv. 5–6).

There's that *righteous* word again. Remember what we learned from Noah? Righteousness isn't about being without faults. *It's about right living in right relationship with God and those around us.*

It took many, many years before old Abraham and Sarah would have a baby, Isaac. We're talking OLD. As old as some great-great-grandparents today! But still, on the night God spoke to him, Abram *believed* it was going to happen as God had said. He trusted that God would do the impossible and give him as many descendants as the stars in the sky. And in time, that promise was fulfilled, but likely much, much later than Abram thought it would. Eventually his family tribe included a lot of people, but think about how many *spiritual* descendants he has as a father of our faith! There are billions of Christians who claim Abraham as their spiritual father, just as there are billions of stars.

> Astronomers think there would have been eight thousand stars visible to the naked eye in Abraham's day. That's a whole lot of kids to think about when you don't have even one!

Imagine This ...
Called Out of a Comfy Life to the Unknown

Maya pulled off her designer boots after school and tossed them onto the stairs. She snagged a soda from the beverage fridge and flopped onto the leather couch in the media room. "Grab a drink, Emma," she shouted, clicking the TV remote.

Maya had a whole separate basement fridge stocked with nothing but Izzes and Cokes and Dr Peppers and fresh-squeezed juices that the family's personal chef made every morning. Emma stood there wishing she had even a minifridge at her house. Nothing tasted better after the ride from school on a hot California afternoon than fresh-squeezed orange juice. She grabbed the pitcher, poured a glass of juice, and took a sip before joining Maya on the couch.

Maya had just logged into Netflix and chosen the latest episode of their favorite show when she turned the volume to mute and cocked her head.

Emma looked over at her. "What?"

"Did you … Did you hear that?"

"What?"

Maya shook her head and then pressed Play and turned up the volume again. Emma settled back in the corner of the couch and spread an afghan over her legs. The well-cooled mansion was a bit chilly for her.

They were only five minutes into the show when Maya abruptly scrambled to her feet, set her can of soda on the table, and ran up the stairs two at a time.

"Maya?" Emma called. "Maya! Want me to pause it?"

But Maya didn't answer.

Frowning, Emma followed her upstairs. She looked around the superclean living room and kitchen—like something out of a magazine—but saw no one.

Just then the chef, Anders, came out of a walk-in pantry. "Looking for our girl?" he asked in a friendly tone. "She went out there," he said, gesturing with his chin to the backyard.

Emma pulled open the sliding-glass door and walked across the cushy green grass, past the pool and Jacuzzi, to where Maya stood. Her backyard stretched to the edge of a cliff. To the east, miles of scrub oak and sage covered rugged hills, not a house in sight.

"Maya?" Emma asked, still puzzled as to what had drawn her friend out here.

Maya glanced at her but appeared dazed, with her lips slightly parted. Her eyes shifted back to the hills. "God spoke to me."

"God," Emma repeated flatly.

Maya nodded. "I'm supposed to go that way ... to leave this place and head out there," she said, motioning toward the wilderness.

"Out there? There's nothing out there but hills and desert until you get to Vegas. Is that what you're saying? You want to go to Vegas? I don't think my parents—"

"No," Maya said, taking Emma's hand. "I'm supposed to go where I've never been before. God spoke to me. He'll show me exactly where once I'm on the road."

"Why?"

"I don't know. I just know I'm supposed to go." She reached up, gripping Emma's arm. "He spoke to me, Emma. I have no choice. I have to go."

"So ... you're talking about running away?" Emma said slowly, trying not to freak out. Was Maya losing it?

"Not at all," Maya replied, looking at Emma with clear eyes, her voice more confident and assured than when she told Emma she was running for class president. "I'm not running away. I'm taking God's hand and letting him lead me."

"To do what?"

She shrugged but smiled, a spark of excitement in her eyes now. "I don't know! But I'm gonna find out."

The Skinny on Genesis 12

- Do you know that African impalas can leap distances of thirty feet and heights of thirteen feet? And yet zookeepers can keep them enclosed behind much shorter walls because they won't jump if they can't see where they'll land.[1] When God asks us to leap, we need to trust that he knows where we'll land.

- God's timing isn't our own. He might *promise* something will happen, but we might not actually *see* it happen. What we're waiting for might come to pass next year or a hundred years from now. Our job is to simply rest in his promises, believe they're true, and trust in his timing.

- Abraham had a problem with lying to protect himself, even though he believed that God could do what he said he was going to do. Just because we're Christians doesn't make us perfect either. Even though we sin, we're not disqualified from doing great things for God.

  God can use all of us to do his good work in the world and fulfill his promises—even when we fail him! That's reassuring and a little crazy too, huh? He takes risks on us, and we can risk trusting him to lead us however and wherever he decides.

WHAT STRUCK YOU IN THIS CHAPTER?

Do you ever think you're not important enough or ready to serve God if he calls you? Do you think only pastors, youth-group leaders, musicians, or stars are the kinds of people he would use?

God calls *all* of us to do his good work in the world right where we are, with all we have at the time (even if we don't think it's "enough"). We're called "his hands and feet"—literally, the *body* of Christ. And bodies move, right? *Moving* might mean leaving our hometowns, like Abraham and Maya did, or serving him right where we are. Wherever God calls you, you can trust him to lead you, even though it might feel risky. You'll be in the best hands ever.

YOUR FUTURE STORY

Do you think God is asking you to step out into unknown territory, trusting him with what will happen? Maybe it's trying out a new youth group or going to a new camp or serving in your community. How is God encouraging you to move today?

> *Go out from your land, your relatives, and your father's*
> *house to the land that I will show you.*
>
> —Genesis 12:1

5

I'll Do It, but I Just Don't Get It
Genesis 22

Don't you hate it when you ask your parents why you have to do something and they say, "Because I said so"? I remember feeling frustrated when my parents did that, and yet I find myself saying similar things to my own kids. Sometimes parents—and God!—have reasons that can't be explained.

Let me give you some examples. I might tell my son he can't buy something, even though he has enough money. I say no because I know someone else plans to give that item to him as a birthday present. Or I'll tell my daughter she can't go to a certain friend's house because I've found out that girl isn't a good influence, but I'm not able to share the specifics. Or I steer my other daughter away from signing up for a church ski trip because I know her friend is planning a surprise party for her the same weekend. My goal as a parent in all three examples is not to make my kids miserable but to lead them to what will be best for them, even though they may not understand it at the time.

Often these types of situations feel like a test of trust with your parents, right? An even bigger act of trust is when God asks you to give up something when it doesn't make sense to you but you just know it's the right thing to do.

That might mean not taking that lawn-mowing job or babysitting gig because you sense God telling you to, even though you're not sure why. You might discover later on that you just needed to spend more time with your family, friends, or God.

Or maybe you're a total drama geek, but you feel like God is asking you not to try out for the school play. Later you might learn that the kid who got the part really, really needed that opportunity to overcome a serious case of stage fright. Or maybe you know you're not supposed to go to camp this summer for some reason, even though you go every year. You might find out later that your folks are struggling financially because of some unexpected bills, but they didn't have the heart to tell you.

Genesis 22 offers one of the most extreme examples in Scripture of following wherever God leads, even when it hurts or doesn't make sense. God told Abraham to take his son Isaac to a mountain and sacrifice him. Say what? You heard right. Sacrifice him. Remember that God promised old Abe that his descendants would be as numerous as the stars (Genesis 15:5; repeated again here in Genesis 22:17). Isaac was his treasured son, the only one born to Sarah and Abe. And now God was asking Abe to kill their precious son?

Taking your child's life would be pretty horrifying, wouldn't it? There wasn't anything warm and fuzzy about it at all. But here's the thing we need to understand about this | Old Abe was ALL-IN. Are you? | father of the faithful: *Abraham was ready to give up his most treasured possession if God asked him to.* Abraham wasn't holding *anything* back. As much as he adored Isaac, Abraham knew that his relationship with God was more important than anything else in his life.

God knew it was going to cost his servant big-time to follow through with what God was asking him to do. The Lord said, "Take your … only son Isaac, whom you love, go to the land of Moriah, and offer him there as a burnt offering on one of the mountains" (Genesis

22:2). God was clearly wanting to find out if Abraham loved him even more than his son.

I think we all breathe a sigh of relief when we get to the part where God intervenes at the last second and provides a ram (a male lamb) to sacrifice instead of Isaac! The angel of the Lord (who is identified with the Lord himself) said, "Do not lay a hand on the boy or do anything to him. For now I know that you fear God, since you have not withheld your only son from me" (v. 12).

Fearing God means giving him respect and trust. That's what he wants from us too.

Imagine This ...
Doing What You're Told, Even When You Don't Want To

"Kam? Kam!" his mother called.

Akamu blinked once and then twice, trying to wake up from a deep sleep.

"C'mon, Kam!" Mom yelled, bursting through his door. "We have to go!"

"What? No," he mumbled as he turned over, thinking his mom's voice was part of a bad dream. He just wanted to sleep.

"Kam, c'mon! Don't you hear it?" Mom flung aside Akamu's covers and yanked him to a sitting position.

It connected then. That siren in the distance.

Tsunami.

"Grab your shoes," Mom said firmly as she rushed toward the hallway. "You can put them on in the car. I'll get Kalea." Kam was twelve; his little sister was only four.

"Where's Dad?"

"Out in the car!" Mom hollered, exiting Kalea's room with the small girl in her arms and then rushing down the hall.

"Wait, Mom! I gotta grab my Xbox!"

"No, Kam! No! Get in the car!"

He paused in the hallway and grimaced, hating to leave behind the game console. It had taken him two years to save the money to buy it. If anything happened to it ... "Mom, why can't I just—"

"Kam, get in the car! Now!" She practically shoved him out the front door.

Outside, the sirens were even louder, with their mournful, menacing cry. A shiver ran down Kam's back. For the first time he understood this wasn't another island drill. Something seriously bad was about to happen.

Dad had their old Chevy going, and he gunned the engine. The car never ran that well until they'd put a few miles on it. *Please, God*, Kam prayed as he ran around to the other side of the car. *Let it work tonight.*

He jumped in the backseat and helped Mom with Kalea's booster belt. His little sis was crying, clinging to the remnants of her old baby blanket. Dad pressed on the gas pedal as soon as Mom's door was shut. The tires skidded a little on the gravel driveway as they rushed out to the main road.

"Wait!" Kam wailed. "We forgot Alani!"

The family cat.

"I looked for her," Dad shouted over his shoulder. "She didn't come when I called."

"Go back!" Kam shrieked over Kalea's cries for Alani. "She always comes when I call!"

"We can't, honey," Mom interrupted. "We have to get to high ground. We might only have a minute or two before the wave hits."

"My monkey!" Kalea cried anew. "I forgot my monkey!"

Kam groaned inside. Kalea never could sleep very well without that old, disgusting stuffed monkey.

Mom reached over and touched Kalea's foot. "Monkey will have to ride out the storm. We can't go back. We can't go back for anything. We have to get to high ground." She turned toward Dad. Kam knew Mom thought he couldn't hear from the backseat when she whispered, "Can you go any faster?"

Mom was scared. Superscared.

"No," Dad said, sounding frustrated. "I've got the gas pedal floored. I'm just thankful the car started." He reached out and laid a hand on the back of Mom's neck. "It's all right. Everything will be all right."

But it wasn't all right. An eighty-foot-high wave, cast ashore by an undersea earthquake, crashed up their valley that night, followed by several more waves, forty to sixty feet high. The surging water smashed some homes and wiped others off their foundations. The massive wall of water rolled cars, tossing them up in tree branches. The fierce current deposited fishing boats in front yards. The tsunami killed hundreds of people, and more than a thousand were declared homeless.

When the flooding receded, Kam's family returned to their neighborhood, hoping to find some of their cherished belongings. But everything was gone, all gone.

Kam's Xbox, Kalea's monkey, Mom and Dad's wedding pictures, even their cat, Alani. The family escaped with only the clothes they'd worn that night. Kam pressed his hand to his head in disbelief that they couldn't find anything. "Not one thing?" he asked his dad. "I thought we'd find something. But it's all gone. We lost everything."

"Not everything," Dad said, wrapping his arm around Kam's shoulder. "We have one another. When something like this happens, it's sad. We lost a lot in that house. Even our wonderful cat. But the most important thing is that we didn't lose one another. Our relationship is what matters most. God saw us through, and that's all that matters."

Kam swallowed hard. Dad was right. They had friends who lost family members that terrible night—little brothers and cousins and fathers and mothers. Five of Kam's school friends were still looking for the bodies of loved ones. But Kam? He had everyone he cared about most. Mom. Dad. Kalea. Despite all he had lost, he knew God had been with them through it all.

And that was all that mattered.

The Skinny on Genesis 22

- The first big thing to remember from this chapter is that Abraham was all about obeying and trusting God rather than trying to second-guess him.

- The second big thing to remember is that there's a difference between God and his gifts. While we want to give thanks for everything God gives us, we're not supposed to worship him just for that. We're to worship him simply because he's God! The One who created this big, beautiful world. The One who breathed life into us. The One who sacrificed his own Son for us. The One we can trust.

- God allows *tests* in our lives to build up our faith and relationship with him. Satan *tempts* us, trying to tear down our faith and relationship with God.

- COOL GEOGRAPHY FACTOIDS: God sent Abe to "the land of Moriah" (Genesis 22:2). King David later established Israel's capital here, in Jerusalem. And it was here at Mount Moriah that David's son Solomon built the massive Jewish temple (2 Chronicles 3:1), which is where Jesus worshipped, taught, and was tempted by Satan.

- Many instances in this story sound vaguely like God's sacrifice of his own Son, huh?

  - Verse 8: "God himself will provide the lamb." God's ultimate, final-and-forever sacrifice was Jesus, "the Lamb of God" (John 1:29).
  - Verse 9: "Abraham … bound his son … and placed him on the altar on top of the wood." And verse 16: "Because you … have not withheld your only son." These images remind us of

God's love and the sacrifice of his only Son, Jesus (John 3:16; Romans 3:22–25).

- Verse 13: "Abraham … took the ram and offered it as a burnt offering in place of his son." Just as the ram died in Isaac's place, Jesus gave his life in our place, "a ransom for many" (Mark 10:45).

WHAT STRUCK YOU IN THIS CHAPTER?

Would you love God and serve him even if he took away everything you love most in life? List the top five things you love most in your life right now:

1.
2.
3.
4.
5.

Is your house, your family, your friends, your clothes, your bike, or your toys on the list?

If you lost all these things and your only joy in life was a friendship with God himself, would you still choose to be faithful? That'd be a challenge, huh? But as our relationship with him deepens, it becomes clearer and clearer that he's more important than anything else in our lives.

YOUR FUTURE STORY

God loves to give us good things, to bless us with great connections with others and awesome opportunities. He wants to bless us with everything we need in life, but most especially he wants to bless us with a growing relationship with him.

What is temporary in your life? Friends? The place you live? The school you go to? What will last forever, no matter what happens in this life? Who will be with you forever?

> *Now I know that you fear God, since you have*
> *not withheld your only son from me.*
> —Genesis 22:12

GOD IS GOOD
WHEN LIFE
GETS MESSY

6

Knowing God by Name
Exodus 3

Are you good at remembering names? I'm not. I had a pastor once who could remember people's names after meeting them just once. His ability to recall names was so cool … because people felt special when he remembered their names the next time they met. Others I've met who are good at this use some sort of detail to recall names. Such as, "Her name is Rae, and she has red hair. R-r-r-red-haired Rae."

The Bible contains hundreds of names, titles, and descriptions for God! Think of your father. You might call him Dad, and your mom probably calls him by his first name (or "honey"—oh, come on, it's not that gross). A baseball team might call him Coach. And your cousins call him Uncle. In the same way, the many names for God in Scripture help describe who he is. Some of the Hebrew names or titles for him mean "the Lord Who Heals" or "the God Who Sees."

Here in Exodus 3, Moses asked what he should call God (v. 13). "God replied to Moses, 'I AM WHO I AM. This is what you are to say to the Israelites: I AM has sent me to you'" (v. 14).

Now I don't know about you, but I picture God saying this in a booming surround-sound sort of voice. (If you've ever seen the movie *The Prince of Egypt*, this scene is perfectly done. If you've never seen it, find it!

It's an awesome retelling of the events in Exodus, when God called Moses to lead his people out of Egypt.)

God went on to tell Moses, "Say this to the Israelites: The LORD, the God of your fathers, the God of Abraham, the God of Isaac, and the God of Jacob, has sent me to you. This is my name forever; this is how I am to be remembered in every generation" (Exodus 3:15).

God wanted his people to know that he was the same God who had led their ancestors in meaningful ways in the past, and the great I AM was on the move again. When God speaks of himself, he calls himself I AM. When we speak of him, we could say HE IS. HE IS always on the move, working, acting. It's an ultimate claim, isn't it? HE IS everything good and mighty and glorious—beyond any name we could come up with for him. HE IS everything we should worship and honor.

Many centuries later, Jesus tied himself to the whole I AM thing. In John 8, Jesus faced off with some Jewish religious leaders (the Pharisees) at the temple in Jerusalem, letting them know that he existed even before Abraham was born. "Truly I tell you, before Abraham was, I am" is how Jesus put it (v. 58).

Those were fightin' words for the Jews. Here was Jesus, a man they said was not yet "fifty years old" (v. 57), and yet he claimed to be older than Abraham. And more than that, he dared to connect himself with God's special name! When the Jews threatened to stone Jesus for what they viewed as blasphemy, he slipped away. But the gospel of John records seven different ways that Jesus referred to himself with "I AM" statements, revealing himself as the one God sent to save us and give us true life.

Imagine This ...
What If You'd Been in Moses's Sandals?

(Note: Write your own name in the blanks before reading. Imagine yourself as the "I" in the following story.)

I stood there, panting and wondering where that stupid goat had gone. Why couldn't he just stay with the rest of the herd? It was always this gray one that sent me climbing over rocks and searching dark caves, trying to find him before nightfall. Sweat dripped down my neck and chest, and I took a precious drink. I had just enough water for the afternoon, but this climb was going to drain my supply before I reached the spring.

I heard the goat bleating from what seemed like just around the corner, so I hurriedly secured my water pouch and attached it to my belt. I climbed, almost fell, and then climbed again, finally finding a small dirt path between the giant red craggy boulders.

I emerged in a clearing of sorts. At first I thought the bush across the way was the setting sun, but then I realized the sun wasn't in that direction. The blazing object before me was as big as a party bonfire. The bush was burning … and yet it wasn't. There wasn't even a withered leaf on the shrub as the flames licked upward, dancing before me in a mix of orange, red, and blue. I walked toward the fire, trying to figure out how this was possible.

Then a voice called to me from the flames, saying my name twice: "_____, _____!"

I paused abruptly. My heart pounded, but I managed to respond. "Here I am."

"Do not come closer," the voice warned. "Remove the sandals from your feet, for the place where you are standing is holy ground."

I practically fell flat on my face. I hurried to unlace my sandals and set them aside. I couldn't rise from my knees. I was terrified.

"_____, I am the God of your father, the God of Abraham, the God of Isaac, and the God of Jacob."

Now I was even more terrified. Was it possible? Was God here? Talking to me? Why?

Then God said, "I have observed the misery of my people in Egypt, and have heard them crying out because of their oppressors. I know about their sufferings, and I have come down to rescue them from the power of the Egyptians and to bring them from that land to a good and spacious land."

I thought back to my years in Egypt. I'd seen what God was talking about. The slaves working from sunup to sundown. The masters with their sticks and whips, beating those poor people. Women with tears streaking their dirty faces. Children carrying impossible loads.

The Lord continued. "I am sending you to Pharaoh so that you may lead my people, the Israelites, out of Egypt."

I dared to glance up at the fire. "M-me, Lord? Who am I that I should go to Pharaoh?"

"I will certainly be with you," God said, "and this will be the sign to you that I am the one who sent you: when you bring the people out of Egypt, you will all worship God at this mountain."

I was shaking my head. What God was saying, what he was asking me to do … it was impossible! Completely impossible! He didn't know Pharaoh. God didn't know how the Egyptians would fight to keep their slaves. I had no army. And the people of Israel … why would they follow me? They'd laugh me out of their camps and villages!

I rose to my knees, my throat dry. "I-if I go t-to the Israelites and say t-to them, 'The God of your fa-fathers has sent me to you,' and they ask me, 'What is his name?' W-what should I tell them?"

God's answer literally blew me backward. His voice was like a rushing wind, like the strongest storm I'd ever faced. "I AM WHO I AM," his voice boomed.

I rolled to my hip and then pushed up with one arm, blinking as I tried to catch my breath. *This is the LORD. The Holy One. The Most High.*

And he had a task for me that I knew I would never be able to escape. For some reason he had chosen me.

I was both honored and horrified. Excited and wishing I could escape. On holy ground with the Holiest One. About to be sent out …

The Skinny on Exodus 3

- Moses's life was about to change again, big-time. When Moses was a baby, his mother and sister set him afloat on the Nile River in a basket, hoping to save him from those coming to kill all Hebrew baby boys. Pharaoh's daughter found him among the reeds and raised Moses as an adopted prince of Egypt. Then one day he murdered an Egyptian and, as a result, fled the country. (You can read the full story in Exodus 2.) Now we see Moses in Exodus 3, a shepherd in the desert, about to be the shepherd of God's people.

- Anytime we sense God's presence, we're on holy ground. As a sign of servitude, slaves in Moses's day weren't allowed to wear shoes. Muslims today still take off their shoes before entering a mosque.

This is like the opposite of that sign that reads No Shoes, No Shirt, No Service! It's as if God was saying, "Show me you're ready to serve me by ditching the shoes!"

- God wanted Moses (and he wants us) to approach him as servants, ready to submit and surrender to his direction and love.

- Moses, like so many heroes of the faith, didn't feel ready to serve God.

  - Moses said, "Who am I?" in Exodus 3:11.
  - Then he said, "What if they won't believe me and will not obey me but say, 'The LORD did not appear to you'?" (4:1).
  - Some people think Moses had a stutter, because he said, "Please, Lord, I have never been eloquent—either in the past or recently or since you have been speaking to your servant—because my mouth and my tongue are sluggish" (v. 10).

    > Sounds like trying to wriggle out of chores, huh?

  - Moses even asked God to "send someone else" (v. 13).

- Learning to know God by name opens up our understanding of who he is, what he's saying to us, and what we're going to do about it!

WHAT STRUCK YOU IN THIS CHAPTER?

While God's all-encompassing name, I AM, might seem a little over-whelming to us, Jesus's use of that name helps us understand God a bit better. Below, mark the statement of Jesus you're most drawn to.

- ❏   I AM the bread of life (John 6:35).
- ❏   I AM the light of the world (John 8:12).
- ❏   I AM the gate (John 10:7).
- ❏   I AM the good shepherd (John 10:11).
- ❏   I AM the resurrection and the life (John 11:25).

❏ I AM the way, the truth, and the life (John 14:6).

❏ I AM the true vine (John 15:1).

What do you think Jesus meant by the I AM statement you marked? (You might want to read the entire chapter referenced beside that one so you can understand it better.) Why do you think that statement stands out to you?

YOUR FUTURE STORY

What do you want to be when you grow up? Do you think you can serve God if you're a teacher, an engineer, a shop clerk, a landscape architect, or a stay-at-home parent?

How can learning all the aspects of God's character lead you into a deeper relationship with him, just like getting to know a person better makes your friendship stronger?

God replied to Moses, "I AM WHO I AM.... This is my name forever; this is how I am to be remembered in every generation."
—Exodus 3:14–15

7

God Leads the Search and Rescue Team
Exodus 14

Moses had seen some big things, impossible things, happen in Egypt. He went where God told him to go and said what he was told to say. Like telling Pharaoh that God said, "Let my people go" (Exodus 5:1), and telling the Israelites that God was going to "rescue [them] from slavery" (Exodus 6:6). Those were some mighty demands and claims for people who were used to the way things had been for many years.

When people get used to things the way they are, they're usually reluctant to change, even if refusing to change will end up costing them. Weird, huh? We humans sometimes *choose discomfort* because it's familiar to us, preferring what we already know and are used to rather than going through some hard things to change.

But God found a way to pry his people loose. He sent plague after plague upon the Egyptians, basically beating Pharaoh down until he agreed to his demands. First the Nile River was turned to blood, then thousands of disgusting frogs poured out of the waters of Egypt and into the streets and people's homes, and then annoying gnats were so thick that they probably stuck inside people's nostrils and eyes—gross! (Exodus 7:14–8:19). But still Pharaoh refused to budge. So God sent swarms of flies; a plague that killed the cows and goats and sheep; a plague of oozing boils on the Egyptians and their animals; thunder, lightning, and hail; locusts (that ate everything); three days of total darkness; and then the worst ... the death of every firstborn son in Egypt (8:20–11:10).

Basically God was letting sin and human self-will run its course. He was going to let these Egyptians go as far as they possibly could to dig their own graves before the big showdown ahead. Remember that for years and years, these guys were abusive toward God's people, keeping them in slavery. God was about to show them just who was BOSS.

For God, having no other gods except him is a big deal. And the Egyptians were all about other gods ... any god, really, other than *the Lord*.

The ten plagues were just the buildup to the big show. In Exodus 14, we see the Egyptians in hot pursuit of the Israelites, bent on recapturing their slave force. But the angel of God appeared as a towering dark cloud (glowing spookily from within) that neither the Egyptians nor the Israelites dared approach that night. Moses lifted up his staff and stretched out his hand—as God instructed—and a path opened through the Red Sea so the Israelites could flee. Once God's people were safely on the other side, those in pursuit drowned.

God's goal in all of this? For all to know that he could deliver his people whenever and however he wanted. Nothing was out of his sight or reach or power to control. At last, everyone—whether Hebrew or Egyptian—knew God's great power, respected him, and believed what he said.

Imagine This ...
On the Run

The Year AD 2284
A chubby baby sat in a muddy street, screaming his head off as people streamed past him. Milas grabbed hold of the little boy's waist and heaved him

up on his hip. Then Milas turned to the crowd of men, women, and children behind him and shouted, "C'mon! Hurry! Leave your things behind!"

He moved over to an old man and yanked at the straps of the heavy bundle on his shoulder. "Leave it!" Milas yelled. "They're going to catch up to you and capture you!"

"But I-I can't," said the man. "It's all I own!"

Milas set down the crying toddler for a second, removed the straps from the old man's shoulders, and replied, "Listen to me! Leave it behind! If you don't hurry, they'll capture you!"

The old man nodded and started walking, this time much faster than before. Milas looked around at his people, hundreds, maybe thousands of people. He picked up the toddler again and held him close, trying to quiet him.

Milas's people were finally being set free after more than a hundred years of slavery.

Terror swirled in his mind even as hope rose in his chest.

Even though the Masborgs had set his people free, word had reached them that the slavers had changed their minds.

The Masborgs were coming after them. To capture them. Or worse, to kill them.

We can't go back. We can't return! Milas vowed. "C'mon!" he shouted at a woman trying to push a heavy cart. "We must make it to the harbor. Run! Run for your lives!"

Milas turned and ran through the crowd, taking the lead. Even in front, he could hear the thundering metallic clang of the Masborg fighters in pursuit. Heavily armed, two stories tall. If four or five of these warriors caught up to Milas's people, they'd surely shrink in fear, and there would be little Milas could do to get them going again.

"This way!" he shouted over the noise. He joined everyone else running down the street.

Two Masborg fighters appeared only three blocks behind the last of the fleeing people. Men were trampling other men, women, and children to get ahead. Milas couldn't stop the panicked mob. He only hoped as many people as possible would make it to the harbor. He'd led them the best he could, as the Lord had instructed him.

Just six more blocks, Milas tried to reassure himself. *Can we make it? But what then? There are no ships, and the people certainly can't swim that distance.*

"What have you done, Milas?" screeched a woman, clutching at his arm and pulling him to a stop. "Have you brought us to the harbor only to die? Why didn't you leave us alone? We would have been better off serving the Masborgs than being killed here in the streets!"

She looked as if she wanted to crumple to the ground right then and there. To give up! If she did, others would surely follow.

"Don't be afraid!" Milas yelled, this time gripping the desperate woman's arm. "Stand firm! You'll see the Lord deliver us this day. He will fight for us!"

The terrible clanking of metal on brick and stone roared through the streets. More women screamed, more men shouted, more children shrieked. More people streamed past Milas, but there were still so many lagging behind. In horror he watched as two more Masborg fighters joined the others. And they were closing in.

"Run!" he ordered, practically pushing the slower people. "Faster! They're coming!"

There was no way every person would live through this.

No way.

But as Milas looked up to the sky, wondering where the Lord was and why he had led them here only to be killed, he saw the clouds above him beginning to swirl. Dark, billowing segments swelled out, turning and twisting. Milas had never witnessed such an eerie green-gray thunderhead streaming downward as if brewing a tornado within. He froze, wondering if the storm mass would suck them all into it. But the clouds divided the people from the Masborg fighters. Milas could see the fighters in the distance, wobbling as if trying to keep their balance against a fierce wind.

Yet on the side of God's people, all was still.

"Lord," Milas whispered. Then he cried "Lord!" in celebration.

"It's an angel! The angel of the Lord!" burst out a woman beside him, arms raised in awe.

"C'mon!" Milas shouted as he turned.

The people ran the rest of the way to the harbor, and Milas pushed to the front through the throngs. He glanced back at the fighters—who would eventually find their way past the Lord's barrier—and then to the sea up ahead and the land on the far side. There was no way Milas and God's people could swim across the open sea. Many didn't even know how to swim. And it was too far.

But the Lord told Milas how to direct the people to safety. In an instant a friend of Milas's tossed him a walking stick. Milas closed his eyes, bowed his head, and lifted both the wooden staff and his hand to the sea.

People gasped as what he had seen began to unfold. He could hear the rush and drip and splash of water—tremendous amounts of water—shifting to form a gigantic wall, and the people crying out ... in praise.

The Skinny on Exodus 14

- God wants us to recognize that no matter what hard things we face, he can be trusted. We have to remember three things when we face big problems:

1. We can trust that God has the situation in hand, even when we can't see how it could possibly work out.

> What is the most frequently repeated command in the Bible? "Do not fear. Do not be afraid. Fear not."

2. Problems come and go. Part of the trick in dealin' with problems is just outlasting them. Keep putting one foot in front of the other; stand firm in trusting God, knowing he'll eventually work everything out.

    > Do you remember your biggest problem from a year ago? Most people can't. Sometimes what seems *HUGE* to us now becomes *tiny* from a distance as time passes.

3. Watch for how God answers your prayers to resolve your problem or helps you heal, and write down or tell someone how he shows up for you.

    > Sometimes God moves in miraculous ways, but more often he works in subtle, quiet ways we might miss if we're not paying attention.

It's important for us to remember how God helped us in the past when we face the next challenge that life, people, or circumstances throw at us!

- The laws of our world—time, space, nature—can't limit God. He controls it *all*. He's so much *BIGGER* than anything we can imagine, and he wants us to remember that!

WHAT STRUCK YOU IN THIS CHAPTER?

It's kind of strange to think that God had to set the stage in Exodus to recapture some of the glory that was his all along. But he describes himself as a jealous God who wants us to be in an active relationship with him—in touch with him—all the time.

Who or what is your own modern-day Egyptian? Who or what is keeping you away from God rather than drawing you closer to him?

YOUR FUTURE STORY

Who do you think is the most powerful person in the world today? Is it

- ❑ The winning team's quarterback in the Super Bowl?
- ❑ The star in the blockbuster movie premiere last week?
- ❑ The Person of the Year on the cover of *Time* magazine?
- ❑ The president of the United States?
- ❑ Other (fill in the blank): _____

Now think about meeting this celebrity, shaking his or her hand, and introducing yourself. How would you feel? What would you be thinking?

How can you treat God with that same sense of awe and respect from this day forward? That's what he wants. And that's what he deserves.

Moses said to the people, "Don't be afraid. Stand firm and see the LORD's salvation that he will accomplish for you today; for the Egyptians you see today, you will never see again. The LORD will fight for you."

—Exodus 14:13–14

8

More Love Than Law
Exodus 20

Quick, name as many of the Ten Commandments as you can!

Done? How'd you do? Why do you think you remembered only one? Or those three? Or all ten? Or maybe this is the first time you've heard of them at all. *"Ten Com-what?"*

When I was a kid in Sunday school, I had to memorize all ten of these special commands found in the Bible. I remember feeling like it was a chore, just something I had to do. After all, how did "Thou shalt not kill" really relate to me? Was I really gonna murder someone? Or what about the one telling us not to steal? I didn't even know an *adult* who had robbed someone. But you have to keep in mind that these were laws given to God's people in order to give us a baseline for living and to protect our hearts.

God's goal wasn't for his people to just follow a bunch of rules. His ultimate goal was for them to live life in a way that would honor his relationship with them and their relationships with one another. The goal of the Old Testament law was love (Romans 13:9–10). By giving his people the Ten Commandments, God continued to reveal himself more and more. He was showing them that he was holy and yet he cared for them, and they were to be set apart for him. Basically, he wanted them to "echo" his holiness, not acting as the people around them did.

That speaks to us still today. We want to be different, in some ways, from those who don't follow Jesus. We want people to notice that we try to live in a way that pleases God, that his joy fills our hearts and helps us love others—because that draws attention. And God is all about drawing attention to himself, even through us. People notice holiness, and God's holiness shone when he revealed his Ten Commandments.

The first four commandments focus on giving God what he deserves:

1. *"Do not have other gods besides me"* (Exodus 20:3)—because God loves us so much, he's fiercely protective of us.

2. *"Do not make an idol for yourself"* (v. 4)—anything we might worship other than God (including video games or a pint of Ben & Jerry's ice cream!)

3. *"Do not misuse the name of the LORD"* (v. 7)—don't be a God follower in name only.

4. *"Remember the Sabbath day, to keep it holy"* (v. 8)—rest at least one day of the week.

The last six commandments focus on what people around us deserve:

5. *"Honor your father and your mother"* (Exodus 20:12)—home is where we need to learn how to do relationships right; begin here.

6. *"Do not murder"* (v. 13)—enough said?

7. *"Do not commit adultery"* (v. 14)—this means sleeping (having sex) with someone besides your husband or wife. You might think this is easy to avoid if you're a younger kid, but there are many ways our minds, hearts, and bodies can be swayed; we need to be on guard against this.

8. *"Do not steal"* (v. 15)—you might have had to return a candy bar to the store manager and apologize when your mom caught you. But watch out for more subtle ways you might be stealing too. Maybe a song or movie online, or someone else's answers to a test at school?

9. *"Do not give false testimony"* (v. 16)—don't lie. Period. No matter how much it hurts to tell the truth.

10. *"Do not covet"* (v. 17)—proof that your mind can do as much evil as your hands. We want to be God's children by being genuinely happy for others who have things or relationships we'd like for ourselves, rather than allowing feelings of jealousy, bitterness, and anger to control us.

Imagine This ...
The Best Teacher in the World

Dylan had either flunked out of or been expelled from five different schools when they sent him to Marion Woldrof's Christian Academy. He expected to check in with his foster dad and be checked out by lunchtime. After all, he knew how to work the system. His goal was to make it so difficult that no school would have him and they'd have to find foster parents willing to homeschool him. And then he'd figure out how to work *them* so he could do school for an hour a day and be a gamer the rest of the time.

With his hand on Dylan's shoulder, his foster dad marched him up the steps of the tiny school half an hour from his work. As they reached the top stair, Dylan shrugged off the man's hand and hurried ahead to open the door. "After you," he said, putting on his best-kid face.

"Well, thanks, Dylan," Grant said, lifting a brow. He was all right as foster dads went. Middle-aged, nice, but tired all the time, as if the world had gotten him down. Dylan's foster mom, Nanci, was like that too. Dylan was just the most recent of about twenty kids they'd fostered over the years, never having had kids of their own.

The door squeaked shut behind them as they stepped into the tall-ceilinged hallway. The building had to be a hundred years old. Dylan didn't know if he'd ever been in a building that ancient. What kind of school was this?

"Now, Dylan, I want you to make the most of this," Grant advised. "It's a drive out here, but I'm willing to do it for you if this is the right …" He paused as if searching for the appropriate word. "If this is the right *situation* for you. I want you to be respectful and listen well and do as they say. This school is a Christian school. They're going to make sure you behave responsibly. Do you understand?"

"I understand," Dylan firmly replied, like a kid who earns citizenship awards. But in his thoughts, he was practically rubbing his hands together and saying, *Oh, I understand, old dude. You have no idea how much I understand. A Christian school? Getting bounced outta here will be ea-sy!*

"Good, good," his foster dad said and patted his shoulder a bit hesitantly, as if he'd caught a glimpse of Dylan's real thoughts. "Dylan?" he asked, leaving the rest of his question unspoken.

"What? I got it, I got it! Trust me." Dylan spread out upturned hands.

"All right …," Grant replied.

They saw through the glass windows at the end of the hall that the principal's office was just ahead to their left. Grant moved ahead of Dylan, glancing back to make sure the boy was following. On the wall straight ahead was a list of the Ten Commandments. *Thou shalt have no other gods before me. Thou shalt not make unto thee any graven image. Thou shalt not bow down thyself to them, nor serve them. Thou shalt not ...*

Dylan stared up at the words with their weird spelling as they waited for the principal. He nudged his foster dad in the side and gestured upward. "Is that in a different language or something?"

"No, son," said a warbly voice from his other side. He jerked and turned, finding the oldest, smallest lady he'd ever seen beside him. What was she, ninety years old? Deep lines crisscrossed her face, and the huge glasses on the tip of her nose magnified her droopy eyelids. "That's King James language. An early English version of the Bible," she added.

"So do we have to memorize that list to get in this school?" asked Dylan. "Or promise not to do any of those things?"

The lady's weathered lips, covered in perfect pink lipstick, turned into a smile that revealed worn, cream-colored teeth. "Well, we hope you don't do any of those things that are bad and do those things that are good. But no, memorization is not required to be part of our school. Come with me," she said, waving for them to follow her back to the office.

Dylan paused in the doorway. "So those Ten Commandments—" he began.

"Dylan! Just let it go," Grant hissed. "Come and sit down!"

"No, no, the boy is curious," insisted the little old lady. She looked at him over the rims of her glasses as if she'd seen a hundred kids just like him.

He squirmed. He liked her kindness. And yet he didn't.

"Dylan, those Ten Commandments are instructions the Lord gave Moses to give to his people. They're a good place to start for us today. But you have to know the secret key."

The principal opened a folder—probably his—and began reading, pen in hand. But there was something in Dylan that wouldn't let this go. He was curious, and that curiosity made him agitated. He felt like he was going to burst out of his own skin.

"The secret key?" he finally asked when it was clear she wasn't going to say more.

"What?" the principal said, blinking at him. "Oh, that," she added with a smile. "Yes. You can learn those commandments easily if you know the secret key."

"Even with all those 'thous' and 'shalt nots'?" he said doubtfully.

Dylan's foster dad shifted in his chair and cleared his throat, clearly getting irritated with him.

"Will you give this school a week if I tell you the secret?" the principal asked, leaning forward, hands folded in front of her on the desk. She stared straight into his eyes. "No games, no trying to get out of things. Just a fair try. That's all I ask."

Dylan gazed back at her, thinking this was like making a deal with a gambler on the street. A gambler who knew a lot more than he did. But there was something about her he liked, something that told him he could give her a week.

"A week, but no more," he said slowly.

"Dylan!" Grant exclaimed, getting red in the face.

But the old principal held up her hand and kept her eyes on Dylan. "Good. So the secret to that long list is to remember it means two things."

She made him ask. "And those are?"

She smiled. A sparkle in her eyes nudged Dylan to smile along with her, even though he didn't really want to. He couldn't help it. "Love God," she said, holding up one finger, "with everything in you." Then she held up a second finger. "And love everyone around you as much as you love yourself. That includes me and your foster dad and the students you're about to meet. Figure out how to do those two things, Dylan. Figure out what those secret keys unlock, and you'll find a path to peace and happiness. I promise you."

Dylan kept his eyes focused on her. *That's some lame kind of secret key*, he thought. And yet to say it that way in his head wasn't quite right either. There was some sort of truth in the old lady's words. Deep down he knew it.

Love God.

Love everyone else.

Were those the two keys to life? A way to peace? Happiness? A way to not have to move to another foster home next month? A way to the smiles this lady passed out like candy?

Dylan stared at her suspiciously but couldn't ignore the spark of hope he sensed. "A week," he said. "But only a week," he reminded her.

"A week is all I need, Dylan," she calmly replied.

The Skinny on Exodus 20

- COOL FACTOID: Why the big ten? Not eight commandments? Or twelve? Because for the ancient Hebrews—the people Moses was talking to—the number ten was the perfect number, an ideal sum.

- God didn't give the commandments to control people but to teach them what loving God and loving others looks like.

  Commandments 1–4: love God!

- John 1:17 says, "The law was given through Moses; grace and truth came through Jesus Christ." Jesus didn't say, "Ignore the Old Testament."

  Commandments 5–10: love people!

  Think of the law as a light, telling us to go, be cautious, or to stop. It's there for a reason and is intended to keep us on a good

track. As the only person to ever obey the law perfectly, Jesus fulfilled the law and ushered in the era of grace.

- Because we live in an "era of grace," our hearts desire to be good citizens of God's kingdom, but when we mess up (sin), Jesus never sends us away. Because of Jesus, we're in a forever relationship with God.

WHAT STRUCK YOU IN THIS CHAPTER?

Isn't it strange to think that God would be jealous (Exodus 20:5)? But God would not put up with his beloved sons and daughters building big statues or carving little idols to hold in their hands, worshipping them instead of him. After all, God was the one who had just rescued them from slavery!

You might feel more thankful for your new dance teacher or coach than your parents (even though they paid for those dance lessons or team fees). Maybe you talk on and on about your teacher or coach as if he or she were a superhero or something. At that point, your parents might feel "jealous" for your love, wanting you to remember all they've given you. Your parents deserve the proper respect and want your relationship with them to take priority in your mind and heart—just like the relationship God wanted with the Hebrews!

YOUR FUTURE STORY

What's more challenging for you—loving God with everything in you or loving people? What could you do this week to take a step forward on that front, learning how to love better?

> *I am the LORD your God, who brought you out of the land of Egypt, out of the place of slavery. Do not have other gods besides me.*
> —Exodus 20:2–3

9

Even Superheroes Have Weaknesses
Judges 16

Okay, so fast-forward. Moses led his people through the desert; Joshua led them into the Promised Land. After Joshua died, there was no rightful leader for God's people, who now lived in Canaan. So for the next three hundred years, God directed a number of "judges" (who were actually the ancient equivalent of action heroes) to lead the Israelite people. One of the last judges was Samson. And he was a whacky character!

When Samson was born to childless parents, an angel visited them and told them not to cut his hair. The boy was to be a "Nazirite to God from birth" who would "save Israel from the power of the Philistines" (Judges 13:5).

> No Great Clips haircuts for the Nazirites!

When Samson was older, he was out and about and saw a Philistine girl he thought was cute. He demanded that his parents get her for him as his wife. (Hint: this dude was seriously spoiled and rude.)

One day Samson was heading back to the town of Timnah, where he'd first seen his bride-to-be, and a lion attacked him. But the Spirit of the Lord came upon Samson, and he tore the lion apart with his bare hands (Judges 14:6)! Even weirder was when Samson went back to marry the girl and stopped by to check out the lion's carcass. He discovered that bees had built a hive in the carcass, and he helped himself to some honey (vv. 8–9).

> Eww! Gross! This guy is a hero of the Bible?

Samson used that experience to weave a gambling riddle for the Philistines. They couldn't answer Samson's brainteaser without pestering his new wife, who then pestered the answer out of him. And that's when Samson got really angry and killed thirty men (Judges 14:10–20).

Judges tells us that he killed people, his enemies killed people, and then Samson killed some more. Back and forth it went in a crazy, ongoing bloodbath.

And *then* came the ladies … Samson fell in love with one named Delilah (Judges 16:4). The Philistines offered her a ton of money to find out the source of Samson's strength and trap him. Three times he lied to Delilah about the source of his power. And three times he fended off his attackers. Why would he do such a thing?

> Samson was physically strong but morally a wimp.

He was playing with Delilah. He thought he was so strong, so smart, and so far from the reach of his enemies that lying was a game to him. Still, he stayed with Delilah, who clearly was trying to trap him. She nagged Samson day after day for the truth, and he finally gave it to her. She lulled Samson to sleep, and a man shaved his head. Instantly the Lord left Samson, draining his supernatural strength, and Samson's enemies quickly overpowered him.

The Philistines gouged out Samson's eyes and forced him to work in their prison. But over time his hair began to grow again. And sometime later, during a drunken celebration, the Philistines had Samson brought out of prison to entertain them. Even though Samson couldn't see, he could feel the pillars of the temple—and he could hear the Philistine leaders and thousands of spectators. Samson cried out, "Lord GOD, please remember me. Strengthen me, God, just once more" (Judges 16:28). Suddenly the temple collapsed, killing Samson with all the Philistines.

———————

Wow. I'm worn out after reading that guy's life story, aren't you? But as tempting as it is to get wrapped up in the drama of his life, we need to remember three key things from Samson's story:

1. His strength wasn't really in his hair; it was in his special relationship with God, represented by his vows. As a Nazirite, Samson couldn't touch a dead body, eat grapes or drink their juice or wine, or cut his hair. Our lives will be full of God's power if we keep our commitments to him. Whenever we compromise, weakness will follow.

2. Samson flirted with temptation. He thought he was so smart and powerful that he could test the limits of his vow to God. It's kind of like playing on the edge of a cliff, right? There's something in us that wants to test our boundaries. But when it takes us into territory that God wouldn't approve of, we're teetering on the edge of disaster.

3. While Samson isn't really the kind of spiritual hero we want to look up to, check out Judges 16:28. As his hair began to grow again, Samson began to grow spiritually, perhaps for the first time. He recognized that his strength didn't come from within; it came from God. This is good news for the rest of us who mess up in life and need to start over. We all fail and have to learn hard lessons. The goal is to continue growing and seeking out God's help in becoming better disciples throughout life.

Imagine This ...
Not Invincible After All

My name is Sam. As long as I can remember, I was the strongest guy around. As a child I could lift boulders much bigger than I was. I tossed balls farther than anyone else. Swam farther. Ran faster. I broke every sports record in grade school, high school, and college.

Over and over people would ask me, "What's the source of your strength, Sam? How can others do what you've done?"

I'd laugh under my breath and then make something up. "It's all in how you eat. The right protein-carb balance, you know." Or "I never touch black pepper. People don't realize how it robs them of their true potential."

My mysterious success prompted journalists to trail me to see my colossal abilities for themselves. My nearest competitors in sports hired private investigators to discover my secrets. Later my enemies in business did the same. My empire expanded with my own chain of hair salons and hair products, as well as a vitamin line. My competitors grew more devious, trying anything they could to discover and copy my secrets or bring me down. Some people even attempted to kill me! Someone hired a man to hit me with his car; he did, but I just got up and walked away. Another jealous rival hired a group of thugs to attack me in an alley, but they were no match for me.

I grew pretty tired of these attempts to destroy me, all by the time I was thirty. And I doubted what my parents told me about the source of my strength and talents. Some promise to God about my hair? What? Maybe I was just the strongest man ever born. Maybe God had just created me this way to bless me.

One night I was stretching out on a leather sofa at my girlfriend's apartment ... I have to tell you, I felt pretty blessed. She cuddled up beside me, looking even more beautiful than usual, and stroked my long hair. "Do you love me, Sam?" Delia asked.

"You know I do," I reassured her, pulling her closer.

"Then tell me your secret," she begged. "No more games. Don't toy with me. If you love me and trust me, confide in me, Sam." She fluttered her long lashes and looked deep into my eyes. "Please?" she whispered.

What's the harm? I thought. What might have started as a seed from God had grown into the giant oak of my strength. It was my power to wield as I wished now. "It began with my hair," I said. "All my life I've never cut it."

Delia's beautiful eyes opened wider, and she reached up to run her fingers down the nearest thick braid. "Your hair?"

"My hair," I murmured. I rested my head in her lap, hoping she would massage my scalp and run her hands over my braids some more. That always felt so good and relaxing.

I smiled as she worked her fingers into my scalp. It felt as if she were reading my thoughts. Gradually I closed my eyes, giving in to a little nap. After a long day I was so tired …

I awoke sometime later.

Something was wrong.

Very wrong.

I tried to lift a hand to my head—which felt oddly light and cold—but my arms were bound. And my feet were too.

My worst enemy, business mogul Phil Stine, smiled down at me with arms crossed, nodding with satisfaction.

My heart lurched. Phil? He was here? How'd he get in? Had he hurt Delia?

But then I saw Delia beside him. She was in on this!

My stomach sank. Again I struggled against my bonds. Why couldn't I break the ropes? I'd burst through *chains* before!

"I told you I'd bring you down one day, Sam," Phil boomed, lifting my cut braids in his fist like a trophy. "And that day has arrived."

The Skinny on Judges 16

- Samson was the last of twelve judges in the book of Judges, some better than others. Unique among them were Deborah (one of the few female leaders in a male-dominated society) and Gideon (who put God to the test with a lamb's fleece).

- God's people kept repeating a five-step cycle throughout Judges:

  1. The people would forget about their commitment to the Lord.
  2. God would try to get their attention by allowing a crisis.
  3. The people would call out to God for rescue.
  4. God would take action.
  5. There'd be peace again.

  This happens in our own spiritual lives too, huh? We're not much different from those old Israelites!

WHAT STRUCK YOU IN THIS CHAPTER?

Is there a part of your life that makes you think, *I rock at this*? While God wants us to be aware of our gifting, he wants us to keep humble hearts, remembering that how we were created and all we've become are *thanks to him*. What are you so good at that you have to be careful you don't become cocky?

YOUR FUTURE STORY

Isn't it interesting that Hebrews 11:32 includes Samson in a list of the faithful? It's probably because his life ended well, at least. It's good encouragement for the rest of us when we make mistakes and fall short of all we know God wants us to be. What are three adjectives (descriptive words) you hope people will use to describe you when your life is over? Write them here:

1. _____
_____

2. _____
_____

3. _____
_____

Lord God, *please remember me. Strengthen me, God, just once more.*
—Judges 16:28

10

Why Hard Times Help Us Grow
1 Samuel 17

Most kids don't think about the battles they face, but the fact is, we all face battles in life. It might be a teacher who has something against you or a bully who won't leave you alone in the halls at school. Or parents who argue too much or a kid who is spreading rumors about you. Think about the battle you're facing right now … or if this is a time of peace for you, think about your *last* battle.

Now try this on for size: what you learn in one battle will prepare you for the next one. David is an example of this. By the time he reached the battlefield and saw the monstrously huge Philistine giant shouting out his challenges to God's people, David had already fought off both a lion and a bear while protecting his sheep (1 Samuel 17:34–36).

That's right, David was nothing but a shepherd boy left behind by his older brothers, who were the "mightier" warriors of the family. But in the end, David's experience fighting off threatening animals, as well as his relationship with God, prepared him to take on this new battle on behalf of all the Israelites.

It's important to note how much David relied on God. Yes, David was a seriously buff little dude, strong in his own right, but his relationship with God made him even stronger. David was the first to announce that the Israelites were allowing the unbelieving Philistines to disgrace the Lord and "defy the armies of the living God" (1 Samuel 17:26).

Still, no one really thought David could beat the giant. His jealous brother chastised him (v. 28), King Saul offered David his armor in the hope that it would help (vv. 38–39), and David's enemy Goliath made fun of David (v. 43).

But David didn't waver. He stayed true to his confidence in the Lord and trusted his past experiences to see him through. And he killed the giant!

Imagine This ...
Superbad Odds

During the state basketball play-offs, Dave's team fought their way to the championship game. Definitely the underdogs in nearly every game, they gradually learned the winning plays their coach taught them. Plus, they learned how to respond to their opponents' plays time and again.

But now Dave's team faced the tall, brawny Philly Middle School dudes, who looked like high schoolers! These opponents looked like they drank oil and ate nails for breakfast.

Dave and his teammates circled up with the coach.

"Did you see those guys?" asked Greg, his eyes wide.

"What, are they on steroids?" added Lucas.

"I think they've all been held back a couple grades," Aman chimed in.

"Can we just forfeit right now, Coach?" Kaleb said. "You know, before they pound us into the floor?"

Coach laughed under his breath and then bent down, hands on knees, and looked around at them. "You've fought hard to get here, boys. You've learned some easy lessons and some hard ones, right?"

"Right, Coach," they all voiced together.

"But the point is, you learned those lessons. They'll serve you well when you hit the court. Those guys, big as they are, aren't likely to bring anything new.

They're probably going to play harder and stronger than other teams you've faced. If they get the ball, you'll likely have a hard time getting it back. But if you're smaller, you're—"

"Faster, Coach," the boys shot back almost in unison.

"And if you're faster, you can keep out of their reach, hold on to that ball, and score and score again." He looked into each of their eyes. "Now you might get knocked down a time or two, but do you think I'd send you out there if I really thought you had no chance or were going to get seriously injured?"

 "No, Coach." Dave knew he believed in them. He'd invested in them, taught them well, and he would not leave their side.

"So there it is," he said matter-of-factly, reaching for the ball at his feet and then straightening. "Rely on what you know about me and what I've taught you. Play smart and—trust me—you can do this."

"Yes, Coach!"

That day Dave's team fought hard for every basket, and Coach helped them rise every time they fell. And bit by bit, they pulled ahead. When the last quarter ended, the buzzer ringing loudly around the court, Dave leaped into Coach's arms, shrieking, "We won! We *won!*"

The Skinny on 1 Samuel 17

- As shepherd boy and future king, David is an important person for us to learn about. Scripture covers his life through sixty-six chapters—more chapters than anyone else in the Bible except for Jesus himself.

- HISTORY FACTOID: The Philistines called for a champion to meet theirs, one way to decide a battle without combat (and potentially losing a ton of men). The Philistines were apparently related to the ancient Greeks, who sometimes did the same thing.

- Saul, the king, had some pretty serious issues with an evil spirit (1 Samuel 16:15–16). So by the time he told David to go to battle, Saul wasn't very stable and had to rely on David for the security of the nation.

- David's chief weapons were his staff (once a shepherd, always a shepherd), his sling, some rocks, and the almighty God (1 Samuel 17:45). Meanwhile, David's enemy was decked out in full battle armor and wielded a honkin' big spear.

  > No matter how big and scary the enemy is, our God is BIGGER!

- Later David used Goliath's sword as his own on other battlefields! This is proof that we can use what we learn and gain from today's battles to fight tomorrow's.

WHAT STRUCK YOU IN THIS CHAPTER?

Look at the ceiling in your house. Most homes have eight-foot ceilings. Goliath was about a foot and a half taller! Now pretend you're David. Even though you've faced down a lion and a bear, do you really think you'd be ready to face down an enemy who is that tall, waving a spear (and a javelin and sword too) in front of you?

How could you find the courage you need to face your enemy? What do you know about God and his care for you that could help?

YOUR FUTURE STORY

What battle are you facing today? Or what was the last hard thing you faced? What do you think God wants you to learn from it and remember for the next battle? (You know there will be one!)

You come against me with a sword, spear, and javelin, but I come against you in the name of the LORD of Armies, the God of the ranks of Israel.

—1 Samuel 17:45

GOD IS BIG

11

When You Lost It ... Big-Time
Job 1

Have you ever wondered why bad things happen to good people? Why does God allow children to get cancer? Why doesn't he stop war? Or car accidents?

Think back to the garden of Eden in Genesis 3. Remember how sin came into the picture and how it continues to echo in our own lives today? Even though we desire to please God and be obedient, we all fall short, don't we? We still have the desire to lie, cheat, and steal. We're drawn to gossip, making ourselves look better, or other things we know are wrong. In other words, we're still pretty far from being what God intended.

And yet God has a way of making the most of our circumstances— even bad ones. Romans 8:28 tells us that God can bring good out of everything. Sometimes we might

> It's like squeezing a lemon and getting apple juice!

not see that happen for a week or a month or a year ... or even until we reach heaven. God doesn't wear an Apple Watch or keep an eye on the calendar like we do. He's more about drawing us closer to him than meeting any deadline.

Seeing the good as we trust God is a big lesson we learn from Job. He wondered why people suffer, much like we ask, "Why do bad things happen to good people?" But God never once answered that question. Job asked why God considered him his enemy (Job 13:24; Job 16). He questioned God's fairness (Job 24:1; 27:2). He was angry at God, pleading his case to him (Job 23), but all he got in return was silence.

Only when Job begins to ask, "Who are you, God? Will you be with me through this? Who will deliver me?" does God respond (Job 38–41).

Job learned to want nothing more than to have God walk with him through his suffering. He turned toward the Lord, wanting to know him better and rest in his power, even in the midst of terrible things happening in his life.

Job lost his children, his servants, his livestock (and therefore his wealth), and even his health. But Job's faith got stronger through all this suffering because he put his trust in God. Even though the Lord gave Job more children and doubled his wealth, I'm pretty sure he would've counted his relationship with God as the best blessing of all.

Imagine This ...
Losing Everything

My name's Grayson, and I want to tell you about one of my best friends. Rob was the middle schooler every kid wanted to be. He had everything a guy could want—a great family, a huge house with a home theater, ATVs, a pool—and he got good grades and had a killer jump shot on the basketball court. To top it all off, Rob was the best kid you could ever meet. Seriously.

Other boys would try to get Rob to fight, but he'd just get them laughing over something until they'd all walk away. The popular kids wanted Rob to eat lunch with them in the cafeteria, but he'd sit with the lonely new kid instead. Rob would pick up trash in the hallway at school and lob it into the can as if it was a game, not some sort of good-citizen chore. He even tutored other kids who were behind in math.

It was awesome to count Rob as one of my friends, but somehow I always felt "less than" when I was around him. He seemed almost too good to be true. One day after basketball practice, I asked Rob point-blank, "What's the deal with you? How can you be so happy all the time?"

Rob squinted at me as if my question confused him. Then he threw up his hands and said, "How can I not? God is on my side, man." Clamping me on the shoulder, he added, "Can't you feel him?" Rob's eyes widened, and he spread out his hands. His grin was unforgettable.

"Here? At school?" I asked, wondering if he was out of his mind.

"Yes! Here at school. Outside school. Everywhere. He's here, with us, dude. Walking with us. Living life with us. And that makes me happy every day."

Rob fist-bumped the rest of the basketball team as they disappeared into the locker room. I stood outside, staring, until the door swung shut.

A week later everything changed. My mom told me, through her own tears, that Rob's parents had been killed in a terrible accident. He and his sisters had been put in foster care—but not all in the same home. Then Rob broke out with the worst case of acne I'd ever seen. The dude was covered from his forehead to his chest and across his back. Many of his friends began ignoring him, whispering that he was cursed or something.

But I didn't. After school one day I followed Rob out to the track and underneath the bleachers. He stood there looking out at the sunset.

"You okay, Rob?" I asked.

"No," he said, choking up a little and shaking his head. "No, I'm not."

"Is it your parents?" I dared. "Are you missing them?"

"Yeah, I miss them a ton," he said, tears now falling down his cheeks. He still looked toward the sunset. "My sisters too. And my house ..." He swallowed hard and then glanced at me. "But you know what I miss most? The sense that God always has my back, that he's with me."

"I know," I said.

We hung out there awhile, me thinking I really didn't have a clue how bad it must be for Rob. Every time I thought about all he'd lost, it made me want to cry. But Rob still showed up every day and tried, even if he only smiled a tenth of what he used to.

I wish I could say it got better for Rob. But then we heard that Rob's sisters had run away from their foster homes and the big house had gone into foreclosure. Rob was having migraines and couldn't focus at school, so his grades were going downhill fast.

"Do you think he's abandoned you?" I asked as we walked to Rob's foster home a couple of weeks later.

"God?" he said, glancing my way.

"Yeah, God."

"Nah," he replied, kicking a rock back where it belonged in front of a house we passed. "I'll never think that. Even though I don't feel him anymore, I know he's still there."

"How are you not mad at God, dude?" I scoffed. "Don't you just want to curse him for all he's let happen to you? If he's out there, all-powerful, wouldn't he have helped you somehow by now? I mean, Rob, what's happened to you … I wouldn't wish on my worst enemy." My face flushed with anger. "You're the best person I know. How can God treat you like this?"

Rob looked at me with such despair that I suddenly wanted to cry. Was he finally going to admit it? How sad he was that God had left him, forgotten him, cursed him?

But instead, Rob assured me, "Bud, the only thing I have left is my relationship with God. If I give up on trusting him, no matter how it looks, I've got nothin'."

I stared at him. "Seriously, man. Are you secretly twenty-five? I mean, what kind of middle schooler thinks like that?"

He laughed a little and then stopped, rubbed his face, and let out a groan, a half cry, a half shout. The look he gave me made me think he was older now. "Let's be real. I'm no Captain America. I pray every day that this sad period of my life will end. But no matter what happens tomorrow, I'm gonna trust that God loves me and has something good for me in the future. It's what I've always believed, and it's what gets me through every day."

"I'll keep praying for you every night, Rob," I promised.

"Thanks, dude," he said as we parted in front of his small, run-down house, so different from his former home.

And I wondered, *Would I hold on to my faith like Rob if I lost so much?*

The Skinny on Job

Rob's story was inspired by Job 1–2. (Check it out if you want to go deeper.) Job quite possibly lived during the time of Abraham, meaning his story took place about two thousand years before Jesus. Job is the guy many people think of when it comes to suffering. Here are some other things to know about him:

- Job was blameless, "a man of complete integrity" (Job 1:1). He chose what was good and rejected evil.

- Job knew God and worshipped him, and God rewarded him big-time: ten children, seven thousand sheep and goats, three thousand camels, one thousand oxen, five hundred donkeys, and a ton of servants (vv. 2–3).

  Whoa. The dude was RICH.

- Enter Satan (whose name means "adversary" or "accuser"). Satan said Job would curse God if God took away all of those blessings (vv. 9–11).

- Then Job lost everything—sheep, goats, camels, oxen, donkeys, servants, and worst of all, his kids (vv. 13–19).

> Job's adversary (Satan) is our adversary too. He always wants to pull us away from God by using any method he can!

- What was Job's response? "The LORD gives, and the LORD takes away. Blessed be the name of the LORD" (v. 21).

- Now Job wasn't perfect. He *did* think a lot about why we suffer and asked about suffering many times throughout the book of Job. But check it out: God never answered his question.

- Job finally asked God the right question: "Who are you, God? Will you be with me through all of this?" Which God answered in a very roundabout way, outlining how he's everywhere and has done everything already—so why would Job even ask that! "Where were you when I established the earth?... Who enclosed the sea behind doors ...when I determined its boundaries and put its bars and doors in place?" (Job 38:4, 8, 10). On and on God went, reminding that HE is the creator and Job was still in his hands.

> Our best shelter in a storm is to trust God, no matter what we face.

- God is in the business of establishing a relationship with us through everything we encounter in life. Circumstances change all the time. But God never changes; he is always and forever constant.

WHAT STRUCK YOU IN THIS CHAPTER?

Have you ever suffered a loss? Maybe a parent's job changed, and you had to move. Or maybe someone close to you died. Just like Job, Rob lost pretty much everything—his wealth, his family, his health. If you'd been in their shoes, how do you think you would have handled such losses? Would you have been angry with God? Would you have turned away from him? Or would you have held on to your faith?

YOUR FUTURE STORY

How can you trust God, no matter what he gives or takes away? Can you trust that he loves you and wants nothing more than a deeper relationship with you? Struggle can be a weird sort of gift if it helps you lean on God more. Kind of like going through tough times with a friend or family member. If you lean toward each other rather than away, your relationship ultimately grows stronger.

The LORD gives, and the LORD takes away. Blessed be the name of the LORD.

—Job 1:21

12

A Sheep, a Shepherd, and You
Psalm 23

I once heard a pastor teach about how we're often compared to sheep in the Bible, with Jesus as our shepherd. The best part was when he shared about Jesus being the "gate" for the sheep (John 10:7). In ancient times shepherds would often create stone pens for their sheep, herd them inside for the night, and then lie down across the opening at the end, literally becoming a gate. The shepherds would sleep with their staffs in their arms, ready to defend their sheep with their lives. Isn't that a reassuring image? Our shepherd, Jesus, is ready to do anything to keep us safe.

David—once a shepherd boy, later a giant killer, and now a king—was thinking about that image when he wrote Psalm 23. The psalms were prayers set to music. God's people once sang these psalms, and some still sing them today. But Psalm 23 has long been a favorite because it reminds us of how God provides what we need (v. 1), restores us when we're weak (v. 3), and rescues us when we're in danger (v. 4).

Imagine This ...

Comfort in the Storm

Julia was terrified. She was sixteen and used to hiking by herself. She usually did twelve miles of trail running every other day during the summer. But today she was already at the top of the peak when she saw a massive cloud bank closing in and realized she hadn't listened for a weather report. Miles wide, the thunderstorm had darkened to black at the center, lightning flashing within.

"Oh no," she groaned, running a hand through her sweat-soaked hair. Drinking steadily from her water bottle, Julia heard the first thunder rumble and started gauging how long she had before it was going to pour. The first gust of wind whipped through the tops of the trees below her and then over the peak and beyond. *Not long.*

Julia guzzled another long drink and then turned back to the trail. If she was lucky, she could make it to the cave halfway down the mountain and find some shelter before the worst of the storm swept in. *Help me, Lord*, Julia prayed, quickly picking her way down the rocky path. *Give me strength. And speed.*

Thunderstorms with intense lightning were always a threat on the mountain. Even along the trail, Julia had noticed several dead, blackened trees split down the middle. And this summer had been so dry. The whole forest was a tinderbox.

Making good time down the trail, Julia passed the first mile marker—a pile of stones her dad had set up at her request. The first raindrops fell. Wind blasted the forest, great gusts making her shiver. The rain felt like ice pellets on her skin. The dark clouds turned the early afternoon into an evening sky. She couldn't see well with the wind whipping her face.

Dad is so gonna kill me. On the way down the mountain, Julia realized she'd checked the weather yesterday, when she was supposed to run, but this morning she just pulled on her shoes and ran out the door, figuring the forecast had to be pretty similar for the rest of the week. It had felt the same outside. Looked the same. But this was mountain territory, where the weather could radically change in an hour's time. She knew that. Everyone knew that.

Despite the pelting rain, Julia picked up her pace while watching the path, trying to steer clear of branches and big pinecones falling among the treacherous rocks at her feet. Her shirt clung to her back and chest. Julia blinked constantly, trying to see in the dim light, and rounded the bend that marked two miles from the top. A second later, lightning and thunder exploded nearby. The heart of the storm was closing in …

I'm not going to make it to the cave, she thought. Another bolt of lightning flashed, and thunder cracked so loud it startled her and she tripped.

Julia felt like she was tumbling in slow motion. Her ankle rolled … her hip lurched … her body careened sideways. She slid off the trail between tree branches and over shrubs. Something tore into her right thigh, and the impact of a pointed rock gouged her left calf.

Finally she twisted to a stop on her back, staring up at the trees frantically waving in the storm. Gingerly Julia took stock of her injuries, slowly moving head, shoulders, arms, hips, legs, and then at last her ankle.

She cried out.

Broken. Definitely broken.

Julia shifted her weight to her elbow, trying to see the trail above her, but it was too far away. She'd slid a good twenty feet down through the brush. If her dad had come up after her, he wouldn't see her down here.

"Dad!" she called out, knowing it was too soon. He wouldn't head up until he saw the rain close in and noticed she wasn't home. A crack of thunder drowned out her fearful cry. The downpour pooled in rivulets around her and then passed her in a race down the mountain.

Julia leaned back, face to the sky, weeping. She was so scared.

But somehow her grandma's words came to mind: *"When you're scared, remember your Savior. He is always near. Concentrate on him, and your fears will fade."*

Through her sobs, Julia began to repeat the psalm she learned from Grandma. "The Lord is my shepherd." *He is my guardian, my protector in the storm.* "He lets me lie down in green pastures." Julia laughed at those words and thought, *Or lets me lie on the sides of mountains.* "Even when I go through the darkest valley, I fear no danger." Julia hiccuped on the last word. Her tears were easing; she was gaining strength from the words and the memory that Jesus was near. "For you are with me." *I'm not alone!*

She closed her eyes, counting as each lightning bolt streaked down and the thunder cracked. The booming was still so loud that it seemed to echo in her chest. But by her count, the storm was moving away. The rain no longer pelted her but fell in soft sheets to the earth. In time the sky lightened.

Julia thought about trying to crawl to the trail, but with a few attempts, she knew that wasn't possible. She'd just have to wait for help to come. "Jesus, stay with me," she whispered. And she smiled when she could practically hear him say, "I'm not leaving you." Her rock, her protector, her shepherd. Julia imagined Jesus sitting on the boulder beside her. Keeping watch. An ear cocked toward the path. Waiting with her as minutes turned to an hour.

"Julia!" came a distant shout at last. "Julia!"

"Dad?" she mumbled. Then she screamed his name, her voice echoing down the canyon. "Dad! Help!"

"I'm coming!" he shouted back.

He was on his way. She would be okay.

But in a weird way, just knowing he was near, she already felt okay.

The Skinny on Psalm 23

- David was a politician, a soldier, an administrator, an architect, a shepherd, and a poet.

Sheesh. Was there anything David couldn't do?

- Another famous sheep-and-shepherd image reads, "We all went astray like sheep; we all have turned to our own way; and the LORD has punished him [Jesus] for the iniquity of us all" (Isaiah 53:6). Jesus had to pay the ultimate price as our shepherd because sin constantly leads us astray, like sheep.

We're so pesky, aren't we? Always leaving the path we're supposed to take!

- Why do shepherds have a staff? Because sheep wander into difficult places looking for their next bite of grass. The crook or bend in a staff allows shepherds to snag and assist sheep in tough places!

- So why do shepherds need a rod too? Remember how David said he had to fight off a lion and a bear (1 Samuel 17:34–35)? Shepherds in David's day carried a club (a "rod") to fight off predators.

WHAT STRUCK YOU ABOUT THIS PSALM?

Can you think of a time when you were sick or sad? Or felt physically weak? When have you ever felt scared or worried for your life? Have you ever looked to Jesus for encouragement or support? What did his encouragement and support feel like?

YOUR FUTURE STORY

Next time you're frightened, for whatever reason, call out in prayer and see what happens. Just a simple, *Be with me, Jesus. Be with me, Protector and Savior*, repeated as many times as you need to, might be just what you need to get through a scary situation!

> *Even when I go through the darkest valley, I fear no danger, for you are with me; your rod and your staff—they comfort me.*
>
> —Psalm 23:4

13

Oh No, You Didn't!
Psalm 51

Oh, David, David, David.

Such a strong start! Protecting your sheep! Slaying a giant! Becoming king!

And then … failure.

Our hero—our *HERO*—slept with a woman he knew was married to one of his own soldiers while that man was off to war. When David found out the woman was pregnant, he had her husband killed, making it look like it happened in battle. At that point David was a sheep on a very bad path. God must have been yelling at him, "No! Don't go there! Get down! That's dangerous territory!" But like a lost sheep, David just did what pleased him.

Have your parents warned you about something or told you not to do something, and you did it anyway? That's called *rebellion*, and David talked about it in Psalm 51:1: "Be gracious to me, God, according to your faithful love; according to your abundant compassion, blot out my rebellion."

> Next time you really mess up with your parents, try those words on your knees! "Be gracious to me, Mom!" How could she resist, right?

David was clearly feeling seriously guilty when he wrote Psalm 51. Not only had he sinned, but he'd also done it on purpose! David's mistake didn't just happen. When he finally realized how far he'd wandered from God's best path, David knew he needed to beg for forgiveness.

The good news is that God—like our parents—wants us to be right with him, and he's always ready to welcome us back with open arms. He is all about grace, mercy, and love, no matter what we've done or how far we've wandered away from him. God just wants us back! He doesn't banish us from his kingdom; he restores us. Over and over he restores us.

In fact, our sins have been wiped clean because of our faith in Jesus. He paid the ultimate sacrifice for us, knowing that we would never be sinless in this life. But we still need to try to make the best decisions possible. And God encourages us to confess our sins when we mess up, knowing that he forgives us. Confession and repentance are part of getting our minds and hearts right so that, hopefully, we won't make the same mistakes again! God wants us to become stronger and stronger as disciples, learning from our mistakes as David did.

Imagine This ...

Confessing to Jesus ... in Person

Spend a moment taking some deep, long breaths. Feel your body relaxing. Think of a place you love, a place Jesus might really like too.

Got it in your mind? Think about what you see ... and hear ... and smell.

Now think about Jesus approaching you from a long way off, just a speck in the distance but getting closer and closer. As he comes near, think about what he might look like.

As Jesus gets closer, note that he is looking at you the whole time. What expression or attitude can you see in his eyes as he looks at you, even before he speaks?

Imagine him standing or sitting right beside you, then taking your hand in his. He's saying your name with only love and kindness in his tone.

Is there something you need to tell him? Something you feel terrible about? Something that fills your heart and mind with guilt or anger or sadness?

Find the words to tell him now. "I'm sorry, Jesus. Sorry that I [fill in your own words]." Tell him about everything that weighs on you.

Now think of how he responds. Does he squeeze your hand? Nod in understanding?

Think of him saying, "I'm glad you confessed this burden. I love you. I'm your savior. You don't need to carry this shame or guilt or sorrow any longer. I died so that you might be free!"

Now thank him in prayer. Tell Jesus you love him and that you want to honor him by doing things differently next time. Then imagine him giving you a big hug.

Take a deep breath and let it out slowly.

Amen.

The Skinny on the Psalms

• The 150 psalms can be divided into three groups:

Group I: Intimacy with God
Group II: Distance from God
Group III: Getting Back Together with God

Our walk with God can feel the same way. Sometimes we feel like he's in our house (intimacy), and sometimes it's as if he's on the moon (distance), right? But he always wants to be close to us (together).

• Sin hurts us and those around us. It's like we're broken. We need to face it and confess it to be the healthiest we can be and live in peace with those around us. This is one of the first steps we take in God's "repair and restoration plan."

- *Repentance* is a big word for "I'm sorry." But we have to *be* genuinely sorry, not just say that we are. We need to ask God to help us make plans to act differently

  David didn't want to be a spiritual wimp! Neither do we!

  next time so we don't end up in the same place again. That's what David was talking about in Psalm 51:10 when he asked God for a "steadfast spirit."

- Seven psalms focus on forgiveness: Psalms 6, 32, 38, 51, 102, 130, and 143. Clearly we're not alone in needing to ask God to forgive us for the ways we fail him and others. We all need Jesus, and turning to him in repentance is a holy habit we all need to develop.

- Sin forms a sort of dam in the river of our relationship with God. When we confess our shortcomings, we find release and relief! And God's life-giving power flows back into us.

WHAT STRUCK YOU ABOUT THIS PSALM?

What's the worst thing you ever did? Did you have to ask God or a person—or both—for forgiveness? Or do you still need to?

YOUR FUTURE STORY

We all need people to call us out if we're acting in a way they know isn't right. Next time a parent, teacher, or friend calls you out, try not to be defensive. Shove aside that pride (something that's hard for all of us to do)! Decide it's going to make you a stronger person and follower of Jesus, and accept the course correction. It might save you a world of hurt (and an even bigger apology) down the road.

God, create a clean heart for me and renew a steadfast spirit within me.
—Psalm 51:10

14

God Is Closer Than You Think
Psalm 139

Isn't it strange how moms and dads seem to literally have eyes in the backs of their heads? You might be sneaking a cookie from the jar—totally silent—and your dad will yell (from upstairs!), "Hey, no cookies before dinner!" Or you might be checking Instagram, and your mom will peek around the corner and say, "No more screen time this afternoon." You think, *How do they know I'm doing something when they can't even see me?*

The cool thing about listening to David in Psalm 139 is that he was inviting God to examine not only his life (like your dad or mom might do with your choices) but also his soul. David stands out in the Scriptures for the way he laid his life—and heart—so bare.

Now the fact is that God knows everything about us, including everything we've ever thought or felt or said or done. I don't know why we think we can hide from him! Back in the garden when Adam and Eve were hiding from God, he called out, "Where are you?" He knew exactly where they were, but he was probably feeling the separation between his heart and the hearts of his children. He felt the rift between himself, as creator, and his precious creations.

Instead of hiding from God, David reached out for his Creator, pouring out his heart in worship. You can almost see him on his knees before an altar, spreading his arms wide, his face turned upward in wonder and prayer. "LORD, you have searched me and known me. You know when I sit down and when I stand up; you understand my thoughts from far away.… Before a word is on my tongue, you know all about it, LORD. You have encircled me; you have placed your hand on me. This wondrous knowledge is beyond me" (Psalm 139:1–2, 4–6).

Beyond me. Meaning, "I can't figure this out, no matter how hard I try." Remember King David in Psalm 51 when he was confessing to God all those evil things he'd done? Here in Psalm 139, David had come to the end of himself and was casting himself at the feet of the Almighty.

> It's as if this earthly king was staring upward in total awe at his heavenly King.

In this psalm David sang in wonder and praise about how God is all-knowing (vv. 1–6), always present (vv. 7–12), and all-seeing (vv. 13–16). And yet it isn't like he was saying that God is some sort of creepy stalker! By inviting God closer, David showed he totally trusted God and wanted to give him 100 percent access: "Search me, God, and know my heart; test me and know my concerns. See if there is any offensive way in me; lead me in the everlasting way" (vv. 23–24).

Clearly King David had turned a good corner and found himself where we would all most benefit from sitting … face-to-face with our King.

Imagine This …
God Is Everywhere

It'd been a long day for Layla. Swim practice before the sun rose, school, and then a long walk home. Mom dropped her at practice in the mornings after her night shift. Afternoons, Layla had to get herself home. Her dad hadn't been a part of the picture for years.

But Layla couldn't wait for swim practice in the morning.

The next day she was up and had mixed her protein shake before Mom even arrived home. They drove to practice in silence. Layla's mind was on other things—a thousand other things. And there was only one thing she wanted to do.

In the locker room, she pulled off her sweats and slipped on her cap and goggles. She uttered "Hey!" to her teammates as she shuffled out to the pool. A shiver of morning breeze set the water rippling in ribbons of silver and blue.

She stepped up on the diving platform, stretched, and took her position. *Good morning, Father*, she prayed silently. *I need to talk to you.*

Coach called, "Three, two, one, go!" He sounded grumpy, like he needed more coffee.

Layla dove into the water, her body reacting to the cold but her heart welcoming the familiar space.

In the pool she could talk to God better than anywhere else.

She needed to talk to him about her *frustrations* … There was never enough money for Mom and her. They'd eaten hot dogs for dinner six out of seven days over the past week. *I'm grateful, sure, Lord, but I'd really like something else.*

About her *fears* … *What if I place in the next race? Mom can't afford to send me to the next meet.* Layla knew that. Coach did too. What was the point? Why work this hard if she couldn't go as far as she could? *Lord, give me the trust I just don't have.*

About her *hopes* … Nichole was so sweet in art class. During ceramics she didn't even laugh at Layla's lame attempt at a coil pot. Every day Nichole said hello, but Layla could barely say hi back. *Lord, give me the courage to reach out to her as a new friend.*

About things she needed to apologize for … Layla just hadn't stepped up this week. She knew she'd missed the chance to help out that kid in pre-algebra who was crashing and burning. That stuff was easy for her.

And she'd resisted giving that homeless woman the last buck she had in her pocket, thinking, *I need it more than you do.* She'd skipped out on youth group, and yesterday she'd stubbornly ignored God during her swim-prayer time. She'd been mad at him.

Mad at God.

The one who walked with her every day, for better or worse.

Lord, I'm sorry. Search me. Help me. Remake me. I want to be yours. But sometimes I'm just so lame at it. I try. I know you see me trying. Help me to be more like you. And rest in you. I know you love me. Help me rest in that.

She knew God loved her. Life was hard, sure. But she had a roof. A mom. A swim team. A school. Clothes—not many, but enough. And with him, it was all enough.

Lord, I praise you. You are my God, the one who brought me into this life, and the one who will welcome me into the next. Make me stronger. Make me more like your Son. Search me, know me, show me. And let me rest in the grace of your unfailing love.

Amen, she prayed, turning her head above the water so she could take a long-awaited breath. *Amen and amen.*

The Skinny on Psalm 139

- We don't have to fear God's ability to know everything about us … if we trust that he loves us and wants the best for us.

- The book of Psalms contains 150 different prayers. For centuries, monks have gathered in their communities for morning prayer. Tradition holds that the first prayer of the day is Psalm 70:1: "God, hurry to rescue me. LORD, hurry to help me!" What a wonderful prayer with which to meet each morning!

- Sometimes we feel distant from God because of our sins. Confession (saying we're sorry for our sins) and praise (loving God in prayer or singing) are two good ways to narrow any gap you feel between you and the One who adores you.

- COOL FACTOID: Psalm 139:21–22 is kind of unusual, huh? What's with all the talk of hating God's enemies? It was actually common in David's time for those who served a king to say an oath like this. David was just doing the same for his King.

WHAT STRUCK YOU ABOUT THIS PSALM?

Are you comfortable with the idea that God knows and sees everything about you? Why or why not?

YOUR FUTURE STORY

Is there a part of your life, heart, or mind that you think you can keep from God or manage on your own? Why not admit that he knows about it too?

Search me, God, and know my heart; test me and know my concerns.

See if there is any offensive way in me; lead me in the everlasting way.

—Psalm 139:23–24

15

Live Smart
Proverbs 1

Let's say you're a new pilot who doesn't totally know how to use the instruments in the cockpit of a single-engine plane. You've gotten pretty good at taking off and holding your own in the air. But now a bad storm is starting to close in. The clouds are so thick that you can't see more than ten feet ahead of you, or anything below. Do you know how long you would keep flying before you crashed?

Minutes.

That's right, minutes. Even experienced pilots crash if they rely on their intuition rather than their instruments to figure out where they think the ground should be and whether their wings are level.

Think of the book of Proverbs as God's instruments, the way to help you grow wiser. We can always learn more about the right way to live better and smarter, as well as discover more about our God. The book of Proverbs is a good place to begin.

Imagine This ...

Living Smarter

Malik had seen it all in his fourteen years. He lost his parents and sisters after militants swept through his country. Hunted by an enemy who wanted him in their army of boys, he fled Africa and ended up in the United States, living in foster home after foster home. A rising soccer star, he never stayed in a home long enough to get to know his coach or teammates, and soon he stopped playing. He spent every afternoon and evening at the mall now, desperate to stay out from under his current parole officer's nose, hoping he wouldn't get in trouble and get kicked out of his foster home. He was at the last stop in the foster-home line; next was the juvenile detention center.

Mike and Jareel, also regulars at the mall, caught his eye as he entered the central plaza; they lifted their chins in welcome. They wore their jeans low on their hips, as he did. But before he could step toward them, Braelin faced off with him, arms crossed.

She wasn't exactly pretty. But there was something about the way she moved, the way she held herself, the way she spoke that always caught him off guard. "Hey, Brae," he said, smiling a little at the rhyme.

"Hey, Malik," she returned. "Where were you today?"

"Uh, I wasn't feeling so hot. I stayed home."

"Home, huh?" Her dark brown eyes searched his. Then she flipped her dyed blonde hair over her slim shoulder. "I could've used your help, *partner.*"

Partner.

Malik groaned inside. They'd been assigned as lab partners in science. He'd totally forgotten today was a lab when he decided to skip school.

"I'm sorry, Braelin," he said. "I should've been there."

"Yeah, you should have," she said. She glanced over her shoulder at Mike and Jareel, who were headed their way. "The way I see it," she said, leaning toward Malik, "you have to make some choices. Get your act together, go to school and complete your assignments, find better friends, and be glad that a family like the Johnsons would take you in. Get on the soccer team. You want that, right? Well, you have to go to school all the time to get on the team."

Malik shifted, feeling agitated. Her words made him angry. But he couldn't deny that she spoke truth.

"Or else keep skipping school and hanging out with guys like this," she went on, hooking a thumb at the guys just behind her, "and you'll sign your own ticket out of town."

She squinted up at Malik, totally ignoring Mike and Jareel, who now stood on either side of her, looking her up and down and making rude comments. "You're smart, Malik Abdulai," she said, tapping him on the chest with her finger. "I just wish you would act like it."

The Skinny on Proverbs

- You can find Psalms in the center of the Bible. Proverbs follows right after Psalms.

- FACTOID: The word *wisdom* appears more than two hundred times in the Bible. Many of those are in Proverbs!

- What's easier? Learning from someone else's mistakes or our own? Mistakes often lead to pain and regret and can hurt us and others around us. Proverbs outlines the mistakes people make and points the way to wiser decisions.

> Well, duh. Who wants to make mistakes? See? You're living smarter already!

- Proverbs 1 also points to discipline, which means practicing what you've learned. If you go to bed on time, you'll be less tired in the morning and better able to learn in school, right? Getting to bed every night on time is an act of discipline.

- The other thing Proverbs 1 points to is insight—seeing things as they truly are, not as they might appear. If you look at an X-ray, you'll mostly see blobs of white against black, right? But your doctor, after years of training and experience, can pick up details that reveal an illness or health issue. Like that experienced doctor, we all want to become insightful people in as many areas of life as possible.

WHAT STRUCK YOU IN THIS CHAPTER?

How are your best friends encouraging you to be a wiser person? Or are they leading you away from good things? Deciding whether to hang with your current friends or find new ones is like going through a maze of decisions. And it's something wise followers of God learn to figure out fast!

YOUR FUTURE STORY

How can you seek out God's wisdom day to day? Hanging out with other believers? Reading the book of Proverbs? Asking a mentor (someone who is further along the faith path than you) about something you're wrestling with?

> *The fear of the LORD is the beginning of knowledge;*
> *fools despise wisdom and discipline.*
> —Proverbs 1:7

TOUGH LOVE, TROUBLED TIMES

16

Jesus Unmasked
Isaiah 53

This passage in Isaiah gets a lot of attention because it was written about seven hundred years before Jesus was born and it pretty much reads as a totally on-point biography of the Savior to come. Isaiah doesn't focus on Jesus's every-man looks but more on his heroic actions.

Jesus's crucifixion—"He was pierced because of our rebellion, crushed because of our iniquities; punishment for our peace was on him, and we are healed by his wounds" (Isaiah 53:5). This verse has Jesus written all over it, doesn't it?

Our need for Jesus's sacrifice—"We all went astray like sheep; we all have turned to our own way; and the LORD has punished him for the iniquity of us all" (v. 6). *All of us.* Those people in Isaiah's time about 2,700 years ago and all of us today. You. Me.

Jesus's burial—"He was assigned a grave with the wicked, but he was with a rich man at his death" (v. 9). Exactly as it went down for Jesus—he was crucified between two criminals and buried in a rich man's tomb.

Jesus's resurrection—"After his anguish, he will see light and be satisfied" (v. 11). In other words, Jesus knew he would conquer death and once again return to heaven. Jesus is not only a memory; his presence is a reality even today.

Two things are interesting about Isaiah's prophecy: (1) God wasn't making things up as he went along. The fact that Jesus came to earth and will come again is all part of God's long-term plan to bring us closer to him. (2) God exists outside our own sense of time; he had no beginning, and he has no end. In order to share this vision with Isaiah, God had to show him what was coming, some seven hundred years before it happened.

Imagine This ...
Glimpsing Jesus in a Vision

Chloe was pretty tired as she walked into the massive old church in Milan, Italy. It was about the hundredth church they'd been in on this trip. The family's month-long tour of Europe seemed to require touring at least ten churches in every city they visited.

At least it's cooler in here, she thought. She blinked, waiting for her eyes to get used to the dim light after the bright summer sunshine outside.

Her big brother brushed by her. "C'mon," he grunted. "Let's get this over with."

They joined the line of about a hundred people, all shuffling forward an inch at a time. What was the deal with this place anyway? Some Shroud of Turin? A big old cloth that supposedly covered Jesus's face after he died?

Yeah, right ...

Chloe thought it'd be way better to head back to the hotel and check out the tiny pool. It was so hot!

Using her church brochure as a fan, she forced herself to smile back at her mom when she looked over her shoulder, eyebrow raised.

A group of Greek tourists in front of them—most at least as old as Chloe's grandma—huddled together, whispering excitedly. They were extremely short; she'd passed them up in height in sixth grade. But that wasn't what made her stare at them. It was their hushed reverence, as if they were in the presence of something holy.

Huh?

The line snaked forward, sometimes hanging there a long time, sometimes jumping forward yards at a time.

Suddenly Chloe's family was in front of the exhibit. A cloth encased in glass was placed above a rather simple altar.

Chloe paused to look at the old linen, wondering if she really could see a face. And then she spotted it: the U shape of a hairline, the spooky eye sockets, the darker shades of a nose, mustache, beard. It was the image of a man long dead.

Chloe sucked in a breath.

She'd studied photography last summer, and it struck her that what she was seeing was a negative. And in her mind's eye, she could see the positive. Yet it wasn't just a positive—a regular photo image. It was more like a 3-D sculpture.

Chloe forced herself to take another breath, and then another. Because now it wasn't just a sculpture before her. It was a full-on living, breathing form of a man.

Sitting up. Rising before her.

"Jesus," Chloe breathed. She fell to her knees.

The man turned to her, eyes so full of love that she started to tear up as he took her hands. Had anyone ever looked at her that way? Even her parents? With such total acceptance? The look in his eyes said, "I see you, Chloe. You are mine. I claim you. I died to save you, and I love you—no matter what you've done."

"Chloe?" her brother said, sounding a little embarrassed. "You okay? C'mon, we have to go."

Chloe looked up at him, blinking, trying to remember where she was and why she was here. Then she gazed back at the shroud, feeling a desperate pang of loss.

Once again it was nothing but a flat piece of tattered, ancient fabric with the dim outline of a face.

The Skinny on Isaiah 53

- Isaiah was one of the biggie prophets, or Major Prophets, as Bible scholars call them—along with Jeremiah, Ezekiel, and Daniel.

Hopefully the MINOR prophets didn't feel bad about not making it to the MAJOR leagues!

- FUN FACTOID: Isaiah's name means "The Lord is salvation." That's a perfect name for a guy who was given so much to tell his people— and us—about God's judgment and salvation!

- The whole book of Isaiah is pretty readable. The dude knew how to use beautiful elements of poetry that sound like songs, as well as personification—giving human attributes to elements of creation (Isaiah 24:23; 35:1)—and even a bit of sarcasm at times (44:9–20).

WHAT STRUCK YOU IN THIS CHAPTER?

Why do you think God revealed who Jesus would be and what he would do seven hundred years before he was born? When Scripture prophesies something fantastic and it actually happens, what does that tell us about Scripture?

YOUR FUTURE STORY

Isaiah's gift was prophecy. Do you know what your own gifting might be based on Romans 12:6–8? Do you think God has uniquely gifted you with (*check all that apply!*)

❑ the gift of prophecy, speaking the truth to people, even if it's hard?
❑ the gift of service, assisting others?
❑ the gift of teaching, helping others learn?
❑ the gift of exhorting, encouraging others?
❑ the gift of giving, living generously?
❑ the gift of leading, directing others well?
❑ the gift of showing mercy, showing kindness to those in need?

Just as God knew what was to come for Jesus, he knows what's ahead for you. As a kid, you might not feel like you're living up to your gifting yet, but God can see you as an adult, using that gift for his glory! He has a plan for his people—including sending his Son to save us. And he has a plan for each of us. That's why we have to pay attention to how he's leading and encouraging us!

We all went astray like sheep; we all have turned to our own way;
and the LORD has punished him for the iniquity of us all.

—Isaiah 53:6

17

Not Me!

Jeremiah 1

It would have been rough being our boy Jeremiah. After David's son King Solomon died, Israel divided into the southern kingdom, known as Judah, and the northern kingdom, known as Israel. (I know—confusing!) The two nations coexisted in an uneasy truce for just over two hundred years until their bad-boy neighbor, Assyria, conquered Israel.

> It'd be kind of like if the USA was divided between north and south, and Canada conquered the north. And then Greenland conquered Canada and had its eyes on the southern USA next.

Then about a century later, Assyria was conquered by its neighbor Babylon. Suddenly Babylon was the biggest, roughest bully on the block and clearly wanted to eat up Judah, Jeremiah's country, too.

Now it was obviously tough in that era on the outside political front. But things weren't awesome on the inside either. Jeremiah took his people to task for their unfaithfulness to God and for worshipping other gods, which—*warning: it's gory*—even included sacrificing their children on the altars of those false gods (Jeremiah 7:30–31). Two of the kings during Jeremiah's lifetime reigned only three months before invaders threw them in prison and set another king in their place.

Getting the picture? It was a highly dangerous time to draw attention to yourself. And Jeremiah was about to draw a lot of attention. God commanded him to speak out against his people's sins and to prophesy of coming conquerors and losses. God instructed Jeremiah to tell his people to submit to the Babylonians—their hated enemy—and not rebel against them, so many Israelites saw him as a traitor. He also prophesied Judah's impending doom, judgment, and punishment. After godly King Josiah died, there wasn't a priest, prophet, or politician who liked our boy Jeremiah for long.

I don't know about you, but if I'd lived during Jeremiah's time, I probably would have avoided him at the lunch table. I might have avoided everyone! But the thing is, God sometimes asks us to speak out in ways that might make us unpopular or even put our lives at risk. We God followers are supposed to be known for our faithful ways, following through on what we believe and living like we believe it.

Sometimes we might feel overwhelmed and like we're not ready to do what God asks us to do. Jeremiah himself protested that he was too young (Jeremiah 1:6). He wasn't alone in trying to talk God out of calling him to do something—we see similar responses from Gideon (Judges 6:15), Moses (Exodus 3:11), and Mary (Luke 1:34). We all have that in common: None of us feel quite ready to serve God in the way he deserves. None of us are perfect. None of us are mature enough, dedicated enough, talented enough, or smart enough. But God somehow fills the gap. If he asks us to do something, we're to be obedient to follow through and trust him with the outcome.

Jeremiah saw many of his prophecies fulfilled during his lifetime. Some happened after he died. But by doing what God asked him to do, when God asked him to do it, Jeremiah became one of our true heroes of the faith.

Imagine This ...
If You Were Friends with an Old Testament Prophet

Jerry stepped up on the plastic bench of the lunch table and then onto the metal top. Everyone at the table stopped eating and talking and looked up at him. Gradually everyone around them did too.

"Oh man," whispered Joaquin, sitting beside Caden. "Not again!" They'd given Jerry the benefit of the doubt, trying to be nice and stuff, and even let him sit with them again during Team 3's lunch period, but now he was about to make things tough again. They could all see it on his face. He looked miserable and yet determined.

"You! Siena!" Jerry called, pointing to the most popular girl in school. "You go to our church, but you haven't been honest. You've been lying to others and spreading rumors! The Lord warns you to stop!"

"Jerry!" Caden whispered, horrified, as Siena's pretty face squinched up in rage. "What are you doing? We talked about this!"

But Jerry ignored him, as usual, and turned instead toward Seth, a big hulk of a kid. Seth had swiped Caden's skateboard from his yard last summer, but there was no way Caden was going to take issue with it. Every day Seth wandered past the lunch benches, lifting Twinkies, sandwiches—anything he thought looked good. But everyone knew that calling him out would mean death. *Death!*

"You, Seth!" Jerry called, pointing again. "You lead the athletes' Bible study, but you know you've stolen what isn't yours! You must return it and apologize!"

Seth rose slowly, fists clenched. From the corner of the room, the teacher assigned lunch duty was finally on the move.

"Jer!"

But he had turned toward Colin, a kid who did drugs and wore a huge pentagram necklace. Colin used to go to their youth group but hadn't come in over a year. He was sitting beside his girlfriend, Darissa, who said she was a Wiccan, or a witch. They sat with four other kids, all wearing shades of gray and black.

"Oh no," Joaquin groaned.

"And you, Colin," Jerry called, horror in his eyes as he looked from the Goth to his friends. "You are far from your Creator. So far! Return to the God who loves you. Worship him as you've been called to do! As we've all been called to do!"

"All right, all right," Mrs. Thompson said, clamping down on Jerry's arm and hauling him down from the table. "That's enough of that. To the principal's office with you."

The Skinny on Jeremiah

- TRIVIA FACTOID: Jeremiah is the longest book in the Bible, if you go by the number of words in the language in which it was written—Hebrew.

- Jeremiah was once King Josiah's friend, but none of Josiah's sons liked him much. So, while Jeremiah probably wandered the palace as a welcome guest at one time, much of his later life was spent in and out of prisons.

  > Bummer for him!

- Life was so bad during Jeremiah's day that God commanded him not to marry or have children because terrible things were coming for Judah's next generation (Jeremiah 16:1–4).

- Jeremiah was asked to call out kings, prophets, and common people alike (Jeremiah 21–24).

  > Whew! That's a lot of speaking out …

- Jeremiah was also commanded to prophesy about God's promise to restore the people of both Israel and Judah in time (Jeremiah 30–33).

WHAT STRUCK YOU IN THIS CHAPTER?

How comfortable are you speaking out when you see someone doing something wrong? What makes you speak out? Or why do you keep silent?

YOUR FUTURE STORY

These days God seldom asks his people to shout out his truths from rooftops and street corners, like the biblical Jeremiah—or our fictional, modern-day "Jerry" in the story above—did. But he *does* ask us to represent Christ so that we are visible reminders to others to turn to the Lord and follow his ways. Are you a living example of a faithful son or daughter? What do you need to do differently to better mirror Jesus?

I chose you before I formed you in the womb;
I set you apart before you were born.
I appointed you a prophet to the nations.

—Jeremiah 1:5

18

Whose Side Is God On?
Daniel 3

About the time things got bad for the prophet Jeremiah, Babylon's ruler, King Nebuchadnezzar (what a name, huh?) invaded Judah. The nation was forced to submit to Babylon, and the invaders carried off some articles from Jerusalem's temple and put them in their own pagan temple in Babylon. Old Neb made it even worse when he forced some of Judah's finest youth—specifically those who were nobles, smart, and handsome—to return with them to Babylon.

Among that popular-kids group were Daniel, Shadrach, Meshach, and Abednego. All four of them soon stood out among the rest of the young men. Daniel could interpret dreams and visions, which was handy, because King Neb seemed to have a lot of dreams and visions that puzzled him. All four served in the king's court, and whenever the king turned to them for counsel, he was greatly impressed with them (Daniel 1:20). This must've made lots of others mad as our four Hebrew boys gained more and more status, especially when Shadrach, Meshach, and Abednego became managers of the province of Babylon. Daniel remained right at King Neb's side, and the king even said, "Your God is indeed God of gods, Lord of kings, and a revealer of mysteries" (2:47).

Wait a sec! A Babylonian king—Nebuchadnezzar, the very one who pillaged the temple of the Holy One in Jerusalem—was now expressing awe for the Israelites' God?

Yup, that king. Well, Babylonian movers and shakers soon figured out how to get old Neb to turn against three of our Fabulous Four. Neb had a pretty famous temper (he murdered the king of Judah's sons in front of him before blinding the man), and he was pretty full of himself. After all, he'd just had a ninety-foot gold-plated statue—probably representing Nebuchadnezzar's favorite "god" Nabu—put up on a hill for all to worship. He'd also announced that anyone who didn't fall down and worship the statue would be thrown into a fiery furnace.

> Ninety feet high! That's as tall as a nine-story building!

Our boys' Babylonian enemies had found their opportunity. They knew that these devout Jews wouldn't worship anything or anyone besides their God. So they pointed them out to the king. And when old Neb found out, he was *really* mad and followed through on his threat, doubting their God was any match for his own power (Daniel 3:13–23).

As you might have read in a Bible storybook, the three Hebrew boys faced that fire without flinching. They said, "If the God we serve exists, then he can rescue us from the furnace of blazing fire, and he can rescue us

> Yeah, this was the same dude who'd expressed awe for the God of Israel after Daniel interpreted his dream. Let's just say King Neb's belief in the one true God didn't last long.

from the power of you, the king. But even if he does not rescue us, we want you as king to know that we will not serve your gods or worship the gold statue you set up" (Daniel 3:17–18). And they did not go alone; a mysterious fourth person joined them in that furnace. When old Neb saw him, he called for them all to come out, but only three emerged, as cool and calm as if they stepped out of an air-conditioned condo. And again, Neb gave praise to their God and promised to punish anyone who spoke against him (vv. 28–29).

What we want to take away from their story is this: the boys didn't assume that because God was on their side, he would automatically save them. They were determined to live as God had told them rather than obey a human ruler. They were dedicated to serving God over man, even if it meant dying for it.

Remember, Jeremiah urged the people of Judah to submit and not rebel against the Babylonians. He knew that someday Judah would be restored. He didn't want his people to physically rebel, but he would have cheered these guys on as they faced the furnace for refusing to worship anything but God. Jeremiah, Daniel, Shadrach, Meshach, and Abednego all knew what they must do … as do we. There is one King, and we must always serve him first, no matter the stakes.

Imagine This …
Facing a Different Kind of Fire

Dad had been in the lead for miles when he paused on the trail and looked back at them. "Do you smell smoke?"

Mom sniffed. Sophie did too, of course. "Yeah," they said together.

Sophie's little sisters set to sniffing like basset hounds, while Mom, Dad, and Sophie took a slow look around. So deep in the trees, they couldn't see where the smell was coming from.

Dad shrugged and set off again. "Best we get to the chalet. We're too deep in to go anywhere else. We'll find out more there."

But as they continued to hike, the wind picked up, hot and dry. Sophie was sweating like a pig when they finally emerged from the trees onto a rocky trail that gave them a panoramic view of the remote Montana valley. To their left was a glacier, with dirty white snow that somehow clung to a jagged mountain peak. To their right was a steep drop-off to the valley floor. At the bottom was a rushing river, tiny in the distance.

Not far from them a column of smoke billowed in a black swirl. As they watched, a plane soared overhead, and six people tumbled out, hurtling downward for a moment before pulling their chutes. They directed themselves down and disappeared among the trees, directly above the fire.

"Cool!" Lily said.

"There you go," Dad said, pumping a fist in the air. "Smoke jumpers! Maybe those guys can stomp out that fire so we're not breathing smoke all night at the chalet."

He set off again, but Mom hesitated. "Wait, Steve. Maybe ... maybe we should sit this out here in the open. If the fire gets close, we can always take refuge up there under the lip of the glacier."

Dad frowned, glanced at his watch, and then pulled out his phone with the trail app and GPS. "We're only a couple miles away, hon," he said.

"Yes, but it's a couple of miles through that forest up there," she replied and then glanced down the valley toward the fire.

"Ahh, we'll be through it before it's even close," he said.

"Likely, yes. But wouldn't rangers find it easier to evacuate us here, if necessary?"

"Evacuate?" Mia shrieked. "We're gonna get evacuated?"

Mom lifted her hands, trying to shush Mia as she listened to Dad.

"Let's get to the chalet," Dad said, already turning back to the trail. "They'll have a landing pad for a chopper, if it comes to that. And if it doesn't, as it likely won't, we're not out the seven hundred bucks for the two rooms."

Mom hesitated a moment more and then set out after him. Sophie's sisters followed, and she brought up the rear. Dad started ringing his bear bell as they entered the forest again, and for the first time, Sophie was actually glad for the threat of grizzly bears to get her mind off the fire.

The little girls were silent, and Sophie was proud of how fast they were moving. Before she knew it, Dad announced they were only a mile away. "We've got this, ladies! We'll have lemonade at the chalet within the hour!" But when he turned back to the trail, he saw a fallen log too late, caught his toe, and tumbled over. Sophie prayed that the sickening crack she'd heard was the wood, but a second later, with one glimpse of his face, she knew it wasn't. It was his leg. The broken bone pressed so close to the skin, it was almost poking through.

They all circled around him, and Mom did her best to make him comfortable. "At least you're not bleeding," Lily said.

"There's that," Dad said through gritted teeth. The veins in his neck stuck out. It was clear he was in a ton of pain. "I'll have to stay here. You girls get to the chalet and send back help."

Mom rose and looked to the trees. Smoke was billowing through them now. Sophie thought she heard the crackle and pop of the fire but told herself it was just her imagination.

"We can't leave you here," Mom said, wringing her hands.

"You can, and you will," Dad said firmly, swallowing hard. "Go, Denise. Take the girls and get them to safety. Then send someone back for me. They'll have a stretcher up there, I bet. Maybe even a ranger or two. But let's not waste any more time debating."

"We can't leave you, Steve. Not alone. With an injury like that, you could go into shock."

"I'll run ahead," Sophie said, shrugging off her pack. "Without the weight, and alone, I'll get to the chalet in what, ten or fifteen minutes?"

She looked to Dad and he nodded, sweat dripping down his temples to his neck. "Stick to the trail, sweetheart. Keep yelling so you don't surprise a bear. Got it?"

Sophie didn't wait for Mom's agreement. She just took off, feeling like this was a race for their lives. And maybe it was.

But the smoke got so thick and the heat so intense that she couldn't keep up her pace for long. She choked on every breath, even with her mouth and nose under the hem of her T-shirt neckline. Her irritated eyes watered so much that she had a hard time seeing the trail. She slowed and blinked, and with a sinking heart, she knew she'd missed a Y in the trail at some point.

What was before her was nothing more than a deer trail that disappeared into the forest. She looked backward. How long ago had she missed the turn?

"Mom!" she shouted. "Mom!"

But only the wind and roar of the approaching fire greeted her. She knew she couldn't just go forward—she might get more lost. She had to go back and find the trail. As she stumbled along, desperately trying to see, she could hear the fire approach. Giant billows seemed to blow the fire along the valley floor, sending it roaring upward.

"Lord God," Sophie prayed through her tears, "be with me! Help us!"

She'd just reached the trail again when she felt a new surge of heat and turned to see a wall of flame. It was coming fast, licking up the trunk of every towering tree before her, crowning the tops, threatening to overtake her.

"Oh, God! God! Where are you?"

Sophie had no choice. She had to leave the trail and run uphill. She was just about to do that when a stern voice shouted, "Wait! Stop right there!"

Sophie glanced over her shoulder, half relieved to not be alone and half in terror to pause even for a second.

A firefighter, dressed in yellow and wearing a helmet, ran up the hill toward her, a silver blanket streaming behind him like a cape. The flames were so close now that she felt the heat burning her skin. The man, panting and gasping for breath, flicked the silver blanket in the wind, and it became a tent. "In! Get in!" he cried. "Tuck in all the edges and pray!"

Sophie did as he told her, instantly aware of her relief over the fire-proof tent. And then she prayed … for Mom and Dad, for her sisters. For herself.

The fire blew through terribly fast. She passed out at some point and awoke coughing. But she could hear people yelling her name.

"I'm here!" Sophie yelled. "I'm here! Over here!"

And then they were there. More firefighters helping her up, assuring her that her family was fine. They were all up at the chalet waiting for her. Sophie wept then, looking at the soot-covered, sweat-streaked faces of the six smoke jumpers that she'd seen tumble from the plane.

But the one who had rescued her wasn't there.

"W-where is the other guy?" Sophie asked the six of them. "The guy who saved me and gave me this tent?"

They all looked at one another and then back to Sophie. "There is no other guy," the leader said. "Just the six of us."

The Skinny on Daniel

- Once Daniel and his friends got to Babylon, they were given new names:

Daniel = Belteshazzar
Hananiah = Shadrach
Mishael = Meshach
Azariah = Abednego

What do you think they would've turned YOUR name into?

- What's up with that mysterious fourth man in the fire? Some think it was an angel; others think it was Jesus. The Bible doesn't explain the mystery.

- God is always near when we face our own "fires." We can be courageous and confident, knowing that we're never alone.

WHAT STRUCK YOU IN THIS CHAPTER?

Have you ever faced a life-threatening fire? An accident? A scary illness? Most kids don't encounter threats to their lives until they're much older. But considering what we would do, even if our choices risked our lives, is important, because it helps us see what is most important to us. For instance, if someone demanded that you worship a false god instead of the one true God—and if you would be put to death if you didn't—would you do it? How do you find the strength to stand up against that kind of pressure?

YOUR FUTURE STORY

Who are the people in your life who can help you stay strong and true to your faith in God, as Shadrach, Meshach, and Abednego likely did for one another? Who could be your spiritual sisters and brothers? We all need a strong spiritual community to face the fires this world brings us. Be on the lookout for people like this when you meet them. They could be the best friends you ever find.

There is no other god who is able to deliver like this.
—Daniel 3:29

19

Stay Cool, Dude
Daniel 6

Daniel had seen a lot in his time. Remember, this was the guy who was buddies with Shadrach, Meshach, and Abednego. He had to have heard about how the Lord had saved them from the fire (Daniel 3), but that was a long time ago. Daniel was probably at least eighty years old when his enemies came up with the scheme to get him thrown to the lions.

You and I might totally forget about God's past faithfulness when we face a threat, but Daniel appears to have remained cool under pressure. You and I might have tried to escape our captors and chains, fighting like crazy not to be thrown into the lions' den, but it seems like Daniel gave right in as the king said, "May your God, whom you continually serve, rescue you!" (Daniel 6:16). Daniel didn't shout out as a stone was rolled over the mouth of the pit, sealing him in with the pacing, prowling lions.

Maybe he was too busy praying.

Because that's the thing about Daniel; he was always praying. Three times a day, facing in the direction of Jerusalem, "just as he had [always] done before" (Daniel 6:10). Even when he knew that it might bring him pain, he chose to honor his God above all else. And in the end, that was what saved him.

Imagine This ...
Facing the Enemies of Your Faith

The Year AD 2182, after World War III

The country your great-great-grandparents knew is long forgotten. The last of the faithful are now prisoners of war marching along a dirt road toward the capital in chains.

But your captors tell your group that you won't reach the capital alive unless you swear allegiance to them. Eat what they eat. Learn to speak their language. Turn from your old ways.

And bow to their god.

You reach camp after miles on the road, but before you're given a drink or shown where you can sleep, you are led to a clearing. At the end of the clearing is a giant statue with the head of a wolf and the body of a man. The sculpture seems to stare right at you with hard, blank eyes, and you shiver.

"That is Janaal," the captain says, nudging your shoulder with the tip of his rifle, pushing you closer. "He is my god, as he will be yours too. Kneel before him. Lie down on your belly and praise his name."

People all around you fall to their knees and then their bellies. But you remain standing. You blink, feeling the nudge of his gun again. You know you should be terrified. If you refuse to bow down and worship the statue, your captor could kill you. He could kill your family or your friends. You've seen him do so over less.

But in that moment you know you can't do what he commands. Even though your mother is sobbing behind you.

A friend reaches up toward you, silently begging you to consider it.

But you worship only one God. The God of all eternity. The God of Abraham, Isaac, and Jacob. The God of Daniel, Shadrach, Meshach, and Abednego.

The God who sent Jesus.

For you. For all those you love. Even for your enemies.

The God who knit you together in your mother's womb. The One who will welcome you into heaven when your life is over. Only him. Always him.

"Kneel! Worship our god!" cries the captain, hitting you harder now, making you sprawl forward.

But you can't. Won't. Not ever.

The Skinny on Daniel 6

* Daniel's name means "God is my judge." He certainly lived like he believed it!

* Daniel's enemies couldn't find anything he was doing wrong to use as an excuse to bring him down. It seemed like Daniel couldn't be trapped. But the only thing

> What your enemies intend for evil, God can use for his own glory.

that made him vulnerable—something that they could use against him—was the way he faithfully worshipped his God.

- Daniel was a man of extreme faithfulness, the same in front of others as he was behind closed doors.

WHAT STRUCK YOU IN THIS CHAPTER?

If someone demanded that you stop praying to God, on pain of death, would you do it? Why or why not?

Many knew that Daniel prayed three times a day. He didn't flaunt it, but he didn't hide it either. For us, prayer is often a silent, private occasion. How does it help us, and others, to know we pray?

YOUR FUTURE STORY

Who are the most faithful people you know and admire? Do they act the same way in front of family and friends as they do in front of strangers? Are they more worried about how they can faithfully serve God than about what anyone else thinks or says? What can you learn about the life of faith from them?

He is the living God, and he endures forever; his kingdom will never be destroyed, and his dominion has no end. He rescues and delivers; he performs signs and wonders in the heavens and on the earth, for he has rescued Daniel from the power of the lions.
—Daniel 6:26–27

20

You Can Run, but You Can't Hide
Jonah 1

Okay, first of all, gross. Wouldn't it be totally disgusting to spend three days in the belly of a big fish? I'm imagining it must have been seriously dark, wet, slippery, and all kinds of stinky. Jonah must have wondered if he'd died. Since he wasn't on the best terms with God, perhaps he even wondered if he'd been sent to a very watery version of hell.

> Check it out! Jesus sure made this fish story sound like death in Matthew 12:40: "For as Jonah was in the belly of the huge fish three days and three nights, so [will I] be in the heart of the earth three days and three nights."

But as much as the whole fish part of the story captivates us, the main point in Jonah is that we don't want to be on the run from God, right? Sure, we like to pretend we're in control, that we can ignore or hide from him. As if we can pull down the shades on a window so he can no longer see us, reach us, or find us!

Jonah shows us that no matter where we go, God is there too. And when God wants us to do something we'd rather not, it's best

> It's kind of like when we ignore our parents when they ask us to do something. What happens? Ignoring them = punishment.

to just sign on for the ride, because God doesn't like to be ignored and he can force us to pay attention to him by making our ride bumpier than it might be otherwise.

In the end Jonah just had to suck it up and do what he didn't want to do. He ultimately chose obedience ... but it was only after he was basically beaten into submission.

I don't know about you, but I'd rather be a willing participant (even if I'm scared) than a punished-into-it participant. Just like in our families, it's usually the happier, more peaceful choice.

Lucky for us, God rarely calls us to do big things like Jonah was instructed to do. I mean, someday he might ask you or me to do something big. But these days he often asks us to do small things that can *feel* like big things. Things like sitting on the bus with the lonely kid rather than with our friends. Or giving our last dollar to the church collection instead of scoring that ninety-nine-cent Slurpee. Or being kind and playing with a super-irritating little sibling who is on our last nerve.

God calls us to do our best, always, so that others will see his best in us. That's how he wants to expand his kingdom ... through us. If we look angry or act mean all the time, not a lot of people will say to themselves, *Hey, I want what that person has in my life too.* Isn't it sad that a lot of Christians look more selfish or mean or cranky than their neighbors who aren't Christians? We don't want to be that kind of Christian. We want to be the sort of Christian others appreciate and admire. Just like we want to be like Jesus.

Imagine This ...
What If God Called You?

Think about if you lived in the Mostly United States, a fragment of what it once was. Instead of Canada being filled with the kindest, most chill people you've ever met, it's totally sketch now, overtaken by soldiers who beat them in a bloody war. The Canadian government has fallen. The soldiers own the streets and are doing horrible things that you used to think only happened in R-rated movies. They cut down anyone who stands in their way or opposes them. They hurt people, including kids. They've killed many and look as if they didn't think twice about it. And now that they own Canada, they're eyeing the Mostly United States, thinking they might as well help themselves to that too.

They're hateful. The worst of the worst.

In the midst of this, God speaks to you.

He says your name so loudly that it practically vibrates in your chest, as if it popped out of a big concert speaker. But there's no big speaker nearby.

You look around, eyes wide. *I didn't just hear that!*

But you did. Because he says your name again.

This time you fall to your knees. You're so scared you're trembling all over.

"Head north," God says, "and tell your enemies how nasty they are. Preach against them! Tell them I see them and hate the evil in them! Tell them to turn from their wicked ways and return to me."

You blink once. Twice.

No, Lord. Not that. Anything but that.

He wants to reach out to them? To try to save them? THEM?

"Yes. Now."

You swallow hard. It grates at you to imagine it. Those soldiers—who have killed so many, lived such terrible lives—God wants to reach *them*? They don't belong with you and your people! They deserve death!

And yet … God has given you clear direction.

Resentful that he would ask you to do something so … *impossible*, you decide to head to Mexico. You burst out your front door and start running south, hoping that God will find someone else and that somehow he won't realize you just took off for the opposite border.

The Skinny on Jonah

- Jonah hightailed it outta town, but God stuck with him, of course. He wanted Jonah to reach out to the Ninevites because he still loved them.

God loves and calls to the lost. Yep! Even THEM. That's a serious sort of love, isn't it? That's how God loves you and me, and he'll stop at nothing to call us to return to him.

- Certain that he couldn't outrun God on land, Jonah took to the sea.

Jonah was kind of a slow learner.

- But who made the sea? Yep. God. So he sent a storm and then a great fish, and through it all, those non-God-following sailors tried to help Jonah, even when they realized he was putting them all at risk.

- Finally Jonah did the stand-up thing and told the sailors to throw him overboard to save themselves.

- And because of Jonah's sacrifice, those sailors' eyes were opened to the power of the God of Israel. Sometimes being a believer costs us. But God will make it count.

WHAT STRUCK YOU IN THIS CHAPTER?

Is God calling you to do something you really don't want to do or change your attitude toward someone? Is selfishness or fear or hatred holding you back? If you felt God calling you to do something that made you angry, how would you respond?

YOUR FUTURE STORY

What kind of kid are you when it comes to your parents and their requests of you? Which best describes you?

- ❑ I do everything my parents ask.
- ❑ I do what my parents ask, most of the time.
- ❑ I try to talk them out of it or make my sister or brother do it for me, most of the time.
- ❑ I pretend I didn't hear my parents and escape out the door before they can ask me again, forgetting I'll eventually have to come home and face them.

Does this help you see how you might respond to God's requests of you? What kind of responder do you want to be as you move forward in life?

Jonah got up to flee to Tarshish from the LORD's presence.
—Jonah 1:3

JESUS HAS JUST ENTERED THE BUILDING

21

Jesus—God with Skin On
John 1

Four gospel books in the Bible record Jesus's life and teachings: Matthew, Mark, Luke, and John. While the first three tell many of the same stories, the gospel of John is 90 percent unique. Mark began his gospel when Jesus was about thirty years old; Luke started his when Jesus was born; and Matthew traced Jesus's lineage back to Abraham. But John? He takes us all the way back to Genesis 1 to help us understand that Jesus was always a part of life: "In the beginning was the Word, and the Word was with God, and the Word was God. He was with God in the beginning. All things were created through him, and apart from him not one thing was created that has been created. In him was life, and that life was the light of men" (John 1:1–4).

Why would John call Jesus the "Word"? It's kind of weird, huh? Well, the ancient Greeks used the term (*logos*) to mean both the spoken word (like what you say out loud) and the unspoken word (like thinking about something, reasoning)—so it was like describing the mouth and mind in action. Jews used *logos* as a way of referring to a sort of "agent" of God, helping him create the world and govern it. So when John used a term for Jesus that *both* Jews and Gentiles (non-Jews) would get, it was perfect, because Jesus came to earth for ALL of us!

Jesus shares equality with God the Father and with the Holy Spirit. Together, we call them the "Trinity." Over time Christians have come up with lots of different analogies to help explain the Trinity, even though none are perfect. That said, you might think of the Trinity like you do an egg—with God the Father as the shell, Jesus the Son as the yolk, and the Holy Spirit as the white. It's all egg, but each element is unique. And yet when you think of an egg, you likely think of a white-shelled orb, right? The whole thing. Jesus and the Spirit, along with the Father, have forever been a part of what Christians call the "Godhead." And God sent his Son— who literally poured himself out—to guarantee our freedom forever.

By the time we get to the last half of John 1, we see Jesus on the move, calling his first disciples. In one chapter, John takes us from creation to calling, which neatly sums up Jesus's life. Jesus created us to be his precious, beloved disciples. And if we listen for his voice and pay attention to how he lived his life, we find the way we should live too.

Imagine This ...
Called Out by Christ

Nate was sitting under a fig tree, waiting out the hottest part of the day, hoping his mother would soon call him home for dinner. Phil was walking down the road, excitedly talking to a couple friends.

"Phil!" Nate called. "How's it going?"

"Nate! You won't believe this!" Phil said, coming closer, another man following behind. "We've found the one Moses wrote about! Jesus, the son of Joseph, from Nazareth!"

Nate frowned. Had he heard Phil right? Surely not the One …

But Phil was practically dancing, he was so excited.

"Nazareth?" Nate said with a scoff. "Nothing good comes out of that town."

His disbelief didn't faze Phil. "Come and see for yourself!" And then he hurried on, apparently not caring whether Nate followed. Nate had to practically run to keep up with the group as they neared the lake.

As soon as he glimpsed the one they called Jesus—already surrounded by a small crowd—Nate knew something was different about him. The way the man moved, the way he looked at each person in his circle, the way he looked at Nate as he approached sent a shiver down Nate's spine. Could it be? Could it really be the One, the Messiah, their king? At long last?

Jesus almost pierced Nate with his brown eyes, as if he could see inside him. Nate glanced nervously at Phil, but Phil was simply waiting on Jesus like the others gathered around. "Here is a true Israelite," Jesus said, taking Nate's arm, "an honest man through and through."

"How can you say that?" Nate asked. "You don't know me." But there was something in his manner that told him he *did*. It wasn't possible! Was it?

"Before Philip called you, when you were under the fig tree, I saw you," Jesus replied.

Nate gasped. That tree was far from where they stood now, beyond where they could see. He hadn't been there long before Phil came by. And yet looking into Jesus's eyes, Nate suddenly knew there was much more to it ...

"Teacher," Nate exclaimed, "you are the Son of God! You are the King of Israel!"

Nate began to kneel. This was the Messiah! But Jesus held Nate's arm firmly and grinned. "Do you believe only because I told you I saw you under the fig tree? You will see greater things than this, brother. Soon you'll see heaven opened and the angels of God ascending and descending on the Son of Man."

Everyone around them took a collective breath and considered what Jesus was saying. *Angels of God? Son of Man?*

At last Jesus released him, and Nate sank to his knees, knowing only one thing. He would be right at Jesus's side, no matter what Jesus did, where he went, or when. There was no other place he could possibly be.

The Skinny on John 1

- John had a thing for a few special words that help us understand Jesus better:

Life: This word is used more often in John than it is in the other three gospels combined. John wanted us to remember that Jesus *is* life—the key to our relationship with God.
  - "I give them eternal life, and they will never perish. No one will snatch them out of my hand" (John 10:28).

    > Dude! Jesus is like the ultimate lifeguard!

  - "I am the way, the truth, and the life. No one comes to the Father except through me" (John 14:6).

Grace: If you look back at human history, it seems like no family counselor could ever have saved our relationship with

God. Humans have always tried to avoid, resist, and run from God—just as most of us do today. God's solution was grace lived out in Jesus, who became the bridge between God and us. No matter how deep the canyon was between us, Jesus forever connected us to God by securing his undeserved favor for us through his sacrifice on the cross.

- "The Word became flesh and dwelt among us. We observed his glory, the glory as the one and only Son from the Father, full of grace and truth" (John 1:14).

Truth: "Reality" is another way to define *truth*. Jesus is God "with flesh on." Think about a man you're close to—your dad, grampa, or maybe a family friend—and how you see him, what you think about him. A stranger might have different thoughts about your father based on what he or she has heard or what Google turned up. But you know the truth about him, right? You know who he is because you know him *personally*. You know the core of his character. Jesus is the core of God's character. The truth.

- "Indeed, we have all received grace upon grace from his fullness, for the law was given through Moses; grace and truth came through Jesus Christ" (John 1:16–17).

> If no one knew your mom or dad, are there parts of you that reflect them?

- "No one has ever seen God. The one and only Son, who is himself God and is at the Father's side—he has revealed him" (John 1:18).

> Jesus called himself "Son of Man" more than eighty times! How's that for giving yourself your own nickname?

- FACTOID: "Son of Man" was Jesus's favorite way to describe himself. Some think he chose this title because he wanted to avoid all the political titles followers would be eager to call him—for example, Messiah, Son of David, King of Israel—and give people the chance to form their own ideas. Start fresh, in a way.

WHAT STRUCK YOU IN THIS CHAPTER?

Many kids think about Jesus being born in a manger and dying on a cross. How does it change your understanding of Jesus to think about him always being a part of God, before and after his life here on earth?

YOUR FUTURE STORY

Sometimes life is hard, even overwhelming. But in the midst of those moments, we must remember that Christ is with us. He is our light in the midst of the darkness. No matter how we feel, we must remember that we are never alone. He is with us.

When you face hard times, can you remember that God knew you from the start, even before you were growing in your mother's womb? Can you remember that you are vital to the kingdom, given a sacred cause? The darkness wants to tell us we are nothing, that we would do best to turn off our light; the Light tells us to shine brightly, to set our lamps where all can see. How can your light shine and encourage others? If it's hidden or in shadow, how can you remove the shade?

> In [Jesus] was life, and that life was the light of
> men. That light shines in the darkness,
> and yet the darkness did not overcome it.
>
> —John 1:4–5

22

Hey, I Know You!
Luke 2

In the last chapter we explored Jesus's divinity. Today we'll look at a chapter of the Bible that focuses more on his humanity.

Jesus started out as lowly as could be. If he'd been born today, he might've been born in an alley

> We use the fancy word *incarnation* to talk about the Son of God becoming flesh—fully human as well as fully divine.

or in a park! There was no fancy hospital or midwife, just Mary and Joseph in a farm animals' stable, which was probably a cave of some sort. The baby Jesus's first visitors were shepherds, who usually weren't considered clean enough to enter the temple, let alone greet the Son of God!

When he was a baby, Jesus cried and peed and pooped, just like we did. And he likely grew up having to do chores and some sort of religious schoolwork. He probably had zits, and his voice cracked as it changed, the way it does for boys going through puberty today. In a typical Jewish community like his, there would have been lots of opportunity to grow relationally—to hang out with neighbors and learn how to deal with the best people ... and the worst. And he was one of seven (or more) children!

> A family with seven kids? Talk about an opportunity to figure out how to deal with people ...

Jesus grew physically and got big enough to help his dad, who was a carpenter. He grew mentally, learning all about Scripture, and he grew spiritually, becoming more and more aware of just whose Son he really was and what that would mean. And yet even with that growing understanding, he was human from birth to death.

Imagine This ...
Missing ... for the Best Reason of All

So when Mary realized that Jesus wasn't with us ...well, let's just say it wasn't good.

We'd been on the road all day from Jerusalem, heading back to Nazareth. My dad had a lot of jobs he had to get to ... as did Joseph. Construction on the outskirts of Nazareth was booming, and to take the week off to attend the Passover was a sacrifice, so we were hurrying back.

But then it became clear that Jesus was missing.

He was about my age, and in seconds I knew where he was—back in the temple, asking questions of the rabbis, gently teasing them with his own knowledge.

So while Mary was in a panic, I did my best to calm her. "Be at peace," I said, bowing in deference. "I know where Jesus is, and no harm has likely come to him."

She gripped my arm. "You know? You know?"

I stared at her, a smile tugging at the corners of my lips. *Where was Jesus? Where did we always find him, even here in town?*

Sure enough, we found him in the temple, asking the teachers challenging questions and then casually stating his own perspective, which no one could seem to argue. Mary was surprised, ashamed even, as she pulled him away.

But Jesus said, "Why were you searching for me? Didn't you know that I had to be in my Father's house?"

Several of the Pharisees drew back at his casual use of language.

But I didn't. They couldn't see what I could—the Son of God *in* the Father's house as we spoke.

He was only twelve years old, but I could see him. Our Savior. All grown up …

The Skinny on Luke 2

- The angels knew from the start that something humongous had just happened. When they told the shepherds, a whole choir of angels cried, "Glory to God in the highest heaven, and peace on earth to people he favors!" (Luke 2:14).

  - This peace the angels were talking about is a peace of mind and soul that we get when we're in a relationship with Jesus.

  - Back in Isaiah 9:6, the prophesied Messiah was called the "Prince of Peace."

    > Check it out! See how Scripture is intertwined?

- Jesus was born for all, and the Spirit awakens us to pay attention when we encounter him. When he was still a baby, his parents took him to the temple to be presented to the Lord. The elderly Simeon, and then Anna, both long on the lookout, recognized him at once as the Messiah.

- While Simeon and Anna got it, Mary and Joseph didn't, even twelve years later. Isn't it wild that Jesus's parents had to go back to Jerusalem and search for him? They were probably

  > Jesus's mom and dad still seemed pretty confused about just WHO their son really was!

seriously freaked out, and there was laid-back, preteen Jesus, hanging out with the teachers, asking questions and "astounding" everyone with his understanding.

WHAT STRUCK YOU IN THIS CHAPTER?

How does God becoming fully human in the person of Jesus help us connect with the all-knowing and all-powerful Creator of the universe? Do you think it would've been strange hanging out with Jesus—God in human flesh and blood … like he was one of your friends? How do you think that felt for him? What might some of his frustrations have been? What inner knowledge might have made him smile as if he had the best secret in the world?

YOUR FUTURE STORY

Think about how Jesus grew up physically, spiritually, mentally, and relationally. He's our role model for every part of our lives. Do you sense God urging you to follow his lead and grow up a little more in some way? Write about it here:

_____

_____

_____

And now ask the Holy Spirit to empower you to grow/change in that way. He will!

Jesus increased in wisdom and stature, and in
favor with God and with people.
—Luke 2:52

23

What Does Jesus Want?
Matthew 5

Jesus doesn't want just the cheese, sauce, rice, or beans. He wants the whole enchilada. He wants all of us.

Think of it this way: we were born subject to the evil force of sin, which twists the way we think, believe, and act. Jesus wants to rescue us from that evil force. He wants to be an ever-present part of our lives, gently, patiently "rewiring" us to be more like God created us to be. Because Jesus died for us, every imperfection, every sin is covered when God looks at us. But that doesn't mean we just sit back and relax. If we put our faith in Jesus, we can be confident that we're covered by grace, that we're saved, but we make it our goal to become more like Jesus with each year we spend on this earth.

And that takes some work. This means we have a lifetime of continuing to learn, modify, grow, and understand what it means to live like Jesus.

When Jesus began preaching the good news to people, he started that "rewiring" business by showing them how mixed up humans had become. He showed them how God can use anything—even the hard, ugly parts of life—to draw us closer to him. God wants us to know that the things that woo us in life, like power and blessings, aren't always the best for us. For instance, being in charge, being rich, being in control *sound* good, right? But these things sometimes lead to the opposite of God's intention for us. God wants to bless us, and Jesus longs for our hearts to find life in him. He loves it when we're gentle, humble, and merciful like him. He wants us to seek peace and *eternal* blessings in this *temporary* world.

The more we can do that, the more we can be "salt"—wise people sharing wisdom with others—and "light"—leading the way by shining brightly ... *so* brightly that others can't ignore Christ within us. (See Matthew 5:13–16 for more.)

Imagine This ...
Meeting a Woman on the Streets

Colton was handing out sandwiches downtown, going from alley to alley to nudge people awake and offer them food and water. Serving others was a thing his church did every other Saturday, and he'd asked his mom to let him go this week. Part of him wanted to see what it was like to help strangers, and part of him felt like God wanted him to do it. He'd never felt this urge inside before. And when he told his mother, she simply nodded with that knowing look she had that made him half irritated and half glad.

He joined two high schoolers and one other middle schooler from their church youth group to cover one downtown block during the food giveaway. They found a zoned-out elderly woman who took hold of a sandwich but never spoke or looked up. The older kids prayed over her and then moved on, finding a young man sitting in the doorway of a closed business. Another guy was asleep behind a garbage Dumpster. Both of them cheered up at the thought of having lunch. One said, "Have a blessed day." The other said, "Keep on keepin' the blessings flowin'." But it was the fourth person Colton met who stuck in his mind six months later.

Robin was about his grandma's age and looked a little like her too …
except that Robin was missing most of her teeth and needed a bath. She
wore four shirt layers, even with it nearly topping ninety that day. Colton
later learned that a lot of homeless people wear all the clothes they own to
prevent others from stealing them. The one high school girl in his group,
Cassie, prayed with Robin, and they were about ready to move on when
the woman interrupted, "Well, I can't eat lunch without company, can I?
Why not sit a spell with me?"

Cassie and Colton decided to stay with Robin, splitting one of the
sandwiches between them so Robin wouldn't have to share hers. The
other two kids continued on. Cassie asked Robin lots of questions, and
Colton just listened. Robin shared that she was widowed and her two
sons had died in an accident. She was kicked out of her home when she
couldn't keep up with the house payments. Without a place to live, she
found it hard to get a job, so she ended up on the streets.

"That's really sad," said Cassie. "I'm sorry all that happened to you."

"I'm not," Robin answered, grinning with her gap-toothed smile.

"You're not?" Cassie asked, blinking in confusion.

"Oh, sure, I miss my boys," Robin said before chewing a bite of sandwich. "I wish they were alive. But I'll see them again come heaven. And
if I hadn't ended up on the streets, I wouldn't have known God's sweet
grace like I do now."

"What do you mean?" Colton wondered aloud.

"Well, sweet thing, I've watched my homeless brothers and sisters steal
from me but also give me their last quarter," Robin explained as she devoured
more of her sandwich. "I've watched good people like you kids come out and
share food with us. I've seen doctors and nurses donate their time to heal us.
I've seen people arrive with blankets on cold nights and others with vans to
take us to shelters. I've seen God's grace day by day through his people. And
if I hadn't been out here on my own, I don't know that I would've ever paid as
much attention to God or how he takes care of us."

Robin reached for Colton's hand and squeezed it. "God loves us so much. Never forget that. Even through the hard times."

"I won't," Colton promised. "Never ever," he added when Robin didn't let go of his hand. He thought she waited to make sure he really meant it.

"Good, sweet thing. Good," Robin said, gripping his fingers a moment longer before releasing them.

The Skinny on Matthew 5

• In the Sermon on the Mount, Jesus encourages his disciples to be merciful, to have pure hearts, and to be peacemakers. If we do those things, Jesus promises that the children of God will receive mercy and will see him in heaven.

• God works through all things if we let him … even the hard stuff. But Jesus also says that we'll be blessed even if we face grief and persecution—in other words, insults or put-downs or teasing.

Wait … what?

• In these challenges we can either have a trusting, open heart, learning more how God sustains and grows us through such experiences, or we can become bitter and angry and turn away from him.

• Think of people like a field and hard times like a plow. How we respond to the plow and the sun and rain will determine what grows in our soil.

• Have you ever had french fries without salt? It's important to get enough salt on them, right? The best moment for adding salt is when french fries are fresh out of the fryer. Wherever we go in this

world, we're supposed to be "salt," sharing needed wisdom from God. To do that, we have to remain connected to him, or we lose our "saltiness" (John 15:1–8).

- Have you ever walked into your house at night when your parents forgot to leave a light on? Isn't it a relief when you turn on that first switch and light warms the room? In the same way, we're supposed to let Jesus's love shine through us, bringing his hope to our dark world.

WHAT STRUCK YOU IN THIS CHAPTER?

Do you think you could ever give thanks to God through the hard times or things you've faced? Why or why not? How do hard times help us?

YOUR FUTURE STORY

Check off the things you struggle with:

❏   Getting angry
❏   Judging others
❏   Wanting to hurt someone who hurt you
❏   Letting others know you're a Christian
❏   Sharing your faith
❏   Loving your enemies

What is God saying to you about those things you checked off? Write your responses here: _____

_____

_____

_____

_____

You have heard that it was said, Love your neighbor and hate your enemy. But I tell you, love your enemies and pray for those who persecute you, so that you may be children of your Father in heaven.
—Matthew 5:43–45

24

Why Worry Never Works
Matthew 6

My son just got back from camp. He's been before a bunch of times and loves the adventure. But this last week I worried about him a ton. I worried he'd have a seizure (sometimes he has seizures at night) and that the camp counselor would panic or the other kids would be mean to him. I worried about my son tackling the high-ropes course. He hates heights, and when I tried that same course, I almost passed out from my own fear. I worried about my boy white-water rafting, because his big sis went rafting once and it was so terrible for her that she vowed to never go again.

Over and over I had to catch myself and turn my worries over to God. "Turning your worries over" means you place them in his hands. You know, God's huge hands. The One who holds it all anyway! I don't know why we think we can control or manage things. There's only so much we can do; at some point we have to let go and trust the God who loves us. He breathed life into us and wants to see us flourish every day.

Instead of worrying about my son, I prayed that God would block the seizures and help Jack manage that high-ropes course. I prayed Jack would have a far different experience rafting than his sister did and love it as much as I do.

I'm happy to report that Jack had a blast at camp. He thought white-water rafting was fun, and he was proud of himself for getting through the high-ropes course. And he didn't have a seizure. By the time I picked him up at camp, he was rocking out in worship, dancing and singing with his cabin buddy and counselor. He was also disgustingly dirty (as all middle school campers tend to be), sunburned, exhausted, and happy.

Now it could have gone differently. Jack could have had seizures—and his counselor and cabin mates would have probably dealt with it just fine. He might have frozen up on the ropes course and found a way to work through his fear. He could've fallen out of the river raft but learned he could get back in.

The point is, Jesus doesn't want us to worry—that accomplishes nothing. He wants us to place our concerns in the Father's hands, and then *trust* the One who loves us through and through (and loves our family and friends too).

Imagine This ...
Talking to God about Your Worries

Take in a deep breath, hold it for a few seconds, and then release it. Repeat that twice more. Imagine yourself in the safest, comfiest room you've ever been in.

Imagine Jesus sitting in a chair beside you, or in front of you, or beside you on the couch. Think of the place that would feel best to you.

Now imagine Jesus taking one of your hands and asking what's on your mind. What you're worried about.

Think of him looking at you with love and tenderness, listening until you're finished telling him everything you're worried about.

Imagine him reminding you that he was with God the Father when the world was created and he'll be there when the world comes to an end. Imagine him gently asking, "Is there anything I can't do?"

Consider your answer and then silently respond to him.

Think of him asking you, "Will you trust me even if your worst fear happens? Will you trust that I have your best in mind and even if you suffer, there will be blessing ahead? Will you trust me, knowing I'll never leave you or ignore you?"

Consider your answer and then silently respond.

Now picture yourself handing Jesus any concern in your life, as though it's contained in a heavy ball. Your worry might be the size of a golf ball or the size of a big heavy bowling ball. Think of Jesus taking that heavy ball. Don't your hands feel lighter now that he's holding your stress instead?

End your prayer time by thanking Jesus for everything you can think of that's good in your life.

Amen.

The Skinny on Matthew 6

- In Matthew 6 Jesus covered

  - the right reason to give to those in need: not so others will think you're great but to honor God (Matthew 6:1–4);
  - a model prayer (a good place to start if you've never been a pray-er before!) teaching people to pray to a God he called "Papa" (vv. 9–13);

    > Addressing God the way a little kid might talk to her daddy? Yep. That's exactly what Jesus was after!

  - an emphasis on forgiveness (vv. 14–15);
  - a warning about fasting to get approval from people instead of God (vv. 16–18);
  - financial advice to store up treasures in heaven instead of on earth (which means to invest in the eternal things

    > Can you have a Ferrari and still go to heaven? Sure. But God urges us to focus on heart things more than physical things.

God loves most rather than some of the things we humans tend to want) (vv. 19–24); and

- reassurance that God will look after our needs (vv. 25–34).

- What do all these lessons have in common? A focus on God through daily living. Honoring him, loving him, trusting him.

WHAT STRUCK YOU IN THIS CHAPTER?

Is there something you tend to worry about? Maybe it's passing math … or art … or PE. Maybe you fear not making it onto a team … or into a club. Maybe you're anxious about friends or your family. What is your most consistent worry? How do you think God can help you with it? What are some surprising ways he might answer that prayer?

YOUR FUTURE STORY

I've heard it said that every time we give in to anxiety, we're actually telling God we don't trust him. Do you trust the God who loves you from the tips of your toes to the top of your head? Do you trust him with every aspect of your life, from your friendships to your future? What daily choices can you make to trust and love God rather than give in to worry?

> *Don't worry about your life, what you will eat or what you*
> *will drink; or about your body, what you will wear. Isn't life*
> *more than food and the body more than clothing?*
> —Matthew 6:25

25

What Should I Do?

Matthew 7

Is your relationship with your closest friend the same today as the first day you met? Of course not.

Lots of things have happened to make that person your closest friend, right? Maybe you've spent nights at each other's houses. Eaten together. Laughed together until you almost couldn't breathe. Maybe you've cried together over a sick or dying grandparent. Perhaps you've even worshipped together at church. But your relationship likely deepened over weeks, months, or years because you chose to be with your friend, enjoying great fun and working through misunderstandings, arguments, and frustrations. Through it all, you've come to trust and like each other even more.

Friendship with God is much the same. If we want to get closer to him—if we want him to be our BFF—then we need to make choices to truly follow him day in and day out. We do that by staying connected to Jesus through the Spirit, not judging others (Matthew 7:1–6), praying often (vv. 7–11), loving and giving (v. 12), and guarding against those who want to pull us from God's best path for us (vv. 13–23). In short, we practice what Jesus preached (vv. 24–27).

Imagine This ...
Judging Someone at Church

Hailey groaned when she saw Alissa from science class.

Alissa, one of the most popular girls at her school.

Alissa, one of the meanest girls alive.

And now she was here in her youth group. They didn't have that big of a church, so it would be impossible to avoid her. Of all the churches in town, why did Alissa have to pick Hailey's?

Still, when they went around the circle, doing that youth-group-icebreaker thing, saying their names and sharing the oddest place they'd ever spent the night (Hailey's was a tree house), Alissa seemed different somehow. Less confident than she was at school. But not because she didn't have a cool place to share—hers was a camper in New Zealand.

Of course her answer was cooler than mine! Hailey grumbled in her thoughts. But it seemed like Alissa didn't really want to be in the group.

She sat with her arms crossed half the time and picked at her nails the other half. When everyone joined in a group game, Alissa ended up in Hailey's smaller group and acknowledged her with a half wave, at least, but that was it. When youth group was over, Alissa was the first one out the door.

Hailey got in the car with her mom and let out a big sigh.

"What's up?" her mother asked, casting her a puzzled look before putting the car into gear. "You usually bounce out of youth group with a grin on your face."

"Yeah, well, Alissa from school showed up today."

"Alissa ... Oh, is she the cute redhead? Jolene's daughter?"

Hailey froze. *Great. Mom knows Alissa's mom?* Next thing she knew, their mothers would be carpooling to youth group, and Hailey would be trapped in a confined space with the world's meanest, most stuck-up girl, with nothing to say, just awkwardly waving at each other. *Ugh.*

"Yeah, I think so," Hailey grudgingly said. "How do you know Alissa's mom?" *May as well get this over with. Maybe I can run interference, make up an excuse as to why carpooling would never work.*

"Jolene volunteers with me at the hospital," her mom said. "They've had a rough year. Alissa's dad died last year. He was a police officer."

Wait. Her dad died?

"Jolene and Alissa moved to our neighborhood to start a new chapter of their lives," Mom went on. "But it's been tough. They don't have much extended family, and a move on top of that kind of grief . . ." She glanced at Hailey. "Hey, what is it?"

"I didn't know Alissa had gone through that. But, Mom, she's the meanest girl at school. I wasn't superexcited when I saw her at youth group. It's hard enough to deal with her at school."

Hailey's mom took a deep breath. "I get it. But don't you see how coming to church and going to youth group might help Alissa? The poor kid has to be hurting. Maybe that's what makes her seem mean."

"She doesn't seem mean, Mom. She *is* mean."

"Hmm. Sometimes stress and grief can bring out the worst in us. Our job is to love the unlovable, babe," she said. "To let Jesus shine through our love and actions. Don't you think on our worst days that we might act a little like Alissa too?"

Hailey thought about that. "Maybe on my worst days," she admitted.

"And yet Jesus's love for you never wavers. Even on your worst days. And doesn't that kind of love encourage you to act better . . . like you want to honor it?"

"I guess . . ."

"This life of being a Jesus follower is challenging sometimes. Loving the way he loves is a tall order. But it means not judging others. Everyone is dealing with things we may not know about. Jesus wants us to look at people with eyes of mercy and grace. If enough of us do, maybe mean people will start to see him too and be less mean."

"You think so?"

"I know so."

Hailey didn't know if her mom was right. She didn't know whether Alissa would ever be a nice person. But knowing some of her story did make Hailey feel a little compassion for her. And her mother's words felt right in her heart, even if her brain was thinking, *Yeah, right ...*

"I'll try, Mom," Hailey finally said.

Mom reached out and stroked Hailey's neck. "That's all any of us can do. Get up and try again each day. That's all Jesus wants from us, and he gives us the power to do it. It's simple, but I know it can be hard. Trust me that if you practice loving others, you'll experience more peace in your life."

The Skinny on Matthew 7

- Jesus wasn't the first to teach what people call the Golden Rule. Confucius, Plato, and a noted Jewish rabbi all said something similar long before Jesus said, "Whatever you want others to do for you, do also the same for them" (Matthew 7:12). But these early philosophers focused on the negative side of this rule: *don't do* what you *don't want* others to do to you. Jesus urged his followers to focus on the positive side.

- Pastor Deron Spoo says, "Jesus invites us to live by intention instead of impulse in our relationships with others." *Living intentionally* means we make good choices about

  - judging others (Matthew 7:1–6),
  - prayerfulness versus prayerlessness (vv. 7–11),
  - how we treat others (v. 12),
  - the path that we choose in life (vv. 13–14),
  - the people we allow to influence us (vv. 15–23), and
  - the kind of foundation we build our spiritual houses on— rock versus sand (vv. 24–27).

WHAT STRUCK YOU IN THIS CHAPTER?

Here's the cool thing: The longer we're Christians, the more we learn about following Christ. And the closer we get to him, the clearer that becomes. Here's the not-so-cool thing: If we're successful at making good choices, we'll be tempted to judge others for not

> Need the secret medicine to stop judging others? Allow the Spirit to awaken *mercy* inside your heart. Follow his lead to see them as God sees them.

doing the same. We'll be tempted to look down our noses at others rather than remembering that no matter how far we've come, we still have ways we could improve. That's why Jesus says to beware of having a "beam of wood" in your own eye when you're pointing out a "splinter" in your friend's eye (Matthew 7:5)!

YOUR FUTURE STORY

When Jesus was finished preaching, "the crowds were astonished ... because he was teaching them like one who had authority, and not like their scribes" (Matthew 7:28–29). Can you imagine what it might have been like for those Jews? Here was a guy not just teaching the law; he was also *commanding* them—like God himself might do. The Jewish people recognized that Jesus was claiming authority like no one else they had ever heard before. Two thousand years later, we basically have the divine cheat sheet: we know we need to heed Jesus's words because we know he was and is the Savior. But are we living as if he has that kind of authority in our lives today? If Jesus was hanging out with us at school, at the gym, or in our homes, would our choices please him?

Whatever you want others to do for you, do also the same for them.

—Matthew 7:12

JESUS WON'T LEAVE US AS WE ARE

26

Jesus Rules
Luke 8

This account of the ministry of Jesus, where he did all sorts of miracles back to back—calming a storm, driving out demons, healing a woman when she touched his robe, and bringing a dead girl back to life—seems pretty BUSY, doesn't it? These days we like to think of Jesus as gentle and calm. But this account shows us that Jesus was that and more. He was megapowerful and on the MOVE!

Jesus was on a mission to nab people's attention, to make them sit up and take notice that there was a new guy in town and he was *holy*. Jesus wanted people who witnessed him at work to have no choice but to believe that God had shown up in the flesh. But he wasn't on some celebrity ego trip, bent on being the center of the gossip machine. Jesus wanted to present an undeniable, amazing story that made everyone whisper in awe, "What was that? I've never seen anything like it in my life!"

Because they hadn't! Jesus wanted them to recognize his power. And later he would bestow that same power on his disciples … the same power that can live in us today.

> Seriously! In us! In you and me!

Now I can see you shifting in your seat, feeling like that's a bit nuts. But it's not. It's truth.

Miracles didn't just occur in the days of Jesus and through the disciples. Miracles are also happening today among Christian disciples around the world. Most of us prefer to keep things "explainable" because it makes us feel more comfortable and secure, but we worship a God who refuses to be entirely explained. He is completely beyond our ability to box him in. He wants us to remember that.

When I was a kid, friends of our family had a little five-year-old, Heather. She had an eye disease that led to multiple surgeries and Coke-bottle-thick glasses, and it was only getting worse. One day a neighbor they barely knew showed up at the family's doorstep. "This is going to sound unbelievable," he said, "but I've been sent here to pray that your daughter will be totally healed."

Now those parents had to do some talking before they gave this man access to their little girl. But eventually they did. And after clearing the house of a Ouija board and some vacation-trip voodoo dolls—which had been purchased as innocent mementos but seemed to have some evil influence—the man prayed with the parents over their little girl.

Right after they laid hands on her, Heather went outside without her glasses and brought in a handful of ants. "Mom! Look at these crawly things!" She'd never seen ants before, but she could then! Her vision had been restored.

Miracles happen today too. Kids with cancer go to their next check-ups and find out their tumors have disappeared. People walk away from serious car accidents. Moms and dads who argue all the time find a way to live together in peace. Jobs are finally found.

But not always, right? Children don't always get healed of cancer. People also die in car accidents, moms and dads sometimes divorce, and families may have to live in a homeless shelter. This is a

> God's not a miracle vending machine. Sometimes praying for a miracle means praying for years!

fallen world, and sometimes we don't understand why God doesn't move in a miraculous way. But the point is, sometimes *he does*. Because God is all-powerful and beyond anything we can imagine, we can pray for the miracles we need in our lives or for others who need them.

Imagine This ...

Seeing Jesus's Miracles Firsthand

My name is Elazar, and I'm young, but everything I'm about to tell you is totally true ...

When we first saw him, Jairus didn't look his usual polished self. Today he wore a dirty, tattered robe that drooped on his shoulders. His graying hair was in tangled knots. He looked as if he hadn't slept in days.

He fell to his knees before Jesus, clutching at his hand. It was then I realized why Jairus's robe was a mess. He'd been kneeling elsewhere.

The disciples tried to pry his fingers off the teacher, but Jesus said, "No. Let him speak."

"Rabbi, my precious little girl is very ill. If what they say is true, you can heal her. Please! Please come to my village, my home! Right away!"

I knew of Jairus's daughter. She was a girl of twelve, about my own age. They lived just a short distance away.

Jesus nodded in agreement, and the crowd fell in around him as he started to make his way there. The throngs of people swarmed around him, and yet he bent his head to listen to one person after another, uttering words I couldn't hear. Some of the people looked confused and some angry. Others appeared relieved. A number of them looked as if they'd just spoken to God himself at the temple.

But when we were partway to the man's house, Jesus halted and stiffened. His head darted from left to right. "Who touched me?"

"Master, everyone is crowding around you," the one named Peter exclaimed. "Anyone might have pressed against you!"

"Someone touched me," Jesus replied, looking intently at one person after another. "I know that power has gone out from me."

After a moment of heavy silence, a woman crouching behind others in the crowd moved forward. With tears streaming down her face, she dropped to Jesus's feet, trembling. "Master, I have been ill for twelve years," she said, "and one touch of your robe healed me."

Jesus reached down to her. I couldn't see over the adults' shoulders in front of me, and I desperately tried to hop up to see what was happening. But a moment later, women were crying out about healing, raising their hands to the sky. Men shouted, eyes wide.

While he was still talking to the woman, a messenger arrived. Jesus looked up, his brow furrowed in concentration. It was almost as if he were … listening?

Word came through the gathering crowd that we were moving toward Jairus's house again. Some whispered that his daughter was dead! I managed to make my way to the front of the crowd. I didn't want to be blocked from the action again. If Jesus could heal someone with a mere touch of his robe, could he possibly help the little girl?

But when I looked down the road, my stomach twisted.

Jairus's wife was outside the house wailing, her forehead touching the ground. Her shrieks carried in the wind.

"Too late," muttered a woman behind me.

"Too late," her companion repeated.

Too late … too late … too late. I'd been so jubilant. So excited to see the rabbi heal this girl next. But we were too late … far too late.

And she was dead.

But Jesus didn't pause. He kept walking toward the house as if everything was perfectly fine. Past the grieving, wailing mother and through the door he went.

Most of us couldn't bear to edge any closer. Coming too near the dead body would make us unclean.

But Jesus remained inside the house for a minute, then two.

The sun grew hot on our heads, but still we stayed. People whispered. Someone coughed. My stomach grumbled.

What was Jesus doing in there? He'd need to spend days performing the rituals of cleansing after being so close to the dead girl. And for what? She was clearly beyond care. Her grieving mother was testimony of that.

I was just thinking about turning and heading for home to get supper when I saw movement inside. Jesus emerged from the house … with Jairus's daughter by his side.

People gasped. I held my breath. Then I lifted my hands to my face, wondering if I was dreaming.

Because she appeared as perfectly alive as I was.

The Skinny on Luke 8

- Luke, the author of this book, accompanied the apostle Paul on some of his missionary journeys and was the author of the book of Acts too. Luke proved to be a faithful and loyal friend to Paul (2 Timothy 4:11).

- Luke was probably born a Gentile, not a Jew. He was well educated and became a doctor (Colossians 4:14).

- These scriptures help us see that Jesus is never too busy to pay attention to us. All-powerful Jesus and his Father notice those in need and are capable of curing us of any illness—including demonic possession!

> Jesus, while fully human, clearly had access to God's own power!

WHAT STRUCK YOU IN THIS CHAPTER?

How would you react to seeing such miracles for yourself? How would that change the way you see Jesus? After reading this chapter, do you have new respect for the power of God?

YOUR FUTURE STORY

Do you need to pray for a miracle for yourself, your family, or your friends? What kind of miracle do you think God would want you to pray for? Is he asking you to believe that he can do the impossible?

Daughter ... your faith has saved you. Go in peace.
—Luke 8:48

27

Jesus: Up Close and Personal
John 3

My daughter had a friend who always texted her one thing: "SUP?" This drove her crazy, because he never asked her anything other than his version of *What's up?* He never got to anything more via text or in real conversations, for that matter. They didn't hang out for long.

Jesus was the opposite of that shallow, simple texter. Jesus was always looking for attentive, "get-to-the-heart-of-things" conversations with everyone he met. It didn't matter if it was a Pharisee (John 3), a Samaritan woman (John 4), a woman caught in adultery (John 8), a man healed of blindness (John 9), or his disciples (John 13–16). Jesus was after reaching everyone with the depth of his message. He wanted to reach every person he could with the good news of God's grace to encourage them to turn to the Father who loved them.

John 3 holds one of the most famous verses in the Bible: "For God loved the world in this way: He gave his one and only Son, so that everyone who believes in him will not perish but have eternal life" (v. 16). Now there are many people who talk about Jesus as a good man and teacher, even if they don't believe in him. But God's Word is superclear on this: Jesus is the only guarantee we have of being forgiven and getting to heaven; we need to accept Christ and become "born again" (John 3:3, 7).

This might seem harsh at a time when the world wants us to think any way but black and white. The world definitely favors gray and statements more like "This is what works for me, but you can believe anything you want."

Here's the thing: salvation—knowing you'll go to heaven because you believe Christ died for your sins and saved you—is a pretty critical issue. And "God did not send his Son into the world to condemn the world, but to save the world through him" (John 3:17). Jesus's goal was to save us, to love us, even though it hurt him big-time to do so.

Think of it this way: At the top of a mountain there was a town about to be destroyed by a volcanic eruption, but someone had built a brand-new bridge over to the next mountain in order to save the townspeople. The people had never seen a bridge before, though, and they didn't know if they could trust it. As the volcano rumbled and spewed smoke and ash, some people ran to the bridge, deciding to rely on it, and others took to the paths down the mountain. When the volcano erupted, everyone still on the mountain died. Those who trusted the bridge were already safe, at home on the new mountain.

Those townspeople are like all of us, really, in the spiritual sense. We have a choice: Will we trust Jesus as our bridge, our Savior, so that when our lives on earth are over, we can get to the other side ... to heaven? Or will we stay on our own path, on our own mountain?

Jesus was so clear about this: trusting him with our eternal lives is the wisest choice we'll ever make.

We don't know whether Nicodemus, the Pharisee who came to talk with Jesus, decided that Jesus was the long-awaited Messiah, because Scripture doesn't record Nicodemus's answer. But the Bible does say that when Jesus died, Nicodemus brought seventy-five pounds of embalming spice for the body (John 19:39). That's a humongous amount of spice.

The only ones who usually got that much spice were kings.

I'm thinking we might get to meet old Nicodemus in heaven someday.

Imagine This ...

Sitting Face-to-Face with Jesus

Sydney liked to squeeze through the scratchy bramble bushes and enter a tiny clearing in the middle of the city park. It was her own special place. A secret place. Surrounded by brush and old trees that climbed to the sky and partially cut out the noise—traffic and crying babies and moms—the space felt holy. A place she could pray and not get interrupted.

She sat down in the center on a rounded boulder that was warm from the sun. She closed her eyes and lifted her face to the sun and waited.

Dear Jesus, I need you, she prayed. *Help me feel your presence.*

Sydney thought about what it would be like to see him here, here in her little clearing. Making his way through the brambles, taking a seat beside her. He was so loving that he might offer to take her hand in his, and Sydney knew his touch would be reassuring.

Thank you for being with me, Lord, she prayed.

She thought about how he'd say her name. With total love in his eyes. For her. As if she was special, even though everyone was special to him. It would be as if he'd known her forever…

Sydney snorted a laugh at herself. *Of course* he'd known her forever. He was God!

In the Bible, Jesus asked Peter, "Who do you say that I am?" Sydney thought about being in Peter's place. She'd been thinking about that ever since they'd gone over it in Sunday school yesterday. *Sydney, who do you say that I am?*

"Jesus, you are the one God sent," she whispered, head bowed. "His Son, to save us from the penalty of our sins. To save me from my sins." Her brow furrowed as she thought of him on a cross. Then she turned her face to the sun again.

Thank you for saving me. Thank you for loving me so much that you would die for me. Thank you for being my Savior. Amen.

The Skinny on John 3

- Jesus was constantly trying to get the Pharisees (Jewish religious leaders) to think beyond the dos and don'ts of religion to the bigger picture: God's passionate love for his people and his desire for a real relationship based on that love, not on duty.

- The kingdom of God = God's rule in the hearts and minds of his people.

> God wants to reign as king in our hearts!

- "Born again" = a launch of a new relationship with God through Jesus, offered to us at any time, no matter what we've done or said in the past. When we are born again, we become a "new creation" in Christ (2 Corinthians 5:17).

- God isn't cold, angry, and distant. Because he loves us so much, he cares about even the smallest details of our lives.

WHAT STRUCK YOU IN THIS CHAPTER?

Would you say that Jesus is the Lord of your life? If you're not sure you can answer yes, would you like to begin a new life with Jesus as your Savior? If so, reach out to a parent or trusted adult who is a Christian. This person will lead you in a prayer to invite Jesus into your heart. Making this commitment aloud will confirm your decision as you begin your new walk of faith!

If you have already been born again, what could you do to honor Jesus as your Lord in some greater way? Like giving him more sway in your decisions? How can you better reflect his love to the world?

And if you're not ready to make this decision yet, that's okay too! God loves you and is reaching out to you every day. How can you keep exploring, learning what it means to have a more dedicated relationship with him?

YOUR FUTURE STORY

Other religions began when a single person had a private idea, private dream, or private encounter with an angel and then that person told the rest of the world about it. Christianity is different; it began with Jesus publicly teaching for three years. At the end of this time, he was publicly executed and buried, and then God raised him from the dead. The risen Christ then appeared to many of his disciples. Those people proclaimed this good news to the world, making Christianity the most verifiable religion ever.

> Jesus claimed he is our savior, sent by God, his Father. Who do you say he is?

Do you believe God loves you so much that he would send his Son to die just for you? Thinking about it in such a personal way helps us understand how much he adores each one of us.

Put your name in the blanks below:

"For God loved _____ in this way: He gave his one and only Son, so that [if] _____ believes in him[, he/she] will not perish but have eternal life" (John 3:16).

Truly I tell you, unless someone is born again,
he cannot see the kingdom of God.
—John 3:3

28

Welcome Home
Luke 15

When you listen to a teacher teach or a preacher preach or a speaker speak, what makes you pay attention and think about what he or she is saying? Stories capture the attention of most of us, and Jesus was really good at reaching people through a particular kind of story—parables. Parables are simple stories about everyday life that help us understand big truths about God.

In Luke 15, Jesus used a one-two-three punch to really drive home the point that every soul matters to God. We might wander away from him for a moment, a day, a month, or even years, but whenever we return to God, we'll find him waiting for us, always ready to welcome us.

These triple-punch parables were stories about a lost sheep (one in a hundred), a lost coin (one in ten), and a lost son (one in two), also known as the Prodigal Son. Jesus started big and broad with the hundred sheep, got a little closer to home with the ten coins, and then really brought the point close to home with the two sons. He wanted people to understand that it doesn't matter whether you're in a crowd of a hundred or are just one of two people—God notices if you're missing.

It's like God sending out his own Amber Alert!

We can wander off the path of faith for a number of reasons. Sometimes it's because we're just clueless or ignorant, like sheep mindlessly wandering from one delicious green blade of grass to the next, until we look up and find out we're WAY far away from home. Sometimes we wander from our faith because everything we want to do or have to do distracts us or because other people who don't put God first turn us away from him. And sometimes we drift spiritually because we have doubts and *decide* to walk away, or we think something else is more important, or we're more interested in pleasing ourselves than our God. *Whatever* pulls us away, God is *always* longing for us and waiting for us to return home, just like the father of the Prodigal Son.

Imagine This ...
Running Away from Home

Gemma had had it. She was sick to death of her mom making her do chores, especially after a long day of school and track afterward. And she was over her dad dragging her to church and making her go to youth group. She was so done with having to be home five nights a week at six o'clock for family dinner. Didn't her parents know that practically all of her friends had cash cards to grab food wherever they wanted, whenever they wanted?

She was finally at the end of her rope. Graduation was tomorrow, and she was ready for the "big talk," the moment when she'd finally tell Mom and Dad her plans. Dad had always said that she and her brother had a set amount of money for college. Well, she was going to take that money and run. There were a thousand ways for a girl to make her way in the world now. And Gemma's dream? Well, she was heading to Hollywood.

Modeling! Acting! It was all about to get real.

Mom cried when Gemma told her. Dad yelled and paced. But Gemma just remained still. She was so proud of herself, not getting all emo with them. They'd see in time that she was right. It was time for her to make her own decisions.

Dad finally sat down on an ottoman in front of her chair, elbows on his thighs, his hands covering his mouth as he stared at her. "So let me get this straight," he finally said. "You want to take everything we've saved for college for you and go and pursue acting in Hollywood."

"Yes," Gemma said, deciding to ignore how he said *acting* and *Hollywood* as if they were curse words. "It's my dream, Dad. College is not my dream."

"But that's what we saved the money for," Mom answered.

"You saved it for me, right? To help me move forward in life? Well, I don't want to be a doctor or a lawyer or a teacher or anything that requires a stupid degree." It was Gemma's turn to stand up and pace. They'd been through it over and over again.

She turned to face them both. "So was the money for me or for you?"

Dad looked as if she'd punched him in the gut. "It was for you. It's always been for you," he said.

"So?" Gemma asked, lifting her hands. "That money will get me the start I need. To get head shots done. Acting lessons. Clothes so I can get the right agent."

"But what if it doesn't work?" Mom asked, wiping her nose. "There must be thousands of girls in Hollywood right now, all with the same dream."

"Yeah, well, it's my dream, not yours," Gemma snapped back, crossing her arms. "And I don't care what the competition is like. I have to try. And now that I'm a legal adult, it's my decision."

Dad shook his head. "You might think you're an adult ..."

Gemma threw up her arms. "I'm old enough to go into the army. I should be old enough to take my money and do what I want with it."

Dad stared at her. "Our money. That we're gifting to you," he said, as if correcting her. "Money we'll never have again. It's taken us years to—"

"Yeah, well, is it my money?" Gemma interrupted. "Or isn't it?"

Dad clamped his lips together. A flash of pain and sorrow went through his eyes, but Gemma shoved away the guilt.

Dad looked to Mom, who was crying harder now, and then to Gemma. "We'll give you the savings, and you can chase your dream, honey." He seemed to be holding back his own tears. "When will you leave?"

Gemma smiled. "Just as soon as I can pack my car."

Gemma didn't look back once she got in that car. She got to California, found an agent, got beautiful head shots—after purchasing on-fleek clothes and getting her hair and makeup done by pros. She also rented a gorgeous apartment. Her roommate was an aspiring actress from Wisconsin. Soon they were partying every weekend with other aspiring actors and models and musicians. No one seemed to care that most of them were underage. They invited everyone over, and someone always brought the booze or the pot or whatever they felt like that night. It was all good, so good. To be reaching for their dreams, talking about casting calls, rehearsals, acting coaches, magazine and catalog shoots. They were inching closer to their dreams, she was sure of it. If she just put in the hard work, invested in the right people, she'd be a star.

Three years later, Gemma's money had evaporated.

She'd been evicted, and she was two months behind on her payments for her Jeep. She was scared to death it would get repossessed.

She sat on the front curb of her beautiful apartment, surrounded by the things she couldn't pawn, wondering how it had come to this. An ex-boyfriend had managed to steal ten thousand dollars before she realized it. Her roommate had gone back to Wisconsin, skipping out on the last three months' rent. Gemma's "manager" had promised he would make her a star, but looking back, she realized he'd done little more than take her out to lunch and talk possibilities … and collect a monthly check. Gemma had even paid for a website so she'd be ready for stardom. She'd purchased an enormous wardrobe, much of which she now had to sell on consignment. And the parties—the catered food, the wine …

All those parties and all those people.

None of whom were returning her IMs now.

"Oh my gosh," she muttered, head in her hands. "What am I going to do now?"

Her first thought was to call her mom and dad.

But there was no way she could do that.

She hadn't talked to them in more than two years. Hadn't returned their calls, messages, or letters. She'd just been too busy.

Guilt flooded through her.

She hadn't wanted to call them. She hadn't wanted to think about how fast the money—once such an enormous sum—had seemed to disappear. She hadn't wanted to think about how Mom and Dad had tried to change her mind about coming here. How she'd been so rude, so demanding, so unloving.

No, she thought, fishing out her phone from her Gucci purse. *I'll try my agent one more time. I'll get a job. Find a new apartment. Start over.*

A month later the auto broker had somehow figured out she was living in a park, sleeping in her Jeep. Two dudes came in the middle of the night and broke the window, hauled her out, tossed her remaining clothes and things to the ground, attached the Jeep to a tow truck, and drove away.

Gemma sat down in the empty parking space and cried. She hadn't found a job. She was starving, literally starving. She'd actually wandered into a Pizza Hut last night, ordered water, and pretended to look at the menu until a nearby family left their table. Then she'd grabbed the half-eaten crusts from their plates and walked out, ignoring the stunned busboy who stood there, ready to clear the table.

She thought again of calling her parents. But how could she? Her cell phone had been shut off. And they didn't want to hear from her anyway. They probably hated her. They'd tell her she should've known better. Should've listened to them. They'd rub her nose in her mistakes.

Gemma's stomach rumbled. She'd have to spend the day outside Wal-Mart, holding a sign and begging for money. Or stop at the soup kitchen five miles away, hoping to get a meal. Or see if a local homeless shelter would take her in.

Or she could just go home.

Beg for her parents' forgiveness.

Take whatever anger they needed to spew.

Wouldn't it be better than this?

It took almost three weeks to hitchhike her way home. Gemma rode with guys who thought she owed them more than her thanks, as well as some nice families, truckers, and teens. By the time Gemma got to her street, she was filthy, not having showered for weeks. Her clothes were disgustingly dirty.

She turned the last corner, only a backpack with her now, the rest of her possessions lost, bartered, or sold. She hesitated, seeing Dad right away, five houses down, watering his flower bed. Gemma tried to will her feet to move, to approach him, but she remained motionless. She knew that nothing she could say or do would make up for what she'd done.

He'd hate her. Blast her for all her stupid decisions. And he'd be right.

Dad moved the hose down the flower bed and then glanced down the street.

He gaped at her, staring as if he couldn't believe his eyes. He let the hose slip to the sidewalk, water still flowing. Weeping, smiling, he shouted her mother's name twice as he was running toward Gemma. *He was weeping and smiling?*

He caught Gemma up in his arms and held her tightly, spinning her around and crying her name. "Oh, Gemma. You're home. You're home. How I've missed you! How we've missed you." She felt as totally free, warm, and welcomed now as she'd been at the age of twelve when she came home from her first solo trip to Gramma's for the summer.

"Dad, Dad," she exclaimed, crying too. "I'm so sorry I haven't called. So sorry I'm such a mess. I've made so many mistakes, Dad. I've lost every penny you gave me," she added as Mom slowly approached, as if uncertain. "I was such a fool. Such a stubborn, terrible, self-focused idiot. Can you ever forgive me?"

Dad took Gemma's face in both of his big hands. "You are forgiven, baby. We love you. Oh, how we love you. All we've ever wanted is for you to return to us. And now you have. You have!" His face broke into a huge grin. "It's time for a party!"

Then she was between them, each of them with an arm around her.

And Gemma knew she was home.

In more ways than one.

The Skinny on Luke 15

- Jesus used common images to help people understand what he was saying. If he were here today, speaking to you and me, he might use a

  - car dealer with a hundred cars (instead of a hundred sheep with a shepherd watching over them);
  - a fifty-dollar bill, about one day's wage (instead of a silver coin);
  - a daughter demanding her college funds for other purposes (instead of a son demanding his part of the family inheritance).

- We walk away from God in big and small ways, but we all walk away at times. It's part of our sinful nature. The call, though, is to return to him.

> God is always waiting to welcome us home, his arms open wide.

- The parable of the prodigal son tells us how crazy in love God is with us! It shows us that he's always willing to cover us with grace—forgiving us and welcoming us home, no matter what we've done or not done.

- You're a sinner. I'm a sinner. All sins get in the way of our relationship with God. Forgiveness and grace are what bring us back to God.

WHAT STRUCK YOU IN THIS CHAPTER?

Jesus told all these stories about going after the lost one. He cared about every single person he met, knowing that connecting with them would mean salvation for them down the road, or at least an opportunity to accept him as Savior. Do you feel his care for you like that? Do you accept that he would come after you alone, even if he had ninety-nine others? Why or why not?

YOUR FUTURE STORY

We all fail on this road of faith. But we can fix those failures by telling God we're sorry, accepting his forgiveness, and then following the Spirit's lead so we don't make the same mistakes again. (The Spirit leads us with gentle nudges to our hearts—telling us what's right or wrong.) Regardless, he always, always loves and forgives us because he wants us to live in freedom. That's the result of Jesus's great gift to us, which covered all our sins. Can you believe that we might be in heaven with murderers, war criminals, terrorists, and robbers? God forgives anyone who truly repents of their sins and puts their trust in him. Anyone. That's what Jesus promises. And that covers you too.

> *"Rejoice with me, because I have found my lost sheep!" I tell you, in the same way, there will be more joy in heaven over one sinner who repents than over ninety-nine righteous people who don't need repentance.*
> —Luke 15:6–7

29

Battle Scars
Mark 15

Have you ever been in a pitch-black room, unable to see the door or lamp or light switch? How did you feel when you finally saw something? Relieved, right? There's something about knowing the uncomfortable experience of true darkness to make us very grateful for true light.

It was the darkest moment in history when Jesus opened his arms and heart and took upon himself the sins of the entire human race (Mark 15). By doing so, the One who had lived in perfect connection with God was momentarily disconnected. The only thing Mark recorded Jesus saying from the cross was, "My God, my God, why have you abandoned me?" (v. 34). The other gospels record additional things he said. But Mark was tuned in to the total wreckage of Jesus's heart in that moment.

The crucifixion itself was brutal, but for Jesus, being separated from his Father was more brutal still. This was why he came, to bear the brunt of our sins, to feel how far it could take us from God, so that we would never be separated from the Father again. We call it *atonement*. Making a terrible wrong right by taking the punishment for our sins.

The angels must have been devastated. The same angels who had gathered en masse to praise God at the King's birth watched as the people mocked him as "King of the Jews" on the way to the cross. They watched him get whipped. Spat on. Laughed at. A crown of thorns pushed onto his head. The angels watched as the Jewish religious leaders mocked him as "the King of Israel" and challenged him to come down from the cross.

Think of that. Jesus, King of Kings, God's own Son, brought to humanity's lowest point. The Romans crucified only the worst of criminals. Nails were driven through the prisoner's wrists and heels, and he was left to await a slow and painful death, hanging from a cross. It was a horrible way to die. And Jesus went through it for you and for me.

He could've called down the angels to rescue him. But he didn't. Because he loves us. He was willing to die to make sure we could always be with God.

Imagine This ...
Bearing the Weight of the World

My name is Henry, and my youth pastor, Jesse, wanted us to get what Jesus did.

I mean, like, really *get* what Jesus did.

He sat all twenty of us in youth group down and said, "What Jesus did was like taking on all the baggage that each of us carries and carrying it himself."

We all stayed quiet.

"You guys are all looking at me like you don't quite understand that," Jesse said. Some of the group looked up. Some of the group looked away. Of course *I* was the loser who stupidly looked him in the eye.

"Henry," he said, standing. "Can you come here?"

I heaved a sigh and walked over to him.

"Now here is what I want you to think about, guys. Think of Henry here like Jesus. No pressure," he said to me with a wink. We all laughed a bit awkwardly. "What I want the rest of you to do is go outside the worship-center doors. You'll see a pile of luggage there. Grab all the suitcases and bags you feel represent your sins today. Some are heavy. Some are light. Go."

The rest of the kids left, giggling and whispering. I took a long, deep breath.

"What you're about to experience, brother," Jesse said quietly, "is something you'll remember the rest of your life."

The kids started flowing back in toward us and standing in front of the altar, all carrying some baggage. One by one Jesse put his hands on the kid in front of him and said these words: "Child of God, you are handing off all the sins of your heart and mind that have been so heavy. Hand them now to your friend Henry as you would to Jesus."

After the first two or three kids dumped their bags on me, I was still smiling.

After the next four or five, I began to get worried.

At first I was holding all the bags, trying to show I was tough and strong.

After they dumped about fifteen more suitcases on me, I was surrounded.

After fifteen more, I was buried.

And still they came, burying me deeper and deeper with layers of baggage.

It was dark. I was worried there wasn't enough oxygen. I was stressed out that the piles would fall and actually hurt me.

Then, through the cracks, I heard Jesse. "See that?" he said. "That's a picture of your Savior buried in your sin. Dead. So you could be free. But you know what?"

What? What? I asked silently.

"He didn't stay dead. Three days later, God raised him to life. Because the price for our sins had been paid. And death couldn't hold him down."

Jesse called, "Henry? Bust loose out of that tomb now. Come out!"

With a roar I pushed and shoved, toppling the mountains of suitcases and duffel bags around me. Then I took a long, deep breath.

I didn't think any breath had ever felt so sweet.

The Skinny on Mark 15

- Mark gives us the feeling of being present, right there with Jesus on that dark day he died for us:

  - Above the cross, where even creation boiled in dark-clouded rage and grief: "Darkness came over the whole land until three in the afternoon" (Mark 15:33).
  - On the cross, when Jesus, feeling totally forsaken, cried out, "My God, my God, why have you abandoned me?" (v. 34).
  - At the foot of the cross, when the hardened Roman centurion recognized something in the way Jesus had "breathed his last" and exclaimed, "Truly this man was the Son of God!" (vv. 37, 39).

- Most of us know about the ark of the covenant from the movie *Raiders of the Lost Ark*. (If not, you can Google it.) Unfortunately the ark was lost during the Babylonian conquest. The ark used to be in a small room at the heart of the Jewish temple called the most holy place, because it represented the presence of God. Only the high priest—the highest ranking priest—got to go in there once a year. He'd enter on the Day of Atonement, when he would offer sacrifices for the sins of all the people. A curtain separated this inner room from everyone and everything else—and it was that same curtain that was torn from top to bottom when Jesus died (Mark 15:38).

> BOOM! Jesus took care of that access-to-God issue. Everyone who believes in him will have access to God forever.

- Who were those angry Sanhedrin guys? The Sanhedrin was the Jews' governing council, and they were superjealous of Jesus. They wanted to kill Jesus, but only the ruling Romans could authorize the death penalty.

WHAT STRUCK YOU IN THIS CHAPTER?

Most of us have gone to church, at least on Christmas and Easter, so we're pretty used to the story of the cross and Christ's death. But have you ever really thought about how much it hurt Jesus? And why he did it? Reading the account this time, did it become more personal to you? How so?

YOUR FUTURE STORY

Jesus didn't die so that we would live in guilt, feeling the weight of his death. He died so that we could be free from our sins, forever connected with the Father, Son, and Holy Spirit. Sometimes we have to experience the darkness to appreciate the light. Jesus deserves our respect and gratitude for what he did for us. Keep that in mind as you praise him in prayer and in worship.

Jesus let out a loud cry and breathed his last.
Then the curtain of the temple was
torn in two from top to bottom. When the centurion,
who was standing opposite him,
saw the way he breathed his last, he said, "Truly
this man was the Son of God!"
—Mark 15:37–39

30

Death Stinks ... and Life Rocks
Matthew 28

So, that day. That terrible day he died. Even thinking about it makes me take a long, deep breath. The angels must have been in deep grief. Devastated. Like the way we feel when we hear our favorite team—the one we knew just *had* to win—lost.

Times a thousand.

Or when someone we hope wins an election but doesn't.

Times a thousand.

Because God's Son, the world's savior, had just been put to death.

Life itself snuffed out, just like that.

He was killed like a common criminal. The Highest of the high treated like the lowest of the low.

You know how you feel when you're losing a game badly? You're so many points behind that there's no hope of coming back. And then miraculously, somehow, something breaks, and you have a *chance*? No, you might even have a chance at a *WIN*!?!

That's how the angels must have felt on the morning Jesus BEAT DEATH and rose from the grave. ALIVE again.

Times a HUNDRED thousand.

Imagine This ...
Witnessing the Empty Tomb

Picture this Jerusalem moment like a movie scene, when all seems lost. LOST!

You are Mary Magdalene, and your Savior, your King, the one you thought would lead the world to a new age, is gone. Put to death. Crucified. Like the worst of criminals.

All of creation seemed to mourn him these past three days, from the darkened skies to the utter stillness of the wind. As if death covered everything.

But as you approach his tomb, even though you know he's gone, you feel a twinge of warning.

An earthquake rattles the ground beneath your feet, and you and your friend hunch down, eyes wide. *What is happening?*

You notice that the enormous stone in front of Jesus's burial cave has been rolled to the side.

Rays of sun stream down between the steel-gray clouds—and you squint up at them, wondering how you can be seeing such a thing at this hour. But the rays are streaming toward ...

The tomb?

After three days of silence, a single musical note seems to ring in your head. High, with a tinge of ... hope?

Slowly you force your legs to move, your body to press forward. Dimly you realize your friend beside you has grabbed onto your dress. She looks as if she's afraid to breathe too. Together you move forward ten paces. Twenty.

Past the guards, who normally look scary-strong and ready to beat you up but now look like terrified kids, squinting up in awe at an angel—bright, *so bright*—who sits on top of the huge stone that had sealed the tomb just days before.

The mouth of the tomb is open. *Open.*

"Don't be afraid!" the angel tells you and your friend. "He is not here! He has been resurrected, just as he said. Come and see."

Could it be? you wonder. *Could it truly be?*

You pass through the mouth of the cave, the place you last glimpsed Jesus's body.

You survey the inner walls. You realize that his body, embalmed with seventy-five pounds of spices, wrapped in perfectly white pristine cloth, and sealed behind a massive boulder … is gone.

GONE!

Three more musical notes sound in your head, each one louder than the last.

You start to feel the stirrings of life again. Hope, sweet hope, fills your heart for the first time since you knew Jesus had been arrested.

The clouds split apart, and the rising sun clears the far horizon, filling the tomb with golden light as you look around once more to make sure this is real.

Yes, it's real. You aren't dreaming.

Jesus isn't here, you think. He really isn't here. *He is risen*. He is risen indeed!

The Skinny on Matthew 28

- Isn't it interesting that the first people to discover the news of Jesus's resurrection were women? Women, at the time, weren't thought to be trustworthy witnesses. They couldn't even testify in court. A common Jewish man's prayer of the time was, "God, thank you that I was not born a Gentile, a dog, or a woman." Wow, right?

- The second group of people who discovered the Big Reveal were the guards. Though they may have been members of the Jewish temple police, it's more likely that they were Roman soldiers. The Jews hated those guys, and yet they got in on the secret next? Go figure!

> Clear on this yet? Jesus invites EVERYONE to accept the truth of who he is!

- Finally, the disciples heard the miraculous news. They saw Jesus, who appeared to them in Galilee. Matthew 28:17 tells us the disciples worshipped him, though some doubted, unable to believe their eyes. But in time all of them got on board.

- Jesus said to his disciples, "All authority has been given to me in heaven and on earth. Go, therefore, and make disciples of all nations, baptizing them in the name of the Father and of the Son and of the Holy Spirit, teaching them to observe everything I have commanded you. And remember, I am with you always, to the end of the age" (Matthew 28:18–20). This is called the Great Commission. It was a big task for the disciples. But it's also what you and I are called to do.

- Wowza! Jesus wasn't talking to the pros of the faith biz, the Pharisees. He was talking to his disciples. Average guys like you and me. He put

their hands on the steering wheel of the ship and pointed ahead, say-

ing, "Go! Do what I did! I give
you my authority to do this!"
He encourages us to do the
same today. It's like being on
his team, about to head out on
the court.

> Leading others to Christ isn't just a pastor or youth-leader gig. YOU have the authority from Jesus to do it too! In fact, you are called to do it!

WHAT STRUCK YOU IN THIS CHAPTER?

Check out any calendar. See how every week begins with Sunday? For the Jews, the seventh day was supposed to be a day of rest and worship—and the seventh day was Saturday. But because Jesus rose on a Sunday, the focus of Christian worship shifted to "the first day of the week" (Matthew 28:1).

We all tend to get used to the routine of worship. But next time you walk into church, think about how you're likely worshipping on a Sunday because for almost two thousand years believers have done so, recognizing it as the day Jesus beat death when God raised him from the grave. In what ways do you think that perspective will change how you view worship? (Even if you're a Saturday-worship attender!)

YOUR FUTURE STORY

Jesus promised to be with his disciples "to the end of the age" (Matthew 28:20). Just as he was with them, he's with you and me, since we're also his disciples. What do you think of his call to go and make other disciples? How can you reach out to others, showing them Jesus's love and grace? What is he asking you to do now, big or small?

I am with you always, to the end of the age.
—Matthew 28:20

FOLLOWING JESUS

31

Jesus Lives ... in Us!
Acts 1

It's no coincidence that Luke—the writer of the gospel of Luke as well as the book of Acts—wrote to a man named Theophilus. Theo's name means "lover of God." So if you love God, you can assume that Acts 1 was written to you too.

Luke gave us a rundown of Jesus's life and ministry in his gospel, but in Acts, Luke really focused on the disciples in action. For them the Big Story had just begun! What Jesus had started, his people could continue. In Acts 1, we see Jesus with his disciples after his resurrection, just as he was about to ascend to heaven.

When Jesus told them they should hang out in Jerusalem because they were about to be baptized with the Holy Spirit (Acts 1:4–5), the disciples got all excited, think-

> Sometimes the disciples were slow to get it.

ing that maybe Jesus was about to restore "the kingdom to Israel" (v. 6).

The disciples couldn't see the kind of kingdom Jesus was building. They were thinking about an earthly kingdom in which their own soldiers had driven out their Roman enemies. He was thinking about the kingdom of *God*, of course. Remember, *kingdom of God* means "God's rule in the hearts and minds of his people."

It's kind of like when you're hoping for one birthday present and your parents have something a hundred times better planned for you! The disciples, like most of the Jewish people, were hoping for the Roman foreigners to be expelled and for the glorious days of David and Solomon to return! But their idea of the restoration of Israel was far different from God's idea. They were thinking about a political kingdom; Jesus was thinking about a spiritual kingdom spreading through the hearts of all believers.

To give you some idea of what came of that:

- Currently Israel is about one-twentieth the size of California.
- Christianity, the kingdom of God in the hearts and minds of his people, has spread *around the world*.
- There are more than eight million people in Israel.
- But there are *two billion Christians* around the world.

Jesus started his plans for his kingdom by encouraging the disciples to tell their neighbors about him. "You will be my witnesses in Jerusalem [think of this as your hometown], in all Judea and Samaria [think of this as your state and country], and to the end of the earth" (Acts 1:8).

Can you imagine what "the end of the earth" sounded like to the disciples? These guys likely hadn't traveled more than a hundred miles from home in their whole lives. The only transportation they had back in Jesus's day were two feet in sandals or, if they were lucky, a donkey. Being Jesus's witness "to the end of the earth" would've sounded pretty overwhelming. (Today it might be like being sent to the South Pole or the jungles of the Amazon.)

But Jesus knows our scaredy-cat hearts. And so he encouraged his disciples to begin at home, just as he encourages you and me to tell fellow students, friends, teammates, and neighbors about him. Once we do that, we find the courage to go a little bit farther and do a little more.

Jerusalem = Your hometown

Imagine This ...
When Faith Is Dangerous

Mosul, Iraq

"They're coming," Mama warned, the cell signal wavering. "ISIS. Just miles away. Come home! We must escape!"

"Okay, Mama," Sara said.

"Fast, baby! As fast as you can!" Mama hadn't wanted Sara to go to the library; she and Papa had been hovering near the radio, wringing their hands, when she slipped out. But they'd been immersed in the radio broadcasts for days, and Sara thought if she didn't get even a moment out of the apartment, she might lose her mind.

Now she feared that her choice might cost her life.

She left the library, just three blocks from their apartment in Mosul. She paused outside, stunned. The city was already in chaos. A jet screamed overhead, another just behind, lower than she'd ever seen. She could hear the distant boom of explosions.

People ran down the street. A family from church ran up to her, already packed and on the move. "Sara!" the father called to her. "Get home! We must all get out!"

"I am!" she called back, running even faster now, the fear in his voice making her heart beat double-time.

People were dragging suitcases and bags to cars, their faces drawn and scared. Now Sara could hear the tinny sound of a loudspeaker proclaiming that the city of Mosul belonged to Islam, not Jesus. Any "infidel dogs"—Christians, like her own family—were to convert to Islam or die.

A stream of Iraqi army jeeps filled with troops roared by Sara as she turned the corner.

They're running away? she thought angrily. *Why do they not stay and fight?*

She heard more bombs, closer now.

She turned another corner, pulled up short, and then peeked around. ISIS soldiers, their heads swathed in black, moved into a building and dragged people out, screaming at a woman and man on their knees in the middle of the street cringing before the Islamist fighters. Sara heard the word *Christian* spit out as if it were a curse word.

Taking a deep breath, she bolted across the street, hoping she'd make it to the other side without attracting any attention. Mama and Papa were already on their motorcycle waiting for her. Sara jumped on and clung to Mama's back as Papa revved the throttle. Each of them carried nothing but a bag. They could barely all fit on the motorbike.

Sara hoped they were free of ISIS as they made their way out of the chaotic city. Papa weaved between streams of wildly honking cars that were already jamming up the road. But as they slowed, they saw what was keeping people from leaving: a checkpoint at the edge of the city. They entered the line of cars, where people had turned off their engines and were pushing their cars forward to conserve gas. They walked the motorcycle forward, wincing every time they heard another bomb or the peppering of machine-gun fire. *It's close, far too close*, Sara worried. Smoke billowed from the center of the city, and more jets screamed overhead. Mama was silently weeping, as were many others in the line.

As scary as the city behind them was, what faced them ahead was far scarier. The checkpoint was close enough for them to see the ISIS soldiers heavily armed with massive guns and long, gleaming swords.

Papa leaned closer to Sara. "They will ask us about our faith. I know it's frightening, but we must stand up for Jesus."

Gulp. They'd talked about this before. A lot. But now it was real. "Papa, I'm so scared."

"Me too, baby," he reassured, pulling her and Mama closer. "But we're not alone. Our God is with us. He will see us through, or he will see us to heaven. Be brave."

The closer they got, the more people started their engines again. Exhaust filled the air, making Sara's eyes and lungs burn. But she would've stayed forever in that cloud if they could've avoided the terrifying soldiers.

The car in front of them pulled away, and it was their turn at last.

Papa stepped forward, and Mama and Sara followed. Mama's tears were dry now, her mouth set in a grim line.

"Who are you?" asked a soldier, lifting his gun toward Papa.

"My family and I are Christians, and now that this is a Muslim city, we must leave."

The soldier stared at Papa coldly. Then the guard turned and waved another soldier forward. The two spoke in undertones for a moment. A third soldier joined them.

The third guard approached them. "You are Christians?" he asked, sounding surprised. Sara guessed that others in the line ahead of them had made up some acceptable excuse for fleeing. But Papa had always said they were to be truthful about their God in good times or bad.

"Yes, we are," Papa stated.

"Then you must convert to Islam, or you, your wife, and your child will be killed. It is simple, no?"

"I cannot," Papa replied. "For my Jesus died for me. Saved me. How can I turn my back on him?"

One of the soldiers pulled out his sword, the sound ringing in Sara's ears.

"No, please," Papa said calmly. He went on to quote passages from the Qur'an that allowed Christians to live if they paid certain *jizya*, or taxes.

Another man stalked toward them. He appeared to be in charge. "What is the holdup?" he asked irritably. "We must get these streets cleared of traffic."

"This man says he and his family are Christians," said the first soldier, raising the gun barrel to Papa's throat.

Sara screamed inside. She didn't want Papa to die. She didn't want to die. *Be with us, Jesus*, she prayed silently. *Save us! We are yours!*

"Wait," commanded the leader, pushing away the soldier's gun. "I know this man." The man giving orders moved to face Papa, and Papa dared to meet his gaze. "You traveled from town to town last year offering help to the widows and orphans, yes? Handing out your Bible of lies?"

Papa nodded slowly, as if admitting this might not help them escape. "We did," he said, glancing to Sara's mother. "Our faith demands that we help those in need, that we show Christ's love to all we meet. Even to you, who might hate us."

With a growl, the first man raised his gun again, and the second wielded his razor-sharp sword.

Sara couldn't help it; she let out a little cry. Mama pulled her closer. Sara squeezed her eyes shut. *Jesus, Jesus, Jesus*, she prayed.

"Wait," the leader interrupted. There was something about him that made Sara think his heart had grown tired of being a loyal ISIS soldier and he was just pretending to be. "You left behind an apartment in the city?"

"We did," Papa said.

"Do you own it?"

"I do."

"Do you carry the deed?"

"I do."

"And you are willing to pay the tax?"

"I am, sir."

In line, Sara had heard others speak of this money deal. The "tax" would mean that ISIS would own the apartment outright. But it didn't matter if it meant getting away from the city and all those who hated them.

The commander pulled out a cell phone and dialed a number. He turned away to have a short conversation as the soldier with the sword continued to circle the family like a lion sniffing its prey.

A minute later the leader returned. "Sign the deed and give it to me. You're being permitted to leave so you can tell your people that we will reign victorious. You leave our land now, but soon all will be ours. We won't stop until the pope himself converts to Islam."

The other two soldiers let out sounds of disgust. One spat on top of Papa's shoe as he passed. Then they turned their attention to the family behind Sara's.

As Papa handed over the deed, the commander leaned close. "One of the women you ministered to was my great-aunt," he said in a whisper. "My aunt said that if it wasn't for you, she would have died that week. She read your Bible and shared it with us. Pray for us who live in secret among your enemies; we do not yet have your courage."

Papa's eyes widened, but he said nothing. To do so could have endangered the man's life.

And as they rode down the paved highway out of town, Sara looked back and prayed for their unlikely angel and Christ's light, burning like an ember inside this compassionate man.[2]

The Skinny on Acts 1

- Jesus knew that with the Holy Spirit soon to arrive, the disciples would have all they needed to establish his kingdom. With his own physical work on earth done, he then ascended to (went up to) heaven.

- Jesus's ascension proves there is a place his followers go when they die: it's heaven. If we belong to Jesus, we'll see him there (John 14:2–3).

- In Acts 1 we see the disciples gathering together again and finding a replacement for Judas, who had betrayed Jesus and then taken his own life out of remorse. The disciples made sure that Judas's replacement was a man who

While our first-century ancestors were focused on filling the coveted number 12 position, the roster expanded over time to millions; you're a disciple of Christ too. *Disciple* means "follower" or "student."

had been following Jesus from his baptism to his ascension—they clearly wanted someone with a "first-person" account! There were two contenders that rose to the top; Matthias won the spot.

- Acts, or the Acts of the Apostles, is about the birth of the church, which began in Jerusalem. Through the apostles (Jesus's inner circle of twelve disciples), the Holy Spirit accomplished amazing things that resulted in thousands of new believers. It didn't take long for the religious elite to have the apostles arrested (chapters 4 and 5), but it took longer for them to find charges that would stick.

WHAT STRUCK YOU IN THIS CHAPTER?

What is the hardest part about being a Christian? While most kids who read this book won't likely be living in a country that is so *physically* against us (like our story from Mosul, Iraq), Christians are starting to see some pushback even in Western societies. Do you think that your friends want to hear about Jesus? Why or why not? Do you ever feel ashamed or scared to share your faith? How is the Spirit encouraging you to be brave?

YOUR FUTURE STORY

After Jesus returned to heaven, the disciples strained their eyes, staring at the sky for any sign of him (Acts 1:9–10). (Wouldn't you totally have done the same?) But an angel basically told them, "People! PEOPLE! Why are you just standing around? He'll be back." I can't help but think of the angel looking at them, arms crossed, as if saying, "Don't you have things to *do*!"

Are you gazing up at heaven, waiting for Jesus to return, or are you on the move, heading out "to the end of the earth" (or maybe beyond!)? What is one thing you feel the Spirit urging you to do as a witness of Christ?

> *You will receive power when the Holy Spirit has come*
> *on you, and you will be my witnesses in Jerusalem, in all*
> *Judea and Samaria, and to the end of the earth.*
>
> —Acts 1:8

32

Happy Birthday to Us
Acts 2

The church was born! Now when I say *church*, I'm not talking about your worship center, school gymnasium, or beautiful old sanctuary. The church isn't just a building; it's the living, breathing BODY of Christ! It's me. It's you. And every believer in Christ we know or have yet to meet.

The church's official birthday was on the day of Pentecost, a Jewish holiday that celebrated the first of the wheat harvest and the gift of God's law to Moses on Mount Sinai. But at this particular harvest festival, things were about to get wild.

A great *spiritual* harvest was about to begin.

Remember that gift of power Jesus had promised his disciples before he ascended to heaven (Acts 1:8)? That outpouring of power was about to arrive.

Think about the strongest wind you've ever experienced. When I was a kid, we vacationed on a lake every summer. Fierce storms surged across the lake with winds so intense that we had to lean at an angle to steady our feet. We loved those amazing storms and how they almost robbed us of breath! Maybe you have experienced even scarier winds, like hurricanes and tornadoes. Sometimes wind can be destructive. But the Greek word for "wind" in Acts 2:2 can also mean "breath." God was breathing life into his church when that wind blew through Jerusalem.

In addition to wind, Pentecost also involved fire, a symbol of power. Where else do we see fire in the Bible? In the burning bush, when God called Moses (Exodus 3). And in the pillar of fire that led God's people in the desert at night (13:21). And when the prophet Elisha saw the prophet Elijah being taken up to heaven in a chariot of fire (2 Kings 2:11–12). These were moments when humans understood they were in God's presence. Now these disciples had flames dancing over their very heads!

As if wind and flame rushing among that original group of believers wasn't enough, the Holy Spirit filled them, and they "began to speak in different [languages], as the Spirit enabled them" (Acts 2:4). Because it was Pentecost, people from distant places were visiting Jerusalem to celebrate. Imagine how amazed these foreign visitors were when they heard Jesus's disciples speaking their languages!

Wow, right?

The more passionately we follow Jesus, the more experiences we'll have like this that we can't totally explain. God wants to be an active, living part of our lives rather than someone who does things we can always explain. He lives beyond the limits of time and space, so it makes sense that he can accomplish things that can't be explained.

Keep deepening your friendship with God, and you'll experience answers to prayers you thought were impossible, coincidences that lead to beautiful blessings, and perhaps even miraculous healings that make doctors shake their heads in disbelief. All of that starts with the Holy Spirit coming to live in you. This is how Christ lives and works through you. Every time you get to be a part of what he's doing, you'll feel incredible wonder and gladness.

We can get a little fidgety giving the Spirit room to do what he wants through us. Our own sinful nature wants to clamp down and be in control. But when we insist on being in control, we aren't allowing God to rule our lives. And in doing so, we're choking the breath out of our part of the kingdom of God.

The apostle Peter preached about Jesus, and three thousand people accepted the message and were baptized that day (Acts 2:41). They committed to learning more about Christ, to hanging out and eating with one another, to praying, and to giving to those in need (vv. 42–47).

On the day of Pentecost the small group of believers became three thousand … and today there are more than two billion Christians around the world.

That was some amazing birthday party, huh?

Imagine This …
Witnessing the Power of God

Avi followed his father down the winding streets of Jerusalem. It was the day of Pentecost, the fiftieth day after Passover, and the Holy City was flooded with pilgrims from very far away and also all the normal residents. At times Avi held on to the back of his father's coat in order not to lose him as they entered a part of the city that he'd never been to before. He looked up at the towering yellow limestone walls that seemed to close in on them, and tripped.

His father turned back to him and frowned, helping him up. "Pay attention, Avi. We're nearing the temple courts!" Then his father took Avi's hand firmly in his and led him onward. They turned and climbed a steep hill, passing merchants selling olives and spices and other things, but Avi kept his gaze firmly on the cobblestone street before him. He would not trip again.

Soon they reached a courtyard where several of his father's friends had gathered, greeting one another and discussing the day's news. At times Avi's father was drawn into a debate. But Avi was drawn toward the cracked door of the building nearby. He'd glimpsed movement and heard laughter and discussion that intrigued him.

Avi eased away from his father and friends and reached the front door. He peeked in and saw a big white-stone room intersected by columns. The men inside seemed like many of his father's friends, but Avi instinctively knew they were different. He recognized one of them, the one they called Peter. He'd heard others say that Peter and his friends were Jesus followers! They were on the other side of the room, while women were setting food and drink on a table to the side. The men appeared to be praying. With a furtive glance back at his father—still in deep discussion—Avi moved to the nearest column, trying to hear them better.

But as soon as he reached the column, the window shutters on the far side of the room began to shake, a wind building beyond them. Avi frowned as the whistle of the wind quickly became a howl. A moment later, the wind blasted open the shuttered windows, banging them against the walls. Everyone's hair was whipped into a tangled mess, head coverings sent flying. Robes flapped about like flags.

What struck Avi most was that no one shouted or cried out, even as his own heart pounded. The men continued to pray, actually drawing nearer to one another.

There's something different about this wind, Avi thought. It wasn't the ordinary wind that pulled and chilled; this one somehow warmed, filled, covered, comforted. It smelled like the earth—of rain and perfect dirt for planting, and sweet flowers and warm spices.

The men who were praying were now practically glowing. Avi blinked as tiny flames flickered around their heads! It was as if each of them were mesmerized by some dazzling treasure, hearing some far-off whisper. They lifted their palms toward the ceiling.

Toward God, Avi realized. *That* was who was in this room, in the wind … The feel of his presence spoke of power and dominion beyond anything he'd experienced before. It was like being before the throne of the mightiest king ever to rule!

Soon the Jesus followers who were praying began to praise God's name. Jews from around the world had come to Jerusalem for Pentecost, and each heard these people speaking in their own language. Avi heard them in his language, Hebrew.

"Praise him, who is the King of Kings!"

"Praise the Holy One, who was and is and is to come!"

"Praise you, Creator, master of everyone here and in all the earth!"

Avi pulled his eyes away to look at the others, hovering in the doorway, who wore the same expression of wonder that had to be on his face too. His father met his gaze, mouth gaping open.

But then they just nodded together and smiled, looking back to the anointed men before them.

In a whisper, Avi began praising God too.

And what poured out of his own mouth sounded like music.

The Skinny on Acts 2

- VOCAB CHECK: Why was this day called Pentecost? It was literally the fiftieth day after Passover. And *pentekonta* means "fifty" in Greek.

- The church: You might be Baptist, Lutheran, Methodist, Presbyterian, Episcopalian, nondenominational, or you might go to a house church. If you believe in Christ, *you are the church*!

> Christians are like different flavors of ice cream; they each have their own unique tastes, but they're all ice cream.

- The first Christians strengthened their faith by doing certain things (Acts 2:42–47):

  - Learning about Jesus
  - Hanging out together

- Eating together and sharing Communion ("the breaking of bread")
- Praying together
- Talking about the wonders of God they could see
- Experiencing miracles
- Sharing what they owned with one another
- Serving others
- Worshipping together
- Praising God

If we do these things too, we'll grow deeper in our faith!

- How do you hear the Holy Spirit when he's not acting like a rushing wind or appearing in tongues of fire? Usually he's much more subtle.

  - A nudge from God's Spirit might be something a friend, a relative, or even someone on a YouTube video says that strikes you as something you need to think over some more, keeping the truth revealed in the Scriptures in mind as you think it through.
  - The Spirit might use a passage you read in the Bible or even a story to point to something you specifically need to pay attention to or change in your life.
  - Or perhaps you'll sense something while you're praying, like God's Spirit whispering to your heart or mind.
  - Whenever, however you feel that twinge or deep urging in your gut or heart, pay attention! That's the way the Spirit talks to us.

- How do you know it's truth from the Spirit and not your own wrong thinking or lies from the Evil One (because he whispers to us too)? Whatever the Spirit tells you would be something Jesus and the Bible would encourage too. If you're hearing something that doesn't match

up with what you think Jesus would encourage you to do, talk to a
parent, pastor, or youth leader.

- Usually the Spirit encourages us to do good things or directs
  us to correct bad choices. His goal is for Jesus to work in and
  through us.
- The Evil One just tries to tear us down and slow us down.
  His goal is to defeat Christ and separate us from Jesus. If the
  whispers we hear would keep us from doing what Jesus would
  want us to do or from getting closer to our Savior, then it's
  the Enemy.
- The good news is that Jesus conquered the Evil One! We can
  just pray those whispers away so we can concentrate on the
  good stuff from the Spirit and keep building up our faith, one
  step at a time, stronger and stronger.

WHAT STRUCK YOU IN THIS CHAPTER?

Kids are often more trusting and open to God's Spirit than adults are. Why do you think that might be? How can you remain open to the Spirit as you get older? What do you think gets in the way for adults?

YOUR FUTURE STORY

Consider J. Oswald Sanders's definition of the Spirit-filled person as one who surrenders to God the entirety of his or her identity—will (what you decide to do), mind (what you decide to believe), emotions (what feelings you give power), and strength (what you can do physically). Based on this definition, are you Spirit filled? Why or why not? Which aspect of your identity from this four-part list do you need to surrender to God today?

> *"Repent and be baptized, each of you, in the name of Jesus Christ for the forgiveness of your sins, and you will receive the gift of the Holy Spirit. For the promise is for you and for your children, and for all who are far off, as many as the Lord our God will call."*

> —Acts 2:38–39

33

Autobots, Roll Out!
Acts 9

He was your worst nightmare. A monster. A hunter. A tracker. With one purpose … to root out and kill as many Christians as he could.

As a Pharisee, Saul of Tarsus knew the Old Testament backward and forward. And he used the ancient writings to trap many new believers who followed Jesus. He was present when Stephen—a godly Christ follower (they didn't call them Christians yet) who was full of the Spirit, wisdom, faith, grace, and power (Acts 6:3, 5, 8)—was stoned to death (7:54–8:1). Saul hunted down believers and threw them in prison (22:4). He tried to make Christ followers say publicly that Jesus is the Son of God—a declaration that could be deemed blasphemy, which was punishable by death (26:10–11).

Saul was lethal. A deadly force.

One day he was traveling to Damascus, in Syria, desperate to get there before any of his horrid enemies spread their Christian "lies" even farther. Saul had to put an end to the nonsense of these Jesus followers.

But then God abruptly interrupted Saul's life.

A blinding flash of light.

A fall to the ground.

Then a booming voice: "Saul, Saul, why are you persecuting me?" (Acts 9:4).

Jesus stepped into Saul's life at that point. Jesus felt his followers' persecution and suffering as his own. Just as he does today. And so he called Saul to face him … to face the Truth.

Recognizing that this was surely the voice of God, Saul asked, "Who are you, Lord?"

"I am Jesus, the one you are persecuting," Jesus firmly replied. "But get up and go into the city, and you will be told what you must do" (Acts 9:5–6).

So began the transformation of one of history's greatest Christian disciples. Saul was the apostle's Jewish name, and Paul was his Roman name. In the midst of his missionary travels in the predominantly Gentile world, he became better known as Paul. He

> This guy went from archenemy to ultimate hero of the faith!

eventually wrote most of nearly half the books in the New Testament. And became a major *defender* of the faith. He would suffer much in the future, just as he made other believers suffer in the past.

If Jesus can transform such a horrendous sinner into a saint, he can do the same with any of us … or anyone we meet. We're all radically transformed when we accept Christ as our Savior, commit to growing stronger in our faith, and allow the Holy Spirit to work in and through us.

Like the Autobots depicted in the movie *Transformers*, a person can begin as one type of warrior but become an entirely new kind of warrior sent out to fight for the good news of Jesus!

So it was for Saul.

Imagine This ...
Called to Fight for the Enemy

Saul paced around the room for the thousandth time. About ten paces wide and ten paces deep, the room held nothing but a mat to sleep on. He'd been blind for three days. And every hour since he arrived in Damascus, on a street named Straight, he'd been praying to God. And yes, *yes*, here and there he'd been praying to Jesus, who had just spoken to him. Over and over Saul asked himself, *Is it really possible? Is this Jesus truly the Messiah? Did the ruling authorities really put God's own Son to death?*

Saul worried that he was going mad. Surely it wasn't possible for Jesus to *really* be God. Or was it? Hadn't Jesus spoken to him on the road to Damascus?

A knock sounded at the door. "Enter," he muttered, his voice thin and raspy from lack of water.

From the sound of it, two men entered the room. One coughed nervously; the other cleared his throat, inhaled deeply, and then left.

"Who is it? Who is there?" Saul asked.

The man who remained pressed his hands on Saul's shoulders. Saul's neck hairs prickled. He could feel the power in this stranger. Saul fell to his knees, instantly recognizing this power ... the same sort of power that struck him blind on the road.

"B-brother Saul," stuttered the man.

Saul felt ashamed. He knew why the visitor was frightened. Had Saul not led many like him to trial? Even to death?

"The-the Lord Jesus," the man went on, "who appeared to you on the road as you were c-coming here, he has sent me so that you may see again and be filled with the Holy Spirit."

As soon as the man's words tumbled out, Saul's heavy eyelids began to lift. Ever since Saul had lost his eyesight, his eyes felt as if they were caked in mud. Saul blinked once, twice. *I can see*, he thought, blinking again. "I can see!" he couldn't help but yell out.

But as Saul focused on Ananias, this man with the healing touch, Saul knew he could "see" in other ways too. The truth seeped down from his mind to his heart, filling him, teaching him, showing him, strengthening him, and making him bold.

Saul had been fighting for the wrong side all along. Now he too was a part of "the Way."

And God's presence and healing were Saul's call to make right what he'd gotten so wrong.

The Skinny on Acts 9

- Do kids in your school call you or other kids mean names? Something that puts you down? Well, in Saul's day, the "mean" name might have been *Christ follower.*

- Early believers called themselves disciples. These first disciples were learning to live under Jesus's leadership.

- Poor Ananias must have been shaking in his sandals when God called him to go to Saul, since he knew that this superscary enemy had come to arrest Christians in his city (Acts 9:13–14).

- When God calls, we're supposed to answer. How does he call?

  - *Through Scripture* (2 Timothy 3:16–17): Remember what we talked about earlier? Do certain Scripture verses call out to you? Does something ever make you want to reread certain Scriptures? Why might that be?
  - *Through other people:* Has somebody said something recently that keeps going through your mind again and again? Why might that be?
  - *Through the circumstances of our lives:* Pay attention to what's happening in your life. Why do you suppose you're experiencing certain circumstances? Do you think God might be trying to tell you something?

WHAT STRUCK YOU IN THIS CHAPTER?

Think about the worst person you know. Do you think God could transform this person into someone who loves God and others? Why or why not? Now think of the worst person you've ever heard about on the news. Do you think God could transform this person? Think about it. Is anyone really beyond the reach of God?

YOUR FUTURE STORY

You might call yourself a Christian, but are you ready to call yourself a disciple? Someone actively learning how to live as Jesus did? Are you ready to be his hands and feet in the world? What's holding you back?

*Saul was with the disciples in Damascus for some time. Immediately he
began proclaiming Jesus in the synagogues: "He is the Son of God." All
who heard him were astounded and said, "Isn't this the man in Jerusalem
who was causing havoc for those who called on this name and came
here for the purpose of taking them as prisoners to the chief priests?"*

—Acts 9:19–21

34

Hardly an Exclusive Club
Acts 10

Do you have cliques at your school? The cool kids? The athletes? The mathletes? The computer geeks?

If the Jews of Jesus's time had had a club of their own, you might have been left out. Because to Jews in ancient Israel, there were only two groups of people: Jews and Gentiles (non-Jews). If you weren't a descendant of Abraham, you were out. In fact, to the Jews, you were more than out; you were God's enemy.

But Jesus changed that. And he left his Jewish friends and followers with a lot of questions. Sure, they'd seen Jesus reach out to Gentile and Jew alike, but most Jesus followers weren't quite ready to do the same. Thankfully his disciples had been called to begin their ministry (to tell others about Jesus) in Jerusalem. In this city Jesus followers could focus their efforts on spreading the good news right there among their own Jewish people.

Acts 10 begins with the apostle Peter staying in the house of a tanner (a person who works with leather), which would have already put him in edgy territory. Jews considered tanners unclean

Cornelius was about as Gentile-y as a Gentile could get!

because they dealt with dead animals and hides. But then Peter was called to the house of Cornelius, a Roman centurion from Italy. That must have made Peter seriously anxious.

Thankfully God used a vision (like a dream) to open Peter's mind and heart and prepare him for a change of perspective. In the vision Peter saw a sheet coming down from heaven. The sheet held all kinds of animals that Jews just didn't eat on their kosher diet (according to Jewish law). A voice commanded, "Get up, Peter; kill and eat" (Acts 10:13).

Peter protested: "No, Lord! ... For I have never eaten anything impure and ritually unclean!"

"Again, a second time, the voice said to him, 'What God has made clean, do not call [unclean]'" (vv. 14–15).

> Note that God used animals to speak to Peter. God can use anything to get our attention!

Before the meaning of the vision was fully revealed to Peter, he was on his way to meet with Cornelius. And before the call of Christ was fully revealed to Cornelius, God heard his prayer (Acts 10:3–5). This shows us that God is at work in many ways and on multiple levels. His aim is to capture the heart of every person he can, whether Gentile or Jew or ... God hater or new Christian.

God wants EVERYONE to hear the good news about Jesus's love and recognize his message as truth. The people who choose to believe in the one true God are his people, regardless of their backgrounds.

Imagine This ...
The Weirdest Christian Club Ever

Imagine yourself in a gym with a hundred high-energy kids. Not one of them is the same. You can't picture more than a few of them ever hanging out together.

People of every race.

Rich kids in clothes you've seen only in magazines.

Kids who live on the street, begging or stealing money.

Track stars and Minecraft scoreboard champs.

A girl who won the state chess tournament, and a guy who barely made it out of third grade.

Guys who wear makeup, and girls who don't.

Mean kids dressed in black leather, looking like they want to hurt somebody. Supersweet kids grinning at everyone around them.

Kids who could be models, and others who never could.

Some kids speaking like educated adults, and other kids speaking in a language you think is English, but you aren't quite sure.

Never have you felt so alone. You feel so different from everybody else in the room.

"I love you," says someone beside you in the gym, "and that makes you one with them." You look up to see it's Jesus, but he's already walking around pointing toward other people. "I love them too. And that makes you all my crazy, beautiful, wonderfully different children, bound by your hearts, if nothing else." Jesus looks back at you. "And trust me, that's enough."

Jesus kindly smiles and motions you forward. "Now come on. Get to know a few of them. You'll see. You have more in common than you think."

The Skinny on Acts 10

- Peter, who saw Jesus minister to Gentile and Jew alike, really preferred to stick with the Jews. Maybe Peter thought he'd deal with the Gentiles later, or maybe he thought someone else would.

- Peter didn't understand how to accept people of all races, so God decided to make sure he got on track:

- God gave Peter a vision (Acts 10:9–16).
- God told Peter that three men had arrived and were looking for him (v. 19).
- Peter went downstairs, and those men told him why they were there (vv. 21–22).
- Peter could see that God was asking him not to count anyone out, so he went with them to Cornelius's house (vv. 23–24).
- Cornelius told Peter that an angel had appeared to him (vv. 30–31).
- Cornelius obeyed the angel's instructions and sent men to find Peter. Then Cornelius gathered a bunch of people to hear from Peter, basically giving him access to them all (vv. 32–33).

> Peter couldn't turn away from an open mic!

- Unless you're Jewish by heritage, you're a Gentile too.

WHAT STRUCK YOU IN THIS CHAPTER?

It's in our nature to be suspicious of people who look or act differently than we do. We might not approve of how other people act or dress, how they think, or what they say. But Jesus wants Christians to be known by our radical love, joy, and peace more than by anything else. If we love people well, we'll attract them to Jesus and the good news. Our kindness may encourage others to say, "I want to be more like them," rather than send them away thinking, *I don't want to be anything like them.*

How can you love others better?

YOUR FUTURE STORY

What about looking at everyone you meet as people God loves? People he wants to know his truth. Sure, there will always be individuals who are stubbornly against God. But we never want to give them a reason to stay that way. People can sense it when we don't love them or even try to like them.

Is there anyone you secretly hate or think bad thoughts about? Tell Jesus about it. Ask him to change your mind and heart so he can work through you to reach that person or group.

> *Peter began to speak: "Now I truly understand that God doesn't show favoritism, but in every nation the person who fears him and does what is right is acceptable to him. He sent the message to the Israelites, proclaiming the good news of peace through Jesus Christ—he is Lord of all."*
>
> —Acts 10:34–36

35

Heaven Is Real
Revelation 22

Hey, I want to share with you a dream I had as a kid at a superimportant moment of my faith life. This may sound more like an "Imagine This" section, but it's what I actually experienced. I hope it will help you think about how God reaches toward us.

It was nighttime in the village of adobe houses. All of them had open doors and open windows. I slipped through a door, and finding the house empty, I crawled through a window and then through the window of the next home. This home was also empty. My agitation was growing. Would I never find it? What was I looking for? I knew at the start, but now I couldn't remember.

I moved from house to house, searching, searching until the flickering light of a fire drew me to the window of the last adobe in the line. There, a circle of people surrounded a campfire.

A man looked up at me.

"Lisa, what are you looking for?"

"The Alpha and the Omega," I said, suddenly remembering what I sought. But as soon as I was saying the words, I knew that the man I was looking at WAS the Alpha and the Omega.

Jesus. Right there before me.

"I am with you," he said. "Just as I always have been and always will be. Why are you looking for me?"

I fell down on my knees.

You know what's weird? I don't recall ever hearing the name Alpha and Omega before I had this dream. I think God first revealed his special name to me in this dream when I

Alpha and Omega = Beginning and End

needed to know he was present with me and always would be.

Like my dream, the book of Revelation is also part encouragement to the church and part dream or vision, written at a superimportant time of the church's beginning. Jesus's people were facing intense persecution; they were being asked to worship the Roman emperor as a god (who was a false god, of course). Some Christians were preaching a compromise between the emperor groupies and the Christian faith. The apostle John was sent to an island prison colony because of his missionary work. But that didn't stop him putting pen on parchment.

John wanted to encourage the faithful and tell people that God and Satan were moving toward a throwdown. John wanted the faithful to stand strong, no matter what Satan aimed at them, even if they faced death. And in the vision John received, he saw a glimpse of heaven that every believer will see.

I don't know about you, but knowing heaven is real is a great comfort to me. God is all about LIFE, and Jesus conquered death so that we can spend eternal life with him.

Imagine This ...
Watching Someone on the Edge of Heaven

My name is Noel, and my gramma was about to die ...

Gramma had been on the "edge of heaven," as Mom called it, for some time. I actually hated to go and visit Gramma in the nursing home these days. But every Saturday without fail, Mom hustled me out of bed, through breakfast, and off to the most depressing place possible.

The care facility's floors were clean and polished, but I breathed through my mouth because I found the mixture of urine and Lysol nauseating. *I hate it here, I hate it here, I hate it here,* I chanted silently. But if I refused to go visit Gramma, Mom would be totally mad at me all day. I'd done that before.

I just had to get through our twenty-minute visit, and I'd be done for another week.

We entered Gramma's room, and I looked around at the framed pictures, Bible verses, and cross on her wall, as I always did before I dragged my eyes over to Gramma. She lay there in bed, mouth partially open, eyes glassy and wide. Mom pulled Gramma's blanket up higher, bent over, and kissed her on the cheek. "Hi, Mother. It's me and Noel. We're here to see you."

As usual, Gramma didn't respond. Her hands were oddly curled inward and didn't move.

"Wouldn't that be weird if she actually said something this time?" I said. "'Hey, girls! Noel! Karla! I've been looking forward to this all week!'"

Mom gave me what hardly passed as a smile before resting her hand on Gramma's shoulder. Mom considered my words, then blinked slowly. "Not until we see her on the other side of heaven, I'm afraid," she said sadly. "There we'll see Gramma as she once was. Young and vibrant. Her mind as clear as a bell."

Mom moved to pull out the dead flowers from the vase we'd brought last week. She ran new water in the vase and then slipped in a fresh bunch of daffodils.

"Why bring her those?" I asked, flopping into the big plastic chair beside Gramma's bed, legs spread apart. "Do you think she even sees them?"

"I don't know," Mom said, arranging the flowers. "I'd like to think she does. And even if there's an off chance, it makes me feel better to know she'd see these beauties and be reminded that she's loved." Mom turned and picked up Gramma's chart. After reading it a moment, she frowned. "Noel, I'll be right back. I need to go talk to the nurses about something."

I sighed but said nothing. Mom knew I didn't like being left alone with Gramma. Not now.

I forced myself to look at Gramma, searching for traces of the person I'd once known. The one who had baked cookies with me and taught me to bait a hook and fish. The one who had cheered at my soccer games. The one she'd been before Alzheimer's robbed her of everything she was, everything I'd loved, leaving a shell of a person who resembled my gramma but acted nothing like her.

While I was studying her profile, Gramma blinked slowly … and then again. Trust me when I tell you, even *that* was an event these days. But then, she turned her face toward me. Her hands uncurled a little, and she lifted her arm—I'm not kidding you; she lifted her arm!—as if reaching for someone beside me.

"Mom," I whispered, half mesmerized, half in terror. *"Mom!"*

Gramma didn't seem to hear me. It was as if she was totally focused on a person beside me. Her wrinkled lips parted into a smile. Her eyes! Her beautiful blue eyes! I hadn't seen Gramma really notice anything in so long, I'd forgotten how pretty her eyes really were.

"Gramma," I said, taking her hand in mine and rising to get closer. "Gramma, it's me, Noel."

"Ah, my sweet Noel," she managed, her voice weak, timid. "Do you see him?" she asked.

"Who? Who, Gramma?" I asked, looking around the room, seeing nothing.

"My Jesus," she said, her smile growing wider. "And his angels. His angels ..."

Gramma's eyes grew wider, her wispy brows arching in surprise. "Oh!" she exclaimed, as if hearing something. "OH!" And then her whole face lit up, like it used to when we spilled out of the car to see her after months away. Only better.

Tingles ran down my arms, and my breath caught.

I knew then what was happening.

What this was.

With Jesus and his angels.

Gramma was *seeing heaven*.

And she was about to enter it.

"Mom!" I cried, finally remembering I should call out to her. "Mom! Come here!"

Mom appeared in the doorway, her hand to her mouth. And I ran to hug her.

She stood there in the doorway, her arm around me. "Is she?"

"She is," I said, crying now.

We raced back to either side of her bed, and Mom held one hand and I held the other.

"We'll see you, Mother," my mom said, tears slipping down her face. "We'll see you there soon."

The Skinny on Revelation 22

- Many kids worry they're going to be bored in heaven. But think about it this way: Consider the most perfect day you've ever had. The day you wished wouldn't end. The day that left

  > I'm thinkin' we won't be bored in heaven!

  you sad because it had to end. The one that even now makes you wish you could experience those twenty-four hours again. Heaven will be *that* kind of day for *eternity*.

- Revelation 22 gives us a peek at what heaven will look like:

  - *A river* (v.1): Thirsty? Need a bath? Want to go swimming? Or float down the river? It's there.

- *A street* (v. 2): Has someone you loved died and gone to heaven before you? I bet you'll meet up with your loved one, and many others you can't wait to meet, on this Main Street of streets!
- *A tree* (v. 2): The Tree of Life, to be specific, bearing different fruit every month. Ever heard of the Fruit of the Month Club that ships a box of pears or apples or oranges to your door every month? It'll be like that but better. This tree speaks to both the variety and the life we'll find in heaven. No one is EVER bored there.
- *A throne* (v. 3): No more wondering where God or Jesus is. You'll be able to approach the throne whenever you wish and join the throng of creation worshipping God and the Lamb.

WHAT STRUCK YOU IN THIS CHAPTER?

Have you ever really thought about where you'll go when you die? If not, stop and think about it right now. Have you thought about heaven? What do you think it will be like? Who are some of the people you'll look forward to seeing again or meeting for the first time?

YOUR FUTURE STORY

If you knew you had one last day on earth, what would you do with it? Whom would you most want to spend time with? What would you say to that person? Life is precious! Most of us will live to be very old, but no matter how long we live, we're called to appreciate every moment. Think about ways you can move beyond *surviving* your days to *thriving*, really appreciating the people on the journey with you and praising God for all the good things surrounding you.

*Look, I am coming soon, and my reward is
with me to repay each person according to his
work. I am the Alpha and the Omega, the first
and the last, the beginning and the end.*
—Revelation 22:12–13

GOD'S MESSAGE
FOR YOU

36

You Were Born to Be God's Kid
Romans 8

Growing up, I always thought it was strange when Christians called one another "sister" or "brother." These Christians weren't from the same family, so why do such a thing? It also made me think of God calling us his children. C'mon! God lives in heaven, right? And I had a mom and dad down here. Why would he call me his child?

But the longer I've walked this earth, the more I understand why God created such language for the body of believers. First, he is our heavenly Father, with a ginormous interest in each of us. Romans 8:14–17 says, "*All those led by God's Spirit are God's sons [and daughters]*. You did not receive a spirit of slavery to fall back into fear. Instead, you received the *Spirit of adoption*, by whom we cry out, '*Abba*, Father!' The Spirit himself testifies together with our spirit that *we are God's children*, and if children, also heirs—*heirs of God and coheirs with Christ*—if indeed we suffer with him so that we may also be glorified with him." (Notice the emphasized words.)

> *Abba* literally means "Daddy." That's what God invites us to call him!

Whoa. So maybe you've been adopted or have an adopted sibling or know someone who has been adopted. Aren't adopted kids as much a part of their families as biological kids? Sure they are! In some ways they're even more celebrated because their adoptive parents sought them out and chose them, just as God chose you and me.

He not only chose us to be in his family, but he also "predestined [us] to be conformed to the image of his Son, so that he would be the first-born among many brothers and sisters" (Romans 8:29). Double that WHOA! God not only adopted us; he also made Jesus our big bro!

> This is just a fancy-shmancy way of saying we're destined to become more like Jesus!

We might have visions of becoming an astronaut or the president or a doctor or a teacher when we grow up, but the best vision of all is to become more like Jesus. God has given us a tool kit to help us know how he'd want to remodel our hearts—the Bible and the Spirit. Knowing Jesus better and better each year helps us the most. After all, if we can see who we want to be like, then we can model our actions after his. Scripture and good teachers and pastors can help us see him in "brothers and sisters" around us. (Yes, that could possibly include your actual brother or sister!) The family of God encourages us to do life the way Jesus did, reaching out to others, serving others, loving others.

But as we *do life*, hard times come. Parents sometimes lose jobs. Siblings sometimes lose their tempers. Relatives get sick, sometimes really sick. Best friends move away. Do you know the best part of being God's kid? "We know that all things work together for the good of those who love God, who are called according to his purpose" (Romans 8:28). Even in those yucky, stressful times, God is at work making us more like his Son, who suffered lots of horrible things and stressful times.

What did Jesus do when he faced hard times? He looked to his Father. Jesus trusted his Abba Daddy even when every fiber of his being recoiled at the thought of what was ahead—his crucifixion (Mark 14:32–36). But

Jesus knew he was never alone. Just like we can know our Abba Daddy is with us forever.

Imagine This ...
Becoming More like Jesus

Pretend that you have the perfect big bro (like—cough—Jesus). He says and does everything God would want him to. Meanwhile, you've been out in the backyard playing in the mud. I mean *really* playing in the mud. There's a huge pile of dirt in the back that construction workers abandoned, and there's been just the right amount of rain to build mud castles and mud forts and mud balls to throw at your sister, brother, friends.

You've been at it for hours. A fresh layer of the earthy goo has dried to your skin, on top of the layer from that last round of mud fighting. This double-thick muck is caked on.

Hearing your dad call, you go in and spot big bro, all flawless in his white linen shirt and pants. Instantly you regret getting so dirty. Everyone has always said you look like your brother, but right now you don't resemble him AT ALL. You look more like a sloppy pig than a human.

Your brother catches sight of you and laughs under his breath. "Stay right there," he advises. Then he goes to grab a bucketful of warm water and a washcloth. When he returns, he bends down in front of you, dips the cloth in steaming water, and wrings it out. "You've been at it, huh?" he asks.

"It seemed fun," you mumble. "At least it was for a while. Not so much now."

He rubs the dried mud until it's down to a couple of layers of streaks and then bare skin. He cleans your forehead and wipes away dirt from your eyebrows first. In the hall mirror, you see that your eyes are like his—more than you ever recognized before. Then he washes off your cheeks and mouth.

Your sister comes in from outside, and you wonder why you didn't stop her from getting so crazy dirty like you. You're HER big brother, after all. You should have taken her to the swings instead of the mud hill. Your big bro crosses his arms and looks at you.

"Sorry," you say. "You can help her before I get done."

"That's something your big bro would say," Daddy comments, leaning against the doorjamb, watching. "You're getting more like him by the day."

"You really think so?" you ask, feeling hope rise in your heart. You've always wanted to be just like your big brother.

"I know so," Daddy says. "Trust me, you'll be just like him someday."

The Skinny on Romans 8

• Paul was writing to a community of believers in Rome whom he hadn't visited yet.

• The main theme in his letter to the Romans is that God has saved us and made us righteous through faith in Christ and we're secure as his children.

• Sometimes Paul's intense language can make it hard to figure out what he's saying. Picture this as you read Romans: superpassionate Paul was speaking fast as his scribe (kind of like an administrative assistant back in his day) madly wrote down Paul's words. Try reading just a bit at a time, pausing and thinking about it. Start with Romans 8:1–2:

    • "Therefore, there is now no condemnation"—the Old Testament law would have condemned us, meaning you and I would fall short if we were judged by it.
    • "for those in Christ Jesus"—that would be us!

- "because the law of the Spirit of life in Christ Jesus"— the Holy Spirit and his laws now rule!
- "has set you free from the law of sin and death"—basically, sin has no hold on us anymore. We're guilty, but Jesus paid the price to free us.

- What's this talk in Romans 8:29 about those God "foreknew"? That means God knew us and loved us before we were even born.

- Our Daddy in heaven is always with us! He has our backs! Romans 8:31 says,

> Our heavenly Daddy is bigger than any other dad in the world.

"What then are we to say about these things? If God is for us, who is against us?"

WHAT STRUCK YOU IN THIS CHAPTER?

God our Father wants us to become more like Jesus, our big bro, every day. What can you do to become a little more like Jesus this week in how you think, act, or speak? What might be hard about this? What might be easy?

YOUR FUTURE STORY

You might have heard someone say that we're princes and princesses because our Daddy in heaven is the King. This is true. We've been adopted into his royal family. What do you think about God choosing you? How does it change how you think about yourself? How does it change how you think about your heavenly Father?

What then are we to say about these things? If
God is for us, who is against us?
—Romans 8:31

37

Choose Love
1 Corinthians 13

You might have had a human biology class in which your teacher talked about our need for touch and connection as we grow. There have been horrible experiments in which monkeys were given water, food, and space but left alone with no communication or touch … and they wasted away.[3] If babies in orphanages don't have adequate touch or connection, they weigh far less, have lower IQs (intelligence), and often develop mental or behavioral problems.[4]

Thankfully these days in Western culture, we've placed orphans in foster care, where they're usually given adequate connection time with people who care for them until they can be adopted. Foster care may be far from perfect, but at least it's a step in the right direction.

God hard-wired a need for love in us. We want not only to BE loved but to also love others in return. Now there are different kinds of love: the physical, "kissy" kind you feel for someone you want to date or marry; the warm, special love you feel for your best friend; the deep, loyal family love you share with your parents and siblings. But the kind of

> Quit squirming! YOU need love too! (Whether you admit it or not!)

love the New Testament talks most about is *agape* love—caring about someone else's interests and needs more than your own.

Sometimes, judging from what we can see, we think people have it all, but they might be wasting away on the inside, wishing for nothing more than love. The computer-software billionaire might have a palace for a house, but if he doesn't have friends who truly love him, he might feel empty. The pop star with the chart-topping album might be surrounded by adoring fans, but if she doesn't have deep, abiding agape love in her life, she might feel lonely. The dude in your class might have everything you could only dream of—a camera-equipped drone, ATVs, a computer with three screens, a pool—but it might feel as if it's all just *stuff* if no one connects with him at home.

There's a reason Jesus left us with two main goals in life—to love our God with everything in us and to love the people around us like we love ourselves. He knew that life is meaningless without love. But we can learn how to love better from the One who IS love by yielding and by obeying his teaching as he transforms us day by day.

Imagine This ...
Your Life without Love

What if love, in every way you experienced it, disappeared from your life?

Think about being left alone in the world.

Your family is gone.

Your friends have drifted away.

Your church has stopped meeting.

Your youth-group leader decided to take a hiatus from his job.

There are people on your street, but no one speaks to you or even looks in your direction.

The clerks at the grocery store only take your money but never speak to you.

Worst of all, you're wondering if God has disappeared. He is silent. You can't feel his presence.

How would you feel? What would life be like? Would you say life was still worth living?

How much more would you appreciate love if your family returned and your house was full of life and chatter and hugs and bickering and laughter again?

What if your friends flooded into your room, playing music, giving you fist bumps, asking how you've been?

What if you went to church and it was full, everybody singing and praising God as well as hugging and praying for one another?

What if your youth-group leader called just to see how things were going for you and invited you out for a Coke with a couple of other kids?

What if the grocery-store clerk made small talk but then recognized you and let you in on a big sale on Gatorade next week?

What if one neighbor brought you a cake and another asked your family over for dinner?

Best of all, what if you got down on your knees that night and realized that God had been with you all along? He had never left you but walked beside you during that dry, dark time.

How would you feel? What would life be like? What would you say about the worth of your life?

The Skinny on 1 Corinthians 13

- Paul was single. Since he traveled a lot, it would've been hard for him to have a wife and kids. After he found Jesus, Paul lived in most places only for a few months before moving on to tell others about Jesus, so it would've been challenging for him to find a long-term place to belong. But through his deep

Have you ever met a friend who was almost instantly a best friend? Someone who just clicked with you? It was probably like that at times for Paul, except his relationships were based on a mutual love for God.

understanding of agape love, Paul found BFFs everywhere he went—
in those who understood God's love too.

- Love doesn't just magically happen for us. It's a series of choices.
  The more we yield to (obey) how the Spirit leads, encourages, and
  challenges, the more love will grow in all areas of our life.

- Let's break down Paul's passionate thoughts about things that look
  like love and success but are nothing without love. Examples today
  could look like these:

  - First Corinthians 13:1: "If I speak human or angelic [lan-
    guages] but do not have love, I am a noisy gong or a clanging

cymbal" = "If I can speak Mandarin Chinese, Italian, and Hindi but don't have love for other people, I sound like a honking goose or vuvuzela (that skinny plastic horn they blow at international soccer matches)."

- Verse 2: "If I have the gift of prophecy and understand all mysteries and all knowledge, and if I have all faith so that I can move mountains but do not have love, I am nothing" = "If I'm the coolest, most amazing religious person you've ever met, a person who understands everything about God and performs miracles that make your jaw drop, I'm still nothing if I don't love others."

- Verse 3: "If I give away all my possessions, and if I give over my body in order to boast but do not have love, I gain nothing" = "If I run a wonderful nonprofit, feeding and giving shelter to thousands, but I don't have love, I've got it all wrong."

WHAT STRUCK YOU IN THIS CHAPTER?

Jesus was the living, breathing, laughing, crying, preaching, caring face and heart of love to everyone he met.

Write the name Jesus in all the blanks below from 1 Corinthians 13:4–8, pausing to think about how he showed each aspect of love:

"_____ is patient, _____ is kind. _____ does not envy, is not boastful, is not arrogant, is not rude, is not self-seeking, is not irritable, and does not keep a record of wrongs. _____ finds no joy in unrighteousness but rejoices in the truth. _____ bears all things, believes all things, hopes all things, endures all things. [The love of] _____ never ends."

YOUR FUTURE STORY

Think about how YOU love others—your family and friends or the kid at school you don't know at all (or wish you didn't). Put a CHECKMARK by the descriptions that you think describe you, and an *X* by those descriptions you think you need to work on. Love is

_____ patient (not impatient) (1 Corinthians 13:4)

_____ kind (not mean) (v. 4)

_____ content (not envious or jealous) (v. 4)

_____ humble (not stuck up or bragging) (v. 4)

_____ polite (not rude) (v. 5)

_____ giving (not selfish) (v. 5)

_____ calm (not irritable) (v. 5)

_____ letting go of hurts (not holding on to them) (v. 5)

_____ truthful (v. 6)

_____ strong and faithful (v. 7)

_____ trusting (v. 7)

_____ hopeful (v. 7)

_____ lasting (v. 7)

Now these three remain: faith, hope, and love—
but the greatest of these is love.
—1 Corinthians 13:13

38

God Works in the Produce Department
Galatians 5

You might have wondered if there's anything more to being a Christian than being good and going to church.

Would it surprise you to know that Jesus said *nothing* about going to church? I'm sure it pleases him to see us making good decisions and worshipping God, but he talked more about producing "fruit." He said, "I am the true vine, and my Father in the gardener. Every branch in me that does not produce fruit he removes, and he prunes every branch that produces fruit so that it will produce more fruit" (John 15:1–2).

> Some Christians still fall into this law trap today. We call that *legalism.*

If you've seen fruit trees or bushes grow in your yard year after year, you might have noticed how pruning can help them produce more the next year. If plants grow too wide or too dense, they might stop growing and even die. In the same way, we sometimes need to check out where we are on the spiritual-fruit scale to see if we need to do some pruning of our own. The goal is for *every* kind of fruit of the Spirit to be visible in our lives: "love, joy, peace, patience, kindness, goodness, faithfulness, gentleness, and self-control" (Galatians 5:22–23).

Back in the apostle Paul's day, our friends in Galatia were getting off track because someone was preaching about how following God's *laws* was how you stayed on God's good side. But that was the *old* way of doing things, figuring out a whole long list of dos and don'ts. Jesus came to free us from the burden of keeping the law in order to have a relationship with God. Paul wrote, "You who are trying to be justified by the law are alienated from Christ; you have fallen from grace" (Galatians 5:4).

> Only faith in Jesus makes us righteous in God's eyes. This is called grace. Most of us are far from being sinless, perfect, law-abiding citizens of God's kingdom. We try, but we always fall short. God showered his grace (total favor) on us by sending Jesus to die for us. THAT ultimate sacrifice secured our future forever!

Yikes. *Alienated*, Paul said. As in, *I'm here on earth, and you are from Mars.* I'd say he thought the Galatians were really off track from where Jesus wanted them to be.

There's something in all of us that likes rules. When we were little kids, we knew that coloring within the lines was the right way to do it. If we did it that way, we'd get a shiny gold star. But living within our own set of rules kind of puts us in God's shoes. We end up relying on ourselves instead of relying on God. And the God who wants nothing more than a great relationship with us wants us to rely on him.

If we're living free in the grace of Jesus's love and are relying on the Spirit to correct and encourage us, we'll eventually produce a huge harvest of fruit to line the shelves of our relational farmer's market—with God (love, joy, peace), with others (patience, kindness, goodness), and with ourselves (faithfulness, gentleness, and self-control).

Imagine This ...
The Fruit of the Spirit in Action

Mrs. Kardovian was elderly, living in a one-hundred-year-old four-story brick building in Boston, Massachusetts. Some of the old brownstones had been remodeled to include air-conditioning. Zoe's had not.

So every summer Mrs. Kardovian and Zoe would hang out on the roof, each of them praying desperately for the heat to break so they could get to sleep that night. Mrs. K was on the third floor; Zoe's family lived on the fourth. But everybody had access to the roof. It was their building's version of a backyard. Only the Smiths from the first floor and the Barockovich family from the second floor never came up on the roof. Everybody else popped up sometime. Maybe lower down, the heat wasn't so oppressive.

Zoe's family came home one day after the downtown festival to find their candles had all melted into sad, snaking humps that warped over and across the dining-room table.

Mom shot Dad a meaningful look, and Dad just shrugged. Mom had been asking him for some time to talk to the landlord about air-conditioning, but Dad wasn't anxious to take on the bigger electric bill that would come with it.

After washing dinner dishes, Zoe grabbed a book and climbed the narrow stairs to the roof. She hoped old Mrs. K wasn't there yet. She was too hot to be happy company for anyone. She'd barely made it through dinner without griping at Mom or arguing with Dad.

But Mrs. K was already there, sitting in an ancient patio chair that Zoe was surprised could still hold her considerable weight.

"Ahh, there you are, my sweet girl," she said in her thick Eastern European accent, waving to the chair beside her.

"Hey, Mrs. K," Zoe muttered, plopping into one of the chairs her dad had recently bought as a peace offering over the AC issue. He'd purchased a hammock too, which they'd strung between a hook on the staircase and another hook on the edge of the roof. The hammock was Zoe's favorite place to sit and read, but what was she supposed to do with Mrs. K sitting there, her round face filled with hope and expectation? *Not* sit in the chair beside her?

I really gotta get another life, Zoe thought with a sigh.

"So," Mrs. K said. "How was your day? What did you do?"

Zoe shoved down a flash of guilt. She knew that Mrs. K rarely got out of the building. Zoe didn't know whether she had any kids, but even her groceries were delivered. "Oh, my mom and dad and I hit that July fest downtown. There were all kinds of art booths and food. You know ...," she finished lamely. *Of course Mrs. K doesn't know. She never gets out!*

"That sounds delightful," Mrs. K said, reaching out to pinch Zoe's cheek lightly the way she'd done since Zoe was seven. "Which was your favorite booth? Which were your favorite three?"

She settled back in her chair and closed her eyes, rubbing her forehead as if preparing her mind to accept Zoe's experience as her own. As if she wanted to live through her experience, kind of like diving into a book and becoming that novel's character.

This had always been their way. Mrs. K asked her questions about life beyond the brownstone, and Zoe answered. Sometimes Zoe wondered if Mrs. K climbed to the roof to hear Zoe's stories more than to find relief from the heat.

"Well, there was an artist who made all kinds of cool things from pipes and faucets and old electric bulbs. They totally looked like steampunk lamps and things."

Mrs. K nodded, even though Zoe doubted she knew what *steampunk* was.

"And then there was this artist who ironed superlight fabric onto huge sheets, and all the layers created shadow and light. He made the face of Benjamin Franklin, and it was as big as that door!"

Mrs. K opened one eye. "And someone would buy such a thing?"

"I guess. It was pretty cool," Zoe continued. "Then there was a guy with no hands and no feet, but he was making these tiny pictures of Boston landmarks by using a calligraphy pen he held in his mouth and dipped in ink. He dropped one dot at a time on his canvas. That was amazing."

Mrs. K nodded. "That would be something to see. You want to read now, yes?" She waved a hand in the air, silently giving Zoe permission, and then closed her eyes again.

But Zoe felt an urge to do something different tonight. To let this night be not just all about her but about Mrs. K too. It'd be good for Zoe to think about Mrs. K for a change.

"Mrs. K," Zoe said, clearing her throat.

The old woman's wrinkled lids blinked open in surprise.

"Do you ever leave the brownstone?"

Mrs. K's eyes narrowed, first in confusion and then in wariness. "Not very often," she admitted.

"Is that because you don't want to?" Zoe asked. "Or because you can't?"

"Why do I need to leave?" she asked with a little shrug. "My groceries and medicines are delivered. I have TV and the QVC to watch. And neighbors like you, sweet girl."

She hadn't answered Zoe's question. Zoe felt this weird encouragement to press again, gently. "Yes, you have what you need," she said quietly. "But don't you miss going out?"

Mrs. K's old eyes widened, and she stared at Zoe for a long moment, as if considering the question. But then her face got supersad, and she turned toward the setting sun. "My husband and daughter were killed in a car crash eighteen years ago. She was a college student studying to be a teacher."

Zoe paused, swallowed hard, waited a moment. She didn't know what to say. "You ... you didn't have any other kids?"

Mrs. K shook her head the tiniest bit and then looked at her hands in her lap.

Zoe didn't want to ask the next question. But she had to.

"Mrs. K, how long has it been since you left your apartment?" she asked, her voice barely a whisper.

"Since the day I returned from their funeral," the old woman whispered back.

They sat there in silence for a long while.

Zoe was praying like crazy, wondering what she was supposed to do next. She was only a kid! How was she supposed to handle something like this? She needed Mom there!

But then it came to her. "Mrs. K, do you think you'd like to go with us to church tomorrow morning? You could ride with us. You know, be with us."

In that moment all she wanted was to fill the gap for Mrs. K. To be her family. Not that they really could, but maybe they could a little.

Mrs. K turned toward Zoe, and her eyes filled with tears. "Do you ... do you think I could?"

She was in her sixties. Zoe was eleven. But in that moment Zoe felt like the grown-up encouraging a kid. "Well, sure," Zoe said. She reached out and took the woman's hand.

"You are so good, sweet child," Mrs. K said, reaching out to pat her cheek while a tear ran down her own.

Zoe knew she wasn't good. Not really. She hadn't wanted to see Mrs. K tonight. She'd wanted to be alone.

But then she'd gone with it. She'd done what her heart had encouraged her to do. What she knew was right. And now, seeing Mrs. K's joy through the tears, Zoe knew this moment was bigger than her.

Somehow this was God working through her.

Her conversation with Mrs. K represented one aspect of the fruit of the Spirit—kindness—in action. Just like her youth pastor had talked about.

God was with her. In her. Right there on that roof.

"Thank you, sweet child," Mrs. K said, patting Zoe's knee. "I don't know if I can go tomorrow, but it's good, so good to be asked."

The Skinny on Galatians 5

- The only way to become a Christian is to be "justified" by faith in Jesus. Once we accept Christ as our Savior, we're part of God's forever family.

- This doesn't mean we live and act like we are *perfect*.

We won't be perfect until we reach heaven!

- Even if we've asked Jesus to be our Savior, we still fight the urge to do whatever pleases us. We all wrestle with sinful desires in our hearts, and that can lead us to do bad things. The apostle Paul outlined some of these in Galatians 5:19–21: hatred, jealousy, selfish ambition, drunkenness, "and anything similar."

- The way we work at driving out what "the flesh desires" is by focusing on growing the "fruit of the Spirit": love, joy, peace,

It's kind of like weed control: grow good stuff to choke out the bad!

patience, kindness, goodness, faithfulness, gentleness, and self-control (vv. 17, 22–23).

WHAT STRUCK YOU IN THIS CHAPTER?

Which aspect of the fruit of the Spirit do you think God wants to produce more of in your life? Take a moment to pray, asking him to show you where you're falling short and where you need some pruning. Then mark which of these qualities jump out at you:

❏ Love	❏ Joy	❏ Peace
❏ Patience	❏ Kindness	❏ Goodness
❏ Faithfulness	❏ Gentleness	❏ Self-Control

Do you see one or two (or nine!) that God is asking you to work on? Pay attention to how those qualities play out in the particular grouping of God, others, or self. All the aspects of the fruit of the Spirit help all relationships, but seeing where your life needs some pruning might help you produce more fruit faster.

YOUR FUTURE STORY

You might be like me and see that list of things you need to work on as a reason to beat yourself up. It's not. Remember to be gentle with yourself! That's one of the characteristics

> Remember, Jesus loves you. He adores you, actually!

of the fruit of the Spirit, right? Take it as encouragement to grow and become more like Jesus, not as judgment.

God already sees you as your perfected self, because where you fail, Jesus fills in the gaps. He's done that for you, and you've accepted that by placing your faith in him. But you honor what Jesus has done and serve him by doing your best to pay attention to where the Spirit is directing you.

So with that in mind, which group (God, others, or self) would you like to see improve in the next year? Which qualities are associated with that group? Take a moment to write down how you'd like to see God produce more of each of those characteristics in your life over the next year.

Example: "Patience"—I'm going to practice counting to three before responding to others when they're on my last nerve.

1. _____

_____

2. _____

_____

3. _____

_____

For freedom, Christ set us free. Stand firm then and don't submit again to a yoke of slavery.… For you were called to be free, brothers and sisters; only don't use this freedom as an opportunity for the flesh, but serve one another through love. For the whole law is fulfilled in one statement: Love your neighbor as yourself.
—Galatians 5:1, 13–14

39

Move It!
James 1

So we talked about Galatians in the previous chapter. Some people call Galatians "Martin Luther's book" because he relied on Galatians so much when he was preaching about grace and being saved by faith, not by works. The funny thing is that Luther wasn't wild about the book of James, because James encouraged believers to *act* on their faith and not just sit around and say, "Yes, I believe in Jesus and all he taught." James wanted us to *show* that our faith is real by our actions.

Martin Luther was the initial leader of the Protestant Reformation, a movement that led to Christians and churches breaking away from the Roman Catholic Church. Luther's followers became known as Lutherans; and the Episcopalians, Presbyterians, Methodists, Baptists, and other Protestant denominations came later.

The trick to appreciating both Galatians *and* James is to keep their core teachings balanced in our minds and hearts.

> TRUTH no. 1 (Galatians): We cannot earn our salvation. Putting our faith in Jesus, who gave up his life for us, is what saves us. End of story. TRUTH no. 2 (James): If we have truly been saved, our lives will reflect Christ's goodness and love; we express our faith through action.

The thing about James is that he was Jesus's half brother, one of the sons of Mary and Joseph. (According to Matthew 13:55–56, Jesus had at least six younger half siblings!) It's interesting that James didn't start his book bragging on the fact that he was family. Wouldn't you be tempted to do so? I would! *"You think you knew Jesus? Well, I ate every meal with him as a kid. I had to share a bedroom with him too! He hogged the covers!"* No, James didn't do that. Instead, he introduced himself as "James, a servant of God and of the Lord Jesus Christ" (James 1:1).

The word James used for "servant" could also be translated "slave." In many households during this era of history, servants and slaves had a unique place in the family. Some eventually were even adopted as heirs. But it's that total, sold-out heart of servanthood James talked about that we want to understand. He didn't approach his life as an entitled sibling; he approached it as a servant of the Savior because he felt he owed Jesus everything.

James was the leader of the Jerusalem church. Living in Jerusalem—sacred to Jews and a powerful Roman stronghold—Christians often faced threats and opposition. They endured constant bullying in their culture, as well as financial hardships. The apostle Paul even wrote about bringing donations from believers elsewhere to support them (1 Corinthians 16:1–3). James noted that he was writing to "the twelve tribes dispersed abroad" (James 1:1), likely a reference to Jewish Christians, who would have had struggles of their own.

Yet James wrote, "Consider it a great joy, my brothers and sisters, whenever you experience various trials, because you know that the testing of your faith produces endurance. And let endurance have its full effect, so that you may be mature and complete, lacking nothing" (James 1:2–4).

James is a great book to read if you're going through tough times. James knew that struggles can make us stronger. Have you heard that a broken bone grows stronger as it heals? Or have you ever noticed after a workout how sore your muscles are? That's because muscles actually break down a little to grow back stronger.

We don't like pain. Most of us would rather avoid it. But remember, God causes "all things [to] work together for the good of those who love [him]" (Romans 8:28). If we believe that, we can learn to appreciate the hard, painful times at least a little. James even encourages us to "consider it a great joy."

> Seriously? Pain is a great JOY? Yes, seriously. Seeing it from the spiritual-development side can lessen the sting. Trust me on this.

I was a freshman in college when my heart was broken. The guy I thought was the one left me for another. I was a total mess. But as I walked and talked with God, pleading for him to bring my boyfriend back to me (which he didn't), I recognized this crazy, growing strength in my relationship with my Father. I started looking to God for validation rather than to my ex-boyfriend. I could feel God sustaining me when I felt like melting. I sensed him building me up from within, telling me that something better was ahead. God felt closer than ever before. So even though my heart was shattered, I could find joy in the trial.

Next time you're struggling, instead of praying, *Lord, take this away from me!* say, *Lord, show me what you want me to learn from this*, and see what happens. When we put our minds and hearts in the mode of trust like James did, no matter what we're facing, we can work through our hard circumstances and deepen our faith. The more our relationship with God develops, the more we'll want to do good works to honor him.

Imagine This ...
Joy in the Trial

Amelia's neighbors had been through a lot. The single mom and her only child, a girl about Amelia's own age, were in and out of hospitals all the time. Because Ashley was constantly sick, she didn't go to the neighborhood middle school with Amelia. Her mother homeschooled her.

Amelia had met the family when they first moved in, and she and Ashley hung out a few times. But after that, they'd just wave when they happened to see each other.

"Why don't you go over there?" Mom asked as Amelia hauled in groceries and glimpsed the neighbors arriving home themselves. "Maybe Ashley wants to play cards or trade books or something."

"Oh, Mom," Amelia said, shifting uncomfortably. "I don't really want to."

"Why not? You used to like playing dolls together."

Amelia just shot her a look. *Dolls?*

"Okay, okay, so you're too big for dolls," Mom said, nudging her with her hip. "But find something else you could do. It's the Christian thing to do."

Amelia sighed heavily as she put the milk in the fridge. "Sometimes being a Christian ..." Amelia dropped the next words, knowing Mom wouldn't like it if she finished her thought.

"'From everyone who has been given much, much will be required,'" Mom said, handing her the OJ.

"Let me guess," Amelia said. "That's from the Bible?"

"Yup. God's given us a lot, right?" She moved past Amelia to put several packs of deli meat in the fridge drawer. "I'm thankful you're a healthy, strong girl and not in Ashley's place. Aren't you?"

"Yeah. Who'd want that?"

"So ... if we're grateful for the life God has given us, then we honor him by acting like it. We do things for others. Help out where we can. Reach out to neighbors—"

"Okay, *okay*, Mom. I'll go over there. But just for a little bit."

Mom smiled. "Ashley might like that new series you've been reading. Her mom says she's as much of a bookworm as you are."

Amelia nodded and then went to her room. She paced around, looking at one thing and then another. Thinking about going next door made her nervous. *What will we talk about? What will we do?*

Her eyes settled on her basket full of nail polish. They could paint their nails! She lifted the basket and slid in the first book of that series her mom had been talking about. Maybe Ashley would have one or two books she could borrow too. It'd be a lot easier to slip over to Ashley's than to get her mom to take her to the library. Amelia grabbed two decks of cards too and then closed her eyes and prayed, *God, make this work. Somehow. Amen.*

Then she pushed out the door and hurried down the stairs before she wimped out.

The Skinny on James 1

- James 1:22, 25 says, "Be doers of the word and not hearers only, deceiving yourselves.... The one who [does good] works—this person will be blessed in what he does." What does it mean to be "doers of the word"? Here are some examples:

  - "Love the LORD your God with all your heart, ... soul, and ... strength" (Deuteronomy 6:5).
  - "Love your enemies" (Matthew 5:44).
  - "Don't worry" (Matthew 6:25).
  - "Do not judge" (Matthew 7:1).
  - "Love your neighbor as yourself" (Mark 12:31).
  - "Share with anyone in need" (Ephesians 4:28).
  - "Look after orphans and widows" (James 1:27).

- Have you heard the phrase "actions speak louder than words"? If you believe God's Word, act on it. Make good choices and act in ways that demonstrate your faith. Others will take notice.

WHAT STRUCK YOU IN THIS CHAPTER?

Sometimes the hardest part of doing something for God is making the first move. If you're anything like me, you feel lazy, or you already have so much to do, you can't imagine adding one more thing to your day. But whenever I push through those feelings, whenever I follow through on what God is calling me to do, it always feels so great. It's kind of like not wanting to go work out (or go to practice) but afterward feeling so much better because you did. What's God encouraging you to do that you're avoiding? Write it down. _____

_____

_____

_____

_____

YOUR FUTURE STORY

There are lots of good, moral people sitting in church (and at home too) but not acting on their faith. We can call them the "frozen chosen"—God's chosen people frozen in place. Jesus called us to break out of the ice, to be the church, to *love*, to *go out* and *teach* others about him (Matthew 28:19–20), and to *look after* the defenseless (James 1:27). Notice all those action words? He didn't call us to just be good people; he called us to be on the move.

What do you think God is calling you to do this week? How are you going to do it? Write down your plan.

_____

_____

_____

Be doers of the word and not hearers only. deceiving yourselves....
But the one who ... is not a forgetful hearer but a doer who
works—this person will be blessed in what he does.
—James 1:22, 25

40

Muddy with Guilt, Washed in Forgiveness
1 John 3

Have you ever seen the ocean? Now that I live in landlocked Colorado, I long to see water of any sort—rivers, lakes, ponds. When I get to the ocean, I can watch the waves for hours. I love it when there's such a broad expanse of water that I can actually see the curvature of the earth. It's one of those times when I realize just how big the world is.

When we finally understand how big, big, BIG the ocean and the earth are beneath our feet, it's like recognizing how much God's love is bigger than our mom's or dad's love. God's love is like all the love we experience from everybody in our lives … times a million.

There's no way we can outrun his love. There's no way we can do anything to make him *not* love us.

By sending Jesus to open the way to a relationship with him, God made sure we'll never be separated from him again. Ever. All of us will sin and fall short in many ways. You might have been like me when I was little. I knew I wasn't supposed to, but I stole a candy bar from the store. My mom made me go back and apologize to the manager and promise not to do it again. In the same way, when we sin, we need to confess it to God and ask him to help us not make the same mistake again.

The Devil, our enemy, *wants* us to sin. He *doesn't* want us to confess when we mess up. He *doesn't* want us to discover how wide and deep and long God's love is for us. Satan *doesn't* want us to rest in God's forgiveness. His whole goal is to separate us from Jesus.

The best way to stay on God's path and not slip onto the Devil's road is to

- pay attention when we're feeling guilty,
- admit to the sin that is making us feel that way,
- confess that sin to God, and
- trust in Jesus to wash us fully clean.

When we meet Jesus in heaven, we'll see that we totally look like we are his little brothers and sisters. His spiritual DNA is in us (1 John 3:9). You might have been born with black curly hair inherited from your dad or dark brown eyes from your mom, but your heart? As you grow closer to Jesus, your heart is gradually becoming a mirror image of Jesus's heart. And when you reach heaven, his love will be shining so clearly through you that there will be no mistaking that you belong to him.

Imagine This ...
Really Accepting Forgiveness

I'd done it all.

Dropped out of high school.

Dropped into drugs.

Run away from home.

Used every person I could when I needed to, stolen from and hurt others. In a hundred different ways.

I was a loser. A failure. A disgrace. That was the worst part, really—thinking of my mama, ashamed of me. Biting her lip, refusing to look me in the eye, shaking her head in regret. Even now, the thought of it made me choke up.

But *he* wasn't, that dark night in the city alley. Jesus wasn't ashamed of me, I mean. He simply stood with me, waiting, hoping.

I was finally at that finish line—so sick of every lie I'd spoken, every sin I'd committed, that I just said it. *I'm sorry. Please forgive me, Jesus.*

I held my breath, thinking how he might respond if he were meeting me at the pearly gates instead of just an intersection in my mind. I braced myself for a lecture. For him to make me feel worse about all I'd done—and not done.

But instead, he spoke to my heart with words that made me blink in surprise. *YOU ARE MINE. YOU ARE LOVED. YOU ARE FORGIVEN. YOU ARE FREE!*

I let out a breath of a laugh. It took me a few minutes to absorb what he'd said to me. But it was as if my heart, so full of dark memories and thoughts, had become this steel-covered orb, and the words *MINE ... LOVED ... FORGIVEN ... FREE* tore chunks of the steel away, letting light flood through. Was it possible? Was it true?

With every passing second, I knew that it was.

And in that moment, alone in that dark city alley, I thanked him for washing me clean. Totally forgiving me. No strings attached. No punishment promised down the road. No lingering shame. It was done. Over. Somehow he'd already forgotten every single thing I'd done wrong. All I felt was welcome, healing, hope.

Thank you, Jesus, I said. *Thank you.* And somehow in those simple words, I'd covered all I needed to say to him.

I turned in a slow circle, feeling lighter and more free than I'd felt in years, and then moved to the mouth of the alley. I looked left, then turned right, walking faster and faster. Toward home.

The Skinny on 1 John 3

- Bible scholars think that the author of this letter is the same John who wrote the gospel of John.

- John knew Jesus's love, perhaps more than any other disciple did. John understood this love when he was a young man in Jesus's company. As an older man writing 1 John, he understood his Master's love even more.

  > Dude! This was the guy who the Bible notes was "the one Jesus loved" (John 13:23).

- While on the cross, Jesus directed these words to his mother, Mary, and his disciple John: "Woman, here is your son.… [John,] here is your mother" (John 19:26–27). It was this John who took Mary home on that terrible day.

- Recognizing how big and wide and deep and long God's love is, John urged his readers to love others in the same way: "This is how we have come to know love: [Jesus] laid down his life for us. We should also lay down our lives for our brothers and sisters. If anyone has this world's goods and sees a fellow believer in need but withholds compassion from him—how does God's love reside in him?" (1 John 3:16–17).

WHAT STRUCK YOU IN THIS CHAPTER?

Think of something you need to apologize for, something to ask forgiveness for. Got it?

Now think of someone you wish would ask *your* forgiveness. Someone who has hurt you or made you sad.

How many times might Jesus point to us and say, "You could have done/said/loved in my name. But you didn't."

Consider those moments. Confess them. Feel God's forgiveness. And then know you are to move out, as a middle schooler, high schooler, or adult … God's agent of change. God's agent of love, forgiveness, mercy, joy, and light.

YOUR FUTURE STORY

Sometimes we mess up and it's hard to move on. We tie ourselves up, bind ourselves with guilt, when Jesus wants nothing more than to free us to do his good works, to love others as ourselves. How can you better absorb how much your Savior wants to free you? Cut loose your bonds? Embrace and walk with you through life? The last thing he wants is for you to feel trapped, tied, stifled. He wants you to accept his forgiveness and then move out, confident in his love. You are his child. There is no way you can escape his love. Is there something you want to confess to him now and be free of it, now and forever?

Do it now. He's waiting to hug you and then send you onward …

This is how we have come to know love: He laid down his life for us.
We should also lay down our lives for our brothers
and sisters. If anyone has this world's
goods and sees a fellow believer in need but withholds
compassion from him—how does God's love reside in him?

—1 John 3:16–17

March 2017

Dear little sister or brother, I SO wish we could sit down together and talk about what God is saying to you and what you're going to do about it. In the end, that's all that matters—God's reach and your response. His call, your answer. It really all boils down to understanding how much your Maker loves, loves, LOVES you.

It is my sincere hope that reading this book is just one step on the long path of faith for you. Because I promise you this: the longer you journey with God, the more you seek him, the more satisfying your life will be. Don't accept "okay" or "fine" on the journey of discipleship, friend. Dive deep. Explore. Feel. Think. Ask questions. Be willing to stand up for what you believe. And be willing to fall into the loving arms of your Savior.

Your life will be richer for it. I promise.

Your big sis,
Lisa

Notes

1. Efrem Smith, *Jump: Into a Life of Further and Higher* (Colorado Springs: David C Cook, 2010), 19–20.

2. Story based on Abu Fadi, "The Day ISIS Arrived in Mosul," in *I Am N: Inspiring Stories of Christians Facing Islamic Extremists* (Colorado Springs: David C Cook, 2016), 23–29.

3. One of these experiments was conducted by Harry Harlow and published in Harry F. Harlow, Robert O. Dodsworth, and Margaret K. Harlow, "Total Social Isolation in Monkeys," *Proceedings of the National Academy of Sciences* 54, no. 1 (1965): 90–97, www.ncbi.nlm.nih.gov/pmc/articles /PMC285801/pdf/pnas00159-0105.pdf.

4. Maia Szalavitz and Bruce D. Perry, *Born for Love: Why Empathy Is Essential— and Endangered* (New York: HarperCollins, 2010), 50–55; Maia Szalavitz, "How Orphanages Kill Babies—and Why No Child under 5 Should Be in One," *Huffington Post*, November 17, 2011, www.huffingtonpost.com /maia-szalavitz/how-orphanages-kill-babie_b_549608.html.

Genesis 1

¹ In the beginning God created the heavens and the earth.

² Now the earth was formless and empty, darkness covered the surface of the watery depths, and the Spirit of God was hovering over the surface of the waters. ³ Then God said, "Let there be light," and there was light. ⁴ God saw that the light was good, and God separated the light from the darkness. ⁵ God called the light "day," and the darkness he called "night." There was an evening, and there was a morning: one day.

⁶ Then God said, "Let there be an expanse between the waters, separating water from water." ⁷ So God made the expanse and separated the water under the expanse from the water above the expanse. And it was so. ⁸ God called the expanse "sky." Evening came and then morning: the second day.

⁹ Then God said, "Let the water under the sky be gathered into one place, and let the dry land appear." And it was so. ¹⁰ God called the dry land "earth," and the gathering of the water he called "seas." And God saw that it was good. ¹¹ Then God said, "Let the earth produce vegetation: seed-bearing plants and fruit trees on the earth bearing fruit with seed in it according to their kinds." And it was so. ¹² The earth produced vegetation: seed-bearing plants according to their kinds and trees bearing fruit with seed in it according to their kinds. And God saw that it was good. ¹³ Evening came and then morning: the third day.

¹⁴ Then God said, "Let there be lights in the expanse of the sky to separate the day from the night. They will serve as signs for seasons and for days and years. ¹⁵ They will be lights in the expanse of the sky to provide light on the earth." And it was so. ¹⁶ God made the two great lights — the greater light to rule over the day and the lesser light to rule over the night — as well as the stars. ¹⁷ God placed them in the expanse of the sky to provide light on the earth, ¹⁸ to rule the day and the night, and to separate light from darkness. And God saw that it was good. ¹⁹ Evening came and then morning: the fourth day.

²⁰ Then God said, "Let the water swarm with living creatures, and let birds fly above the earth across the expanse of the sky." ²¹ So God created the large sea-creatures and every living creature that moves and swarms in the water, according to their kinds. He also created every winged creature according to its kind. And God saw that it was good. ²² God blessed them: "Be fruitful, multiply, and fill the waters of the seas, and let the birds multiply on the earth." ²³ Evening came and then morning: the fifth day.

²⁴ Then God said, "Let the earth produce living creatures according to their kinds: livestock, creatures that crawl, and the wildlife of the earth according to their kinds." And it was so. ²⁵ So God made the wildlife of the earth according to their kinds, the livestock according to their kinds, and all the creatures that crawl on the ground according to their kinds. And God saw that it was good.

²⁶ Then God said, "Let us make man in our image, according to our likeness. They will rule the fish of the sea, the birds of the sky, the livestock, the whole earth, and the creatures that crawl on the earth."

²⁷ So God created man in his own image;
he created him in the image of God;
he created them male and female.

²⁸ God blessed them, and God said to them, "Be fruitful, multiply, fill the earth, and subdue it. Rule the fish of the sea, the birds of the sky, and every creature that crawls on the earth." ²⁹ God also said, "Look, I have given you every seed-bearing plant on the surface of the entire earth and every tree whose fruit contains seed. This will be food for you, ³⁰ for all the wildlife of the earth, for every bird of the sky, and for every creature that crawls on the earth — everything having the breath of life in it — I have given every green plant for food." And it was so. ³¹ God saw all that he had made, and it was very good indeed. Evening came and then morning: the sixth day.

Genesis 3

¹ Now the serpent was the most cunning of all the wild animals that the LORD God had made. He said to the woman, "Did God really say, 'You can't eat from any tree in the garden'?"

² The woman said to the serpent, "We may eat the fruit from the trees in the garden. ³ But about the fruit of the tree in the middle of the garden, God said, 'You must not eat it or touch it, or you will die.'"

⁴ "No! You will not die," the serpent said to the woman. ⁵ "In fact, God knows that when you eat it your eyes will be opened and you will be like God, knowing good and evil." ⁶ The woman saw that the tree was good for food and delightful to look at, and that it was desirable for obtaining wisdom. So she took some of its fruit and ate it; she also gave some to her husband, who was with her, and he ate it. ⁷ Then the eyes of both of them were opened, and they knew they were naked; so they sewed fig leaves together and made coverings for themselves.

⁸ Then the man and his wife heard the sound of the LORD God walking in the garden at the time of the evening breeze, and they hid from the LORD God among the trees of the garden. ⁹ So the LORD God called out to the man and said to him, "Where are you?"

¹⁰ And he said, "I heard you in the garden, and I was afraid because I was naked, so I hid."

¹¹ Then he asked, "Who told you that you were naked? Did you eat from the tree that I commanded you not to eat from?"

¹² The man replied, "The woman you gave to be with me — she gave me some fruit from the tree, and I ate."

¹³ So the LORD God asked the woman, "What is this you have done?"

And the woman said, "The serpent deceived me, and I ate."

¹⁴ So the LORD God said to the serpent:

Because you have done this,
you are cursed more than any livestock
and more than any wild animal.
You will move on your belly
and eat dust all the days of your life.
¹⁵ I will put hostility between you and the woman,
and between your offspring and her offspring.
He will strike your head,
and you will strike his heel.

¹⁶ He said to the woman:

I will intensify your labor pains;
you will bear children with painful effort.
Your desire will be for your husband,
yet he will rule over you.

¹⁷ And he said to the man, "Because you listened to your wife and ate from the tree about which I commanded you, 'Do not eat from it':

The ground is cursed because of you.
You will eat from it by means of painful labor
all the days of your life.
¹⁸ It will produce thorns and thistles for you,
and you will eat the plants of the field.
¹⁹ You will eat bread by the sweat of your brow
until you return to the ground,
since you were taken from it.
For you are dust,
and you will return to dust."

²⁰ The man named his wife Eve because she was the mother of all the living. ²¹ The LORD God made clothing from skins for the man and his wife, and he clothed them.

²² The LORD God said, "Since the man has become like one of us, knowing good and evil, he must not reach out, take from the tree of life, eat, and live forever." ²³ So the LORD God sent him away from the garden of Eden to work the ground from which he was taken. ²⁴ He drove the man out and stationed the cherubim and the flaming, whirling sword east of the garden of Eden to guard the way to the tree of life.

Genesis 6

¹ When mankind began to multiply on the earth and daughters were born to them, ² the sons of God saw that the daughters of mankind were beautiful, and they took any they chose as wives for themselves. ³ And the LORD said, "My Spirit will not remain with mankind forever, because they are corrupt. Their days will be 120 years." ⁴ The Nephilim were on the earth both in those days and afterward, when the sons of God came to the daughters of mankind, who bore children to them. They were the powerful men of old, the famous men.

⁵ When the LORD saw that human wickedness was widespread on the earth and that every inclination of the human mind was nothing but evil all the time, ⁶ the LORD regretted that he had made man on the earth, and he was deeply grieved. ⁷ Then the LORD said, "I will wipe mankind, whom I created, off the face of the earth, together with the animals, creatures that crawl, and birds of the sky — for I regret that I made them." ⁸ Noah, however, found favor with the LORD.

⁹ These are the family records of Noah. Noah was a righteous man, blameless among his contemporaries; Noah walked with God. ¹⁰ And Noah fathered three sons: Shem, Ham, and Japheth.

¹¹ Now the earth was corrupt in God's sight, and the earth was filled with wickedness. ¹² God saw how corrupt the earth was, for every creature had corrupted its way on the earth. ¹³ Then God said to Noah, "I have decided to put an end to every creature, for the earth is filled with wickedness because of them; therefore I am going to destroy them along with the earth.

¹⁴ "Make yourself an ark of gopher wood. Make rooms in the ark, and cover it with pitch inside and outside. ¹⁵ This is how you are to make it: The ark will be 450 feet long, 75 feet wide, and 45 feet high. ¹⁶ You are to make a roof, finishing the sides of the ark to within eighteen inches of the roof. You are to put a door in the side of the ark. Make it with lower, middle, and upper decks.

¹⁷ "Understand that I am bringing a flood — floodwaters on the earth to destroy every creature under heaven with the breath of life in it. Everything on earth will perish. ¹⁸ But I will establish my covenant with you, and you will enter the ark with your sons, your wife, and your sons' wives. ¹⁹ You are also to bring into the ark two of all

the living creatures, male and female, to keep them alive with you. [20] Two of everything — from the birds according to their kinds, from the livestock according to their kinds, and from the animals that crawl on the ground according to their kinds — will come to you so that you can keep them alive. [21] Take with you every kind of food that is eaten; gather it as food for you and for them." [22] And Noah did this. He did everything that God had commanded him.

Genesis 12

¹ The LORD said to Abram:

> Go out from your land,
> your relatives,
> and your father's house
> to the land that I will show you.
> ² I will make you into a great nation,
> I will bless you,
> I will make your name great,
> and you will be a blessing.
> ³ I will bless those who bless you,
> I will curse anyone who treats you with contempt,
> and all the peoples on earth
> will be blessed through you.

⁴ So Abram went, as the LORD had told him, and Lot went with him. Abram was seventy-five years old when he left Haran. ⁵ He took his wife Sarai, his nephew Lot, all the possessions they had accumulated, and the people they had acquired in Haran, and they set out for the land of Canaan. When they came to the land of Canaan, ⁶ Abram passed through the land to the site of Shechem, at the oak of Moreh. (At that time the Canaanites were in the land.) ⁷ The LORD appeared to Abram and said, "To your offspring I will give this land." So he built an altar there to the LORD who had appeared to him. ⁸ From there he moved on to the hill country east of Bethel and pitched his tent, with Bethel on the west and Ai on the east. He built an altar to the LORD there, and he called on the name of the LORD. ⁹ Then Abram journeyed by stages to the Negev.

¹⁰ There was a famine in the land, so Abram went down to Egypt to stay there for a while because the famine in the land was severe. ¹¹ When he was about to enter Egypt, he said to his wife Sarai, "Look, I know what a beautiful woman you are. ¹² When the Egyptians see you, they will say, 'This is his wife.' They will kill me but let you live. ¹³ Please say you're my sister so it will go well for me because of you, and my life will be spared on your account." ¹⁴ When Abram entered Egypt, the Egyptians saw that the woman was very beautiful. ¹⁵ Pharaoh's officials saw her and praised her to Pharaoh, so the woman was taken to Pharaoh's household. ¹⁶ He

treated Abram well because of her, and Abram acquired flocks and herds, male and female donkeys, male and female slaves, and camels.

[17] But the LORD struck Pharaoh and his household with severe plagues because of Abram's wife Sarai. [18] So Pharaoh sent for Abram and said, "What have you done to me? Why didn't you tell me she was your wife? [19] Why did you say, 'She's my sister,' so that I took her as my wife? Now, here is your wife. Take her and go!" [20] Then Pharaoh gave his men orders about him, and they sent him away with his wife and all he had.

Genesis 22

¹ After these things God tested Abraham and said to him, "Abraham!"

"Here I am," he answered.

² "Take your son," he said, "your only son Isaac, whom you love, go to the land of Moriah, and offer him there as a burnt offering on one of the mountains I will tell you about."

³ So Abraham got up early in the morning, saddled his donkey, and took with him two of his young men and his son Isaac. He split wood for a burnt offering and set out to go to the place God had told him about. ⁴ On the third day Abraham looked up and saw the place in the distance. ⁵ Then Abraham said to his young men, "Stay here with the donkey. The boy and I will go over there to worship; then we'll come back to you." ⁶ Abraham took the wood for the burnt offering and laid it on his son Isaac. In his hand he took the fire and the knife, and the two of them walked on together.

⁷ Then Isaac spoke to his father Abraham and said, "My father."

And he replied, "Here I am, my son."

Isaac said, "The fire and the wood are here, but where is the lamb for the burnt offering?"

⁸ Abraham answered, "God himself will provide the lamb for the burnt offering, my son." Then the two of them walked on together.

⁹ When they arrived at the place that God had told him about, Abraham built the altar there and arranged the wood. He bound his son Isaac and placed him on the altar on top of the wood. ¹⁰ Then Abraham reached out and took the knife to slaughter his son.

¹¹ But the angel of the LORD called to him from heaven and said, "Abraham, Abraham!"

He replied, "Here I am."

¹² Then he said, "Do not lay a hand on the boy or do anything to him. For now I know that you fear God, since you have not withheld your only son from me." ¹³ Abraham looked up and saw a ram caught in the thicket by its horns. So Abraham went and took the ram and offered it as a burnt offering in place of his son. ¹⁴ And Abraham named that place The LORD Will Provide, so today it is said: "It will be provided on the LORD's mountain."

¹⁵ Then the angel of the LORD called to Abraham a second time from heaven ¹⁶ and said, "By myself I have sworn," this is the LORD's declaration: "Because you have done this thing and have not withheld your only son,

[17] I will indeed bless you and make your offspring as numerous as the stars of the sky and the sand on the seashore. Your offspring will possess the city gates of their enemies. [18] And all the nations of the earth will be blessed by your offspring because you have obeyed my command."

[19] Abraham went back to his young men, and they got up and went together to Beer-sheba. And Abraham settled in Beer-sheba.

[20] Now after these things Abraham was told, "Milcah also has borne sons to your brother Nahor: [21] Uz his firstborn, his brother Buz, Kemuel the father of Aram, [22] Chesed, Hazo, Pildash, Jidlaph, and Bethuel." [23] And Bethuel fathered Rebekah. Milcah bore these eight to Nahor, Abraham's brother. [24] His concubine, whose name was Reumah, also bore Tebah, Gaham, Tahash, and Maacah.

Exodus 3

¹ Meanwhile, Moses was shepherding the flock of his father-in-law Jethro, the priest of Midian. He led the flock to the far side of the wilderness and came to Horeb, the mountain of God. ² Then the angel of the LORD appeared to him in a flame of fire within a bush. As Moses looked, he saw that the bush was on fire but was not consumed. ³ So Moses thought, "I must go over and look at this remarkable sight. Why isn't the bush burning up?"

⁴ When the LORD saw that he had gone over to look, God called out to him from the bush, "Moses, Moses!"

"Here I am," he answered.

⁵ "Do not come closer," he said. "Remove the sandals from your feet, for the place where you are standing is holy ground." ⁶ Then he continued, "I am the God of your father, the God of Abraham, the God of Isaac, and the God of Jacob." Moses hid his face because he was afraid to look at God.

⁷ Then the LORD said, "I have observed the misery of my people in Egypt, and have heard them crying out because of their oppressors. I know about their sufferings, ⁸ and I have come down to rescue them from the power of the Egyptians and to bring them from that land to a good and spacious land, a land flowing with milk and honey — the territory of the Canaanites, Hethites, Amorites, Perizzites, Hivites, and Jebusites. ⁹ So because the Israelites' cry for help has come to me, and I have also seen the way the Egyptians are oppressing them, ¹⁰ therefore, go. I am sending you to Pharaoh so that you may lead my people, the Israelites, out of Egypt."

¹¹ But Moses asked God, "Who am I that I should go to Pharaoh and that I should bring the Israelites out of Egypt?"

¹² He answered, "I will certainly be with you, and this will be the sign to you that I am the one who sent you: when you bring the people out of Egypt, you will all worship God at this mountain."

¹³ Then Moses asked God, "If I go to the Israelites and say to them, 'The God of your fathers has sent me to you,' and they ask me, 'What is his name?' what should I tell them?"

¹⁴ God replied to Moses, "I AM WHO I AM. This is what you are to say to the Israelites: I AM has sent me to you." ¹⁵ God also said to Moses, "Say this to the Israelites: The LORD, the God of your fathers, the God of Abraham, the God of Isaac, and the God of Jacob, has sent me to you.

This is my name forever; this is how I am to be remembered in every generation.

[16] "Go and assemble the elders of Israel and say to them: The LORD, the God of your fathers, the God of Abraham, Isaac, and Jacob, has appeared to me and said: I have paid close attention to you and to what has been done to you in Egypt. [17] And I have promised you that I will bring you up from the misery of Egypt to the land of the Canaanites, Hethites, Amorites, Perizzites, Hivites, and Jebusites — a land flowing with milk and honey. [18] They will listen to what you say. Then you, along with the elders of Israel, must go to the king of Egypt and say to him: The LORD, the God of the Hebrews, has met with us. Now please let us go on a three-day trip into the wilderness so that we may sacrifice to the LORD our God.

[19] "However, I know that the king of Egypt will not allow you to go, even under force from a strong hand. [20] But when I stretch out my hand and strike Egypt with all my miracles that I will perform in it, after that, he will let you go. [21] And I will give these people such favor with the Egyptians that when you go, you will not go empty-handed. [22] Each woman will ask her neighbor and any woman staying in her house for silver and gold jewelry, and clothing, and you will put them on your sons and daughters. So you will plunder the Egyptians."

Exodus 14

¹ Then the LORD spoke to Moses: ² "Tell the Israelites to turn back and camp in front of Pi-hahiroth, between Migdol and the sea; you must camp in front of Baal-zephon, facing it by the sea. ³ Pharaoh will say of the Israelites: They are wandering around the land in confusion; the wilderness has boxed them in. ⁴ I will harden Pharaoh's heart so that he will pursue them. Then I will receive glory by means of Pharaoh and all his army, and the Egyptians will know that I am the LORD." So the Israelites did this.

⁵ When the king of Egypt was told that the people had fled, Pharaoh and his officials changed their minds about the people and said: "What have we done? We have released Israel from serving us." ⁶ So he got his chariot ready and took his troops with him; ⁷ he took six hundred of the best chariots and all the rest of the chariots of Egypt, with officers in each one. ⁸ The LORD hardened the heart of Pharaoh king of Egypt, and he pursued the Israelites, who were going out defiantly. ⁹ The Egyptians — all Pharaoh's horses and chariots, his horsemen, and his army — chased after them and caught up with them as they camped by the sea beside Pi-hahiroth, in front of Baal-zephon.

¹⁰ As Pharaoh approached, the Israelites looked up and there were the Egyptians coming after them! The Israelites were terrified and cried out to the LORD for help. ¹¹ They said to Moses: "Is it because there are no graves in Egypt that you have taken us away to die in the wilderness? What have you done to us by bringing us out of Egypt? ¹² Isn't this what we told you in Egypt: Leave us alone so that we may serve the Egyptians? It would have been better for us to serve the Egyptians than to die in the wilderness."

¹³ But Moses said to the people, "Don't be afraid. Stand firm and see the LORD's salvation that he will accomplish for you today; for the Egyptians you see today, you will never see again. ¹⁴ The LORD will fight for you, and you must be quiet."

¹⁵ The LORD said to Moses, "Why are you crying out to me? Tell the Israelites to break camp. ¹⁶ As for you, lift up your staff, stretch out your hand over the sea, and divide it so that the Israelites can go through the sea on dry ground. ¹⁷ As for me, I am going to harden the hearts of the Egyptians so that they will go in after them, and I will receive glory by

means of Pharaoh, all his army, and his chariots and horsemen. [18] The Egyptians will know that I am the LORD when I receive glory through Pharaoh, his chariots, and his horsemen."

[19] Then the angel of God, who was going in front of the Israelite forces, moved and went behind them. The pillar of cloud moved from in front of them and stood behind them. [20] It came between the Egyptian and Israelite forces. There was cloud and darkness, it lit up the night, and neither group came near the other all night long.

[21] Then Moses stretched out his hand over the sea. The LORD drove the sea back with a powerful east wind all that night and turned the sea into dry land. So the waters were divided, [22] and the Israelites went through the sea on dry ground, with the waters like a wall to them on their right and their left.

[23] The Egyptians set out in pursuit — all Pharaoh's horses, his chariots, and his horsemen — and went into the sea after them. [24] During the morning watch, the LORD looked down at the Egyptian forces from the pillar of fire and cloud, and threw the Egyptian forces into confusion. [25] He caused their chariot wheels to swerve and made them drive with difficulty. "Let's get away from Israel," the Egyptians said, "because the LORD is fighting for them against Egypt!"

[26] Then the LORD said to Moses, "Stretch out your hand over the sea so that the water may come back on the Egyptians, on their chariots and horsemen." [27] So Moses stretched out his hand over the sea, and at daybreak the sea returned to its normal depth. While the Egyptians were trying to escape from it, the LORD threw them into the sea. [28] The water came back and covered the chariots and horsemen, plus the entire army of Pharaoh that had gone after them into the sea. Not even one of them survived.

[29] But the Israelites had walked through the sea on dry ground, with the waters like a wall to them on their right and their left. [30] That day the LORD saved Israel from the power of the Egyptians, and Israel saw the Egyptians dead on the seashore. [31] When Israel saw the great power that the LORD used against the Egyptians, the people feared the LORD and believed in him and in his servant Moses.

Exodus 20

¹ Then God spoke all these words:

² I am the LORD your God, who brought you out of the land of Egypt, out of the place of slavery.

³ Do not have other gods besides me.

⁴ Do not make an idol for yourself, whether in the shape of anything in the heavens above or on the earth below or in the waters under the earth. ⁵ Do not bow in worship to them, and do not serve them; for I, the LORD your God, am a jealous God, punishing the children for the fathers' iniquity, to the third and fourth generations of those who hate me, ⁶ but showing faithful love to a thousand generations of those who love me and keep my commands.

⁷ Do not misuse the name of the LORD your God, because the LORD will not leave anyone unpunished who misuses his name.

⁸ Remember the Sabbath day, to keep it holy: ⁹ You are to labor six days and do all your work, ¹⁰ but the seventh day is a Sabbath to the LORD your God. You must not do any work — you, your son or daughter, your male or female servant, your livestock, or the resident alien who is within your city gates. ¹¹ For the LORD made the heavens and the earth, the sea, and everything in them in six days; then he rested on the seventh day. Therefore the LORD blessed the Sabbath day and declared it holy.

¹² Honor your father and your mother so that you may have a long life in the land that the LORD your God is giving you.

¹³ Do not murder.

¹⁴ Do not commit adultery.

¹⁵ Do not steal.

¹⁶ Do not give false testimony against your neighbor.

¹⁷ Do not covet your neighbor's house. Do not covet your neighbor's wife, his male or female servant, his ox or donkey, or anything that belongs to your neighbor.

¹⁸ All the people witnessed the thunder and lightning, the sound of the trumpet, and the mountain surrounded by smoke. When the people saw it they trembled and stood at a distance. ¹⁹ "You speak to us, and we will listen," they said to Moses, "but don't let God speak to us, or we will die."

²⁰ Moses responded to the people, "Don't be afraid, for God has come to test you, so that you will fear him and will not sin." ²¹ And the people

remained standing at a distance as Moses approached the total darkness where God was.

[22] Then the LORD told Moses, "This is what you are to say to the Israelites:
You have seen that I have spoken to you from heaven. [23] Do not make
gods of silver to rival me; do not make gods of gold for yourselves.

[24] "Make an earthen altar for me, and sacrifice on it your burnt offerings and fellowship offerings, your flocks and herds. I will come to you
and bless you in every place where I cause my name to be remembered.
[25] If you make a stone altar for me, do not build it out of cut stones. If you
use your chisel on it, you will defile it. [26] Do not go up to my altar on steps,
so that your nakedness is not exposed on it."

Judges 16

¹ Samson went to Gaza, where he saw a prostitute and went to bed with her. ² When the Gazites heard that Samson was there, they surrounded the place and waited in ambush for him all that night at the city gate. They kept quiet all night, saying, "Let's wait until dawn; then we will kill him." ³ But Samson stayed in bed only until midnight. Then he got up, took hold of the doors of the city gate along with the two gateposts, and pulled them out, bar and all. He put them on his shoulders and took them to the top of the mountain overlooking Hebron.

⁴ Some time later, he fell in love with a woman named Delilah, who lived in the Sorek Valley. ⁵ The Philistine leaders went to her and said, "Persuade him to tell you where his great strength comes from, so we can overpower him, tie him up, and make him helpless. Each of us will then give you 1,100 pieces of silver."

⁶ So Delilah said to Samson, "Please tell me, where does your great strength come from? How could someone tie you up and make you helpless?"

⁷ Samson told her, "If they tie me up with seven fresh bowstrings that have not been dried, I will become weak and be like any other man."

⁸ The Philistine leaders brought her seven fresh bowstrings that had not been dried, and she tied him up with them. ⁹ While the men in ambush were waiting in her room, she called out to him, "Samson, the Philistines are here!" But he snapped the bowstrings as a strand of yarn snaps when it touches fire. The secret of his strength remained unknown.

¹⁰ Then Delilah said to Samson, "You have mocked me and told me lies! Won't you please tell me how you can be tied up?"

¹¹ He told her, "If they tie me up with new ropes that have never been used, I will become weak and be like any other man."

¹² Delilah took new ropes, tied him up with them, and shouted, "Samson, the Philistines are here!" But while the men in ambush were waiting in her room, he snapped the ropes off his arms like a thread.

¹³ Then Delilah said to Samson, "You have mocked me all along and told me lies! Tell me how you can be tied up."

He told her, "If you weave the seven braids on my head into the fabric on a loom—"

¹⁴ She fastened the braids with a pin and called to him, "Samson, the Philistines are here!" He awoke from his sleep and pulled out the pin, with the loom and the web.

¹⁵ "How can you say, 'I love you,'" she told him, "when your heart is not with me? This is the third time you have mocked me and not told me what makes your strength so great!"

¹⁶ Because she nagged him day after day and pleaded with him until she wore him out, ¹⁷ he told her the whole truth and said to her, "My hair has never been cut, because I am a Nazirite to God from birth. If I am shaved, my strength will leave me, and I will become weak and be like any other man."

¹⁸ When Delilah realized that he had told her the whole truth, she sent this message to the Philistine leaders: "Come one more time, for he has told me the whole truth." The Philistine leaders came to her and brought the silver with them.

¹⁹ Then she let him fall asleep on her lap and called a man to shave off the seven braids on his head. In this way, she made him helpless, and his strength left him. ²⁰ Then she cried, "Samson, the Philistines are here!" When he awoke from his sleep, he said, "I will escape as I did before and shake myself free." But he did not know that the LORD had left him.

²¹ The Philistines seized him and gouged out his eyes. They brought him down to Gaza and bound him with bronze shackles, and he was forced to grind grain in the prison. ²² But his hair began to grow back after it had been shaved.

²³ Now the Philistine leaders gathered together to offer a great sacrifice to their god Dagon. They rejoiced and said:

Our god has handed over
our enemy Samson to us.

²⁴ When the people saw him, they praised their god and said:

Our god has handed over to us
our enemy who destroyed our land
and who multiplied our dead.

²⁵ When they were in good spirits, they said, "Bring Samson here to entertain us." So they brought Samson from prison, and he entertained them. They had him stand between the pillars.

²⁶ Samson said to the young man who was leading him by the hand, "Lead me where I can feel the pillars supporting the temple, so I can lean

against them." ²⁷ The temple was full of men and women; all the leaders of the Philistines were there, and about three thousand men and women were on the roof watching Samson entertain them. ²⁸ He called out to the LORD: "Lord GOD, please remember me. Strengthen me, God, just once more. With one act of vengeance, let me pay back the Philistines for my two eyes." ²⁹ Samson took hold of the two middle pillars supporting the temple and leaned against them, one on his right hand and the other on his left. ³⁰ Samson said, "Let me die with the Philistines." He pushed with all his might, and the temple fell on the leaders and all the people in it. And those he killed at his death were more than those he had killed in his life.

³¹ Then his brothers and all his father's family came down, carried him back, and buried him between Zorah and Eshtaol in the tomb of his father Manoah. So he judged Israel twenty years.

1 Samuel 17

¹ The Philistines gathered their forces for war at Socoh in Judah and camped between Socoh and Azekah in Ephes-dammim. ² Saul and the men of Israel gathered and camped in the Valley of Elah; then they lined up in battle formation to face the Philistines.

³ The Philistines were standing on one hill, and the Israelites were standing on another hill with a ravine between them. ⁴ Then a champion named Goliath, from Gath, came out from the Philistine camp. He was nine feet, nine inches tall ⁵ and wore a bronze helmet and bronze scale armor that weighed one hundred twenty-five pounds. ⁶ There was bronze armor on his shins, and a bronze javelin was slung between his shoulders. ⁷ His spear shaft was like a weaver's beam, and the iron point of his spear weighed fifteen pounds. In addition, a shield-bearer was walking in front of him.

⁸ He stood and shouted to the Israelite battle formations: "Why do you come out to line up in battle formation?" He asked them, "Am I not a Philistine and are you not servants of Saul? Choose one of your men and have him come down against me. ⁹ If he wins in a fight against me and kills me, we will be your servants. But if I win against him and kill him, then you will be our servants and serve us." ¹⁰ Then the Philistine said, "I defy the ranks of Israel today. Send me a man so we can fight each other!" ¹¹ When Saul and all Israel heard these words from the Philistine, they lost their courage and were terrified.

¹² Now David was the son of the Ephrathite from Bethlehem of Judah named Jesse. Jesse had eight sons and during Saul's reign was already an old man. ¹³ Jesse's three oldest sons had followed Saul to the war, and their names were Eliab, the firstborn, Abinadab, the next, and Shammah, the third, ¹⁴ and David was the youngest. The three oldest had followed Saul, ¹⁵ but David kept going back and forth from Saul to tend his father's flock in Bethlehem.

¹⁶ Every morning and evening for forty days the Philistine came forward and took his stand. ¹⁷ One day Jesse had told his son David: "Take this half-bushel of roasted grain along with these ten loaves of bread for your brothers and hurry to their camp. ¹⁸ Also take these ten portions of cheese to the field commander. Check on the well-being of your brothers and bring a confirmation from them. ¹⁹ They are with Saul and all the men of Israel in the Valley of Elah fighting with the Philistines."

²⁰ So David got up early in the morning, left the flock with someone to keep it, loaded up, and set out as Jesse had charged him.

He arrived at the perimeter of the camp as the army was marching out to its battle formation shouting their battle cry. ²¹ Israel and the Philistines lined up in battle formation facing each other. ²² David left his supplies in the care of the quartermaster and ran to the battle line. When he arrived, he asked his brothers how they were. ²³ While he was speaking with them, suddenly the champion named Goliath, the Philistine from Gath, came forward from the Philistine battle line and shouted his usual words, which David heard. ²⁴ When all the Israelite men saw Goliath, they retreated from him terrified.

²⁵ Previously, an Israelite man had declared: "Do you see this man who keeps coming out? He comes to defy Israel. The king will make the man who kills him very rich and will give him his daughter. The king will also make the family of that man's father exempt from paying taxes in Israel."

²⁶ David spoke to the men who were standing with him: "What will be done for the man who kills that Philistine and removes this disgrace from Israel? Just who is this uncircumcised Philistine that he should defy the armies of the living God?"

²⁷ The troops told him about the offer, concluding, "That is what will be done for the man who kills him."

²⁸ David's oldest brother Eliab listened as he spoke to the men, and he became angry with him. "Why did you come down here?" he asked. "Who did you leave those few sheep with in the wilderness? I know your arrogance and your evil heart — you came down to see the battle!"

²⁹ "What have I done now?" protested David. "It was just a question." ³⁰ Then he turned from those beside him to others in front of him and asked about the offer. The people gave him the same answer as before.

³¹ What David said was overheard and reported to Saul, so he had David brought to him. ³² David said to Saul, "Don't let anyone be discouraged by him; your servant will go and fight this Philistine!"

³³ But Saul replied, "You can't go fight this Philistine. You're just a youth, and he's been a warrior since he was young."

³⁴ David answered Saul: "Your servant has been tending his father's sheep. Whenever a lion or a bear came and carried off a lamb from the flock, ³⁵ I went after it, struck it down, and rescued the lamb from its mouth. If it reared up against me, I would grab it by its fur, strike it down, and kill it. ³⁶ Your servant has killed lions and bears; this uncircumcised Philistine will be like one of them, for he has defied the armies of the

living God." ³⁷ Then David said, "The LORD who rescued me from the paw of the lion and the paw of the bear will rescue me from the hand of this Philistine."

Saul said to David, "Go, and may the LORD be with you."

³⁸ Then Saul had his own military clothes put on David. He put a bronze helmet on David's head and had him put on armor. ³⁹ David strapped his sword on over the military clothes and tried to walk, but he was not used to them. "I can't walk in these," David said to Saul, "I'm not used to them." So David took them off. ⁴⁰ Instead, he took his staff in his hand and chose five smooth stones from the wadi and put them in the pouch, in his shepherd's bag. Then, with his sling in his hand, he approached the Philistine.

⁴¹ The Philistine came closer and closer to David, with the shield-bearer in front of him. ⁴² When the Philistine looked and saw David, he despised him because he was just a youth, healthy and handsome. ⁴³ He said to David, "Am I a dog that you come against me with sticks?" Then he cursed David by his gods. ⁴⁴ "Come here," the Philistine called to David, "and I'll give your flesh to the birds of the sky and the wild beasts!"

⁴⁵ David said to the Philistine: "You come against me with a sword, spear, and javelin, but I come against you in the name of the LORD of Armies, the God of the ranks of Israel — you have defied him. ⁴⁶ Today, the LORD will hand you over to me. Today, I'll strike you down, remove your head, and give the corpses of the Philistine camp to the birds of the sky and the wild creatures of the earth. Then all the world will know that Israel has a God, ⁴⁷ and this whole assembly will know that it is not by sword or by spear that the LORD saves, for the battle is the LORD's. He will hand you over to us."

⁴⁸ When the Philistine started forward to attack him, David ran quickly to the battle line to meet the Philistine. ⁴⁹ David put his hand in the bag, took out a stone, slung it, and hit the Philistine on his forehead. The stone sank into his forehead, and he fell facedown to the ground. ⁵⁰ David defeated the Philistine with a sling and a stone. David overpowered the Philistine and killed him without having a sword. ⁵¹ David ran and stood over him. He grabbed the Philistine's sword, pulled it from its sheath, and used it to kill him. Then he cut off his head. When the Philistines saw that their hero was dead, they fled. ⁵² The men of Israel and Judah rallied, shouting their battle cry, and chased the Philistines to the entrance of the valley and to the gates of Ekron. Philistine bodies were strewn all along the Shaaraim road to Gath and Ekron.

[53] When the Israelites returned from the pursuit of the Philistines, they plundered their camps. [54] David took Goliath's head and brought it to Jerusalem, but he put Goliath's weapons in his own tent.

[55] When Saul had seen David going out to confront the Philistine, he asked Abner the commander of the army, "Whose son is this youth, Abner?"

"Your Majesty, as surely as you live, I don't know," Abner replied.

[56] The king said, "Find out whose son this young man is!"

[57] When David returned from killing the Philistine, Abner took him and brought him before Saul with the Philistine's head still in his hand. [58] Saul said to him, "Whose son are you, young man?"

"The son of your servant Jesse of Bethlehem," David answered.

Job 1

¹ There was a man in the country of Uz named Job. He was a man of complete integrity, who feared God and turned away from evil. ² He had seven sons and three daughters. ³ His estate included seven thousand sheep and goats, three thousand camels, five hundred yoke of oxen, five hundred female donkeys, and a very large number of servants. Job was the greatest man among all the people of the east.

⁴ His sons used to take turns having banquets at their homes. They would send an invitation to their three sisters to eat and drink with them. ⁵ Whenever a round of banqueting was over, Job would send for his children and purify them, rising early in the morning to offer burnt offerings for all of them. For Job thought, "Perhaps my children have sinned, having cursed God in their hearts." This was Job's regular practice.

⁶ One day the sons of God came to present themselves before the LORD, and Satan also came with them. ⁷ The LORD asked Satan, "Where have you come from?"

"From roaming through the earth," Satan answered him, "and walking around on it."

⁸ Then the LORD said to Satan, "Have you considered my servant Job? No one else on earth is like him, a man of perfect integrity, who fears God and turns away from evil."

⁹ Satan answered the LORD, "Does Job fear God for nothing? ¹⁰ Haven't you placed a hedge around him, his household, and everything he owns? You have blessed the work of his hands, and his possessions have increased in the land. ¹¹ But stretch out your hand and strike everything he owns, and he will surely curse you to your face."

¹² "Very well," the LORD told Satan, "everything he owns is in your power. However, do not lay a hand on Job himself." So Satan left the LORD's presence.

¹³ One day when Job's sons and daughters were eating and drinking wine in their oldest brother's house, ¹⁴ a messenger came to Job and reported: "While the oxen were plowing and the donkeys grazing nearby, ¹⁵ the Sabeans swooped down and took them away. They struck down the servants with the sword, and I alone have escaped to tell you!"

¹⁶ He was still speaking when another messenger came and reported: "God's fire fell from heaven. It burned the sheep and the servants and devoured them, and I alone have escaped to tell you!"

¹⁷ That messenger was still speaking when yet another came and reported: "The Chaldeans formed three bands, made a raid on the camels, and took them away. They struck down the servants with the sword, and I alone have escaped to tell you!"

¹⁸ He was still speaking when another messenger came and reported: "Your sons and daughters were eating and drinking wine in their oldest brother's house. ¹⁹ Suddenly a powerful wind swept in from the desert and struck the four corners of the house. It collapsed on the young people so that they died, and I alone have escaped to tell you!"

²⁰ Then Job stood up, tore his robe, and shaved his head. He fell to the ground and worshiped, ²¹ saying:

> Naked I came from my mother's womb,
> and naked I will leave this life.
> The LORD gives, and the LORD takes away.
> Blessed be the name of the LORD.

²² Throughout all this Job did not sin or blame God for anything.

Psalm 23

A psalm of David.

[1] The LORD is my shepherd;
I have what I need.
[2] He lets me lie down in green pastures;
he leads me beside quiet waters.
[3] He renews my life;
he leads me along the right paths
for his name's sake.
[4] Even when I go through the darkest valley,
I fear no danger,
for you are with me;
your rod and your staff — they comfort me.

[5] You prepare a table before me
in the presence of my enemies;
you anoint my head with oil;
my cup overflows.
[6] Only goodness and faithful love will pursue me
all the days of my life,
and I will dwell in the house of the LORD
as long as I live.

Psalm 51

For the choir director. A psalm of David, when the prophet Nathan came to him after he had gone to Bathsheba.

1 Be gracious to me, God,
according to your faithful love;
according to your abundant compassion,
blot out my rebellion.
2 Completely wash away my guilt
and cleanse me from my sin.
3 For I am conscious of my rebellion,
and my sin is always before me.
4 Against you — you alone — I have sinned
and done this evil in your sight.
So you are right when you pass sentence;
you are blameless when you judge.
5 Indeed, I was guilty when I was born;
I was sinful when my mother conceived me.

6 Surely you desire integrity in the inner self,
and you teach me wisdom deep within.
7 Purify me with hyssop, and I will be clean;
wash me, and I will be whiter than snow.
8 Let me hear joy and gladness;
let the bones you have crushed rejoice.
9 Turn your face away from my sins
and blot out all my guilt.

10 God, create a clean heart for me
and renew a steadfast spirit within me.
11 Do not banish me from your presence
or take your Holy Spirit from me.
12 Restore the joy of your salvation to me,
and sustain me by giving me a willing spirit.
13 Then I will teach the rebellious your ways,
and sinners will return to you.

14 Save me from the guilt of bloodshed, God —
God of my salvation —

and my tongue will sing of your righteousness.
¹⁵ Lord, open my lips,
and my mouth will declare your praise.
¹⁶ You do not want a sacrifice, or I would give it;
you are not pleased with a burnt offering.
¹⁷ The sacrifice pleasing to God is a broken spirit.
You will not despise a broken and humbled heart, God.

¹⁸ In your good pleasure, cause Zion to prosper;
build the walls of Jerusalem.
¹⁹ Then you will delight in righteous sacrifices,
whole burnt offerings;
then bulls will be offered on your altar.

Psalm 139

For the choir director. A psalm of David.

¹ LORD, you have searched me and known me.
² You know when I sit down and when I stand up;
you understand my thoughts from far away.
³ You observe my travels and my rest;
you are aware of all my ways.
⁴ Before a word is on my tongue,
you know all about it, LORD.
⁵ You have encircled me;
you have placed your hand on me.
⁶ This wondrous knowledge is beyond me.
It is lofty; I am unable to reach it.

⁷ Where can I go to escape your Spirit?
Where can I flee from your presence?
⁸ If I go up to heaven, you are there;
if I make my bed in Sheol, you are there.
⁹ If I live at the eastern horizon
or settle at the western limits,
¹⁰ even there your hand will lead me;
your right hand will hold on to me.
¹¹ If I say, "Surely the darkness will hide me,
and the light around me will be night" —
¹² even the darkness is not dark to you.
The night shines like the day;
darkness and light are alike to you.

¹³ For it was you who created my inward parts;
you knit me together in my mother's womb.
¹⁴ I will praise you
because I have been remarkably and wondrously made.
Your works are wondrous,
and I know this very well.
¹⁵ My bones were not hidden from you
when I was made in secret,
when I was formed in the depths of the earth.

[16] Your eyes saw me when I was formless;
all my days were written in your book and planned
before a single one of them began.

[17] God, how precious your thoughts are
to me;
how vast their sum is!
[18] If I counted them,
they would outnumber the grains of sand;
when I wake up, I am still with you.

[19] God, if only you would kill the wicked —
you bloodthirsty men, stay away from me —
[20] who invoke you deceitfully.
Your enemies swear by you falsely.
[21] LORD, don't I hate those who hate you,
and detest those who rebel against you?
[22] I hate them with extreme hatred;
I consider them my enemies.

[23] Search me, God, and know my heart;
test me and know my concerns.
[24] See if there is any offensive way in me;
lead me in the everlasting way.

Proverbs 1

¹ The proverbs of Solomon son of David, king of Israel:
² For learning wisdom and discipline;
for understanding insightful sayings;
³ for receiving prudent instruction
in righteousness, justice, and integrity;
⁴ for teaching shrewdness to the inexperienced,
knowledge and discretion to a young man —
⁵ let a wise person listen and increase learning,
and let a discerning person obtain guidance —
⁶ for understanding a proverb or a parable,
the words of the wise, and their riddles.

⁷ The fear of the LORD
is the beginning of knowledge;
fools despise wisdom and discipline.

⁸ Listen, my son, to your father's instruction,
and don't reject your mother's teaching,
⁹ for they will be a garland of favor on your head
and pendants around your neck.
¹⁰ My son, if sinners entice you,
don't be persuaded.
¹¹ If they say — "Come with us!
Let's set an ambush and kill someone.
Let's attack some innocent person just for fun!
¹² Let's swallow them alive, like Sheol,
whole, like those who go down to the Pit.
¹³ We'll find all kinds of valuable property
and fill our houses with plunder.
¹⁴ Throw in your lot with us,
and we'll all share the loot" —
¹⁵ my son, don't travel that road with them
or set foot on their path,
¹⁶ because their feet run toward evil
and they hurry to shed blood.
¹⁷ It is useless to spread a net
where any bird can see it,

¹⁸ but they set an ambush to kill themselves;
they attack their own lives.
¹⁹ Such are the paths of all who make profit dishonestly;
it takes the lives of those who receive it.

²⁰ Wisdom calls out in the street;
she makes her voice heard in the public squares.
²¹ She cries out above the commotion;
she speaks at the entrance of the city gates:
²² "How long, inexperienced ones, will you love ignorance?
How long will you mockers enjoy mocking
and you fools hate knowledge?
²³ If you respond to my warning,
then I will pour out my spirit on you
and teach you my words.
²⁴ Since I called out and you refused,
extended my hand and no one paid attention,
²⁵ since you neglected all my counsel
and did not accept my correction,
²⁶ I, in turn, will laugh at your calamity.
I will mock when terror strikes you,
²⁷ when terror strikes you like a storm
and your calamity comes like a whirlwind,
when trouble and stress overcome you.
²⁸ Then they will call me, but I won't answer;
they will search for me, but won't find me.
²⁹ Because they hated knowledge,
didn't choose to fear the LORD,
³⁰ were not interested in my counsel,
and rejected all my correction,
³¹ they will eat the fruit of their way
and be glutted with their own schemes.
³² For the apostasy of the inexperienced will kill them,
and the complacency of fools will destroy them.
³³ But whoever listens to me will live securely
and be undisturbed by the dread of danger."

Isaiah 53

¹ Who has believed what we have heard?
And to whom has the arm of the LORD been revealed?
² He grew up before him like a young plant
and like a root out of dry ground.
He didn't have an impressive form
or majesty that we should look at him,
no appearance that we should desire him.
³ He was despised and rejected by men,
a man of suffering who knew what sickness was.
He was like someone people turned away from;
he was despised, and we didn't value him.

⁴ Yet he himself bore our sicknesses,
and he carried our pains;
but we in turn regarded him stricken,
struck down by God, and afflicted.
⁵ But he was pierced because of our rebellion,
crushed because of our iniquities;
punishment for our peace was on him,
and we are healed by his wounds.
⁶ We all went astray like sheep;
we all have turned to our own way;
and the LORD has punished him
for the iniquity of us all.

⁷ He was oppressed and afflicted,
yet he did not open his mouth.
Like a lamb led to the slaughter
and like a sheep silent before her shearers,
he did not open his mouth.
⁸ He was taken away because of oppression and judgment;
and who considered his fate?
For he was cut off from the land of the living;
he was struck because of my people's rebellion.
⁹ He was assigned a grave with the wicked,
but he was with a rich man at his death,
because he had done no violence
and had not spoken deceitfully.

[10] Yet the LORD was pleased to crush him severely.
When you make him a guilt offering,
he will see his seed, he will prolong his days,
and by his hand, the LORD's pleasure will be accomplished.
[11] After his anguish,
he will see light and be satisfied.
By his knowledge,
my righteous servant will justify many,
and he will carry their iniquities.
[12] Therefore I will give him the many as a portion,
and he will receive the mighty as spoil,
because he willingly submitted to death,
and was counted among the rebels;
yet he bore the sin of many
and interceded for the rebels.

Jeremiah 1

¹ The words of Jeremiah, the son of Hilkiah, one of the priests living in Anathoth in the territory of Benjamin. ² The word of the LORD came to him in the thirteenth year of the reign of Josiah son of Amon, king of Judah. ³ It also came throughout the days of Jehoiakim son of Josiah, king of Judah, until the fifth month of the eleventh year of Zedekiah son of Josiah, king of Judah, when the people of Jerusalem went into exile.

⁴ The word of the LORD came to me:

⁵ I chose you before I formed you in the womb;
I set you apart before you were born.
I appointed you a prophet to the nations.

⁶ But I protested, "Oh no, Lord GOD! Look, I don't know how to speak since I am only a youth."
⁷ Then the LORD said to me:

Do not say, "I am only a youth,"
for you will go to everyone I send you to
and speak whatever I tell you.
⁸ Do not be afraid of anyone,
for I will be with you to rescue you.
This is the LORD's declaration.

⁹ Then the LORD reached out his hand, touched my mouth, and told me:

I have now filled your mouth with my words.
¹⁰ See, I have appointed you today
over nations and kingdoms
to uproot and tear down,
to destroy and demolish,
to build and plant.

¹¹ Then the word of the LORD came to me, asking, "What do you see, Jeremiah?"
I replied, "I see a branch of an almond tree."

¹² The LORD said to me, "You have seen correctly, for I watch over my word to accomplish it." ¹³ Again the word of the LORD came to me asking, "What do you see?"

And I replied, "I see a boiling pot, its lip tilted from the north to the south."

¹⁴ Then the LORD said to me, "Disaster will be poured out from the north on all who live in the land. ¹⁵ Indeed, I am about to summon all the clans and kingdoms of the north."

This is the LORD's declaration.

They will come, and each king will set up his throne
at the entrance to Jerusalem's gates.
They will attack all her surrounding walls
and all the other cities of Judah.

¹⁶ "I will pronounce my judgments against them for all the evil they did when they abandoned me to burn incense to other gods and to worship the works of their own hands.

¹⁷ "Now, get ready. Stand up and tell them everything that I command you. Do not be intimidated by them or I will cause you to cower before them. ¹⁸ Today, I am the one who has made you a fortified city, an iron pillar, and bronze walls against the whole land — against the kings of Judah, its officials, its priests, and the population. ¹⁹ They will fight against you but never prevail over you, since I am with you to rescue you."

This is the LORD's declaration.

Daniel 3

¹ King Nebuchadnezzar made a gold statue, ninety feet high and nine feet wide. He set it up on the plain of Dura in the province of Babylon. ² King Nebuchadnezzar sent word to assemble the satraps, prefects, governors, advisers, treasurers, judges, magistrates, and all the rulers of the provinces to attend the dedication of the statue King Nebuchadnezzar had set up. ³ So the satraps, prefects, governors, advisers, treasurers, judges, magistrates, and all the rulers of the provinces assembled for the dedication of the statue the king had set up. Then they stood before the statue Nebuchadnezzar had set up.

⁴ A herald loudly proclaimed, "People of every nation and language, you are commanded: ⁵ When you hear the sound of the horn, flute, zither, lyre, harp, drum, and every kind of music, you are to fall facedown and worship the gold statue that King Nebuchadnezzar has set up. ⁶ But whoever does not fall down and worship will immediately be thrown into a furnace of blazing fire."

⁷ Therefore, when all the people heard the sound of the horn, flute, zither, lyre, harp, and every kind of music, people of every nation and language fell down and worshiped the gold statue that King Nebuchadnezzar had set up.

⁸ Some Chaldeans took this occasion to come forward and maliciously accuse the Jews. ⁹ They said to King Nebuchadnezzar, "May the king live forever. ¹⁰ You as king have issued a decree that everyone who hears the sound of the horn, flute, zither, lyre, harp, drum, and every kind of music must fall down and worship the gold statue. ¹¹ Whoever does not fall down and worship will be thrown into a furnace of blazing fire. ¹² There are some Jews you have appointed to manage the province of Babylon: Shadrach, Meshach, and Abednego. These men have ignored you, the king; they do not serve your gods or worship the gold statue you have set up."

¹³ Then in a furious rage Nebuchadnezzar gave orders to bring in Shadrach, Meshach, and Abednego. So these men were brought before the king. ¹⁴ Nebuchadnezzar asked them, "Shadrach, Meshach, and Abednego, is it true that you don't serve my gods or worship the gold statue I have set up? ¹⁵ Now if you're ready, when you hear the sound of the horn, flute, zither, lyre, harp, drum, and every kind of music, fall down and worship the statue I made. But if you don't worship it, you will immediately be thrown into a furnace of blazing fire — and who is the god who can rescue you from my power?"

¹⁶ Shadrach, Meshach, and Abednego replied to the king, "Nebuchadnezzar, we don't need to give you an answer to this question. ¹⁷ If the God we serve exists, then he can rescue us from the furnace of blazing fire, and he can rescue us from the power of you, the king. ¹⁸ But even if he does not rescue us, we want you as king to know that we will not serve your gods or worship the gold statue you set up."

¹⁹ Then Nebuchadnezzar was filled with rage, and the expression on his face changed toward Shadrach, Meshach, and Abednego. He gave orders to heat the furnace seven times more than was customary, ²⁰ and he commanded some of the best soldiers in his army to tie up Shadrach, Meshach, and Abednego and throw them into the furnace of blazing fire. ²¹ So these men, in their trousers, robes, head coverings, and other clothes, were tied up and thrown into the furnace of blazing fire. ²² Since the king's command was so urgent and the furnace extremely hot, the raging flames killed those men who carried Shadrach, Meshach, and Abednego up. ²³ And these three men, Shadrach, Meshach, and Abednego fell, bound, into the furnace of blazing fire.

²⁴ Then King Nebuchadnezzar jumped up in alarm. He said to his advisers, "Didn't we throw three men, bound, into the fire?"

"Yes, of course, Your Majesty," they replied to the king.

²⁵ He exclaimed, "Look! I see four men, not tied, walking around in the fire unharmed; and the fourth looks like a son of the gods."

²⁶ Nebuchadnezzar then approached the door of the furnace of blazing fire and called: "Shadrach, Meshach, and Abednego, you servants of the Most High God — come out!" So Shadrach, Meshach, and Abednego came out of the fire. ²⁷ When the satraps, prefects, governors, and the king's advisers gathered around, they saw that the fire had no effect on the bodies of these men: not a hair of their heads was singed, their robes were unaffected, and there was no smell of fire on them. ²⁸ Nebuchadnezzar exclaimed, "Praise to the God of Shadrach, Meshach, and Abednego! He sent his angel and rescued his servants who trusted in him. They violated the king's command and risked their lives rather than serve or worship any god except their own God. ²⁹ Therefore I issue a decree that anyone of any people, nation, or language who says anything offensive against the God of Shadrach, Meshach, and Abednego will be torn limb from limb and his house made a garbage dump. For there is no other god who is able to deliver like this." ³⁰ Then the king rewarded Shadrach, Meshach, and Abednego in the province of Babylon.

Daniel 6

¹ Darius decided to appoint 120 satraps over the kingdom, stationed throughout the realm, ² and over them three administrators, including Daniel. These satraps would be accountable to them so that the king would not be defrauded. ³ Daniel distinguished himself above the administrators and satraps because he had an extraordinary spirit, so the king planned to set him over the whole realm. ⁴ The administrators and satraps, therefore, kept trying to find a charge against Daniel regarding the kingdom. But they could find no charge or corruption, for he was trustworthy, and no negligence or corruption was found in him. ⁵ Then these men said, "We will never find any charge against this Daniel unless we find something against him concerning the law of his God."

⁶ So the administrators and satraps went together to the king and said to him, "May King Darius live forever. ⁷ All the administrators of the kingdom, the prefects, satraps, advisers, and governors have agreed that the king should establish an ordinance and enforce an edict that for thirty days, anyone who petitions any god or man except you, the king, will be thrown into the lions' den. ⁸ Therefore, Your Majesty, establish the edict and sign the document so that, as a law of the Medes and Persians, it is irrevocable and cannot be changed." ⁹ So King Darius signed the written edict.

¹⁰ When Daniel learned that the document had been signed, he went into his house. The windows in its upstairs room opened toward Jerusalem, and three times a day he got down on his knees, prayed, and gave thanks to his God, just as he had done before. ¹¹ Then these men went as a group and found Daniel petitioning and imploring his God. ¹² So they approached the king and asked about his edict: "Didn't you sign an edict that for thirty days any person who petitions any god or man except you, the king, will be thrown into the lions' den?"

The king answered, "As a law of the Medes and Persians, the order stands and is irrevocable."

¹³ Then they replied to the king, "Daniel, one of the Judean exiles, has ignored you, the king, and the edict you signed, for he prays three times a day." ¹⁴ As soon as the king heard this, he was very displeased; he set his mind on rescuing Daniel and made every effort until sundown to deliver him.

¹⁵ Then these men went together to the king and said to him, "You know, Your Majesty, that it is a law of the Medes and Persians that no edict or ordinance the king establishes can be changed."

¹⁶ So the king gave the order, and they brought Daniel and threw him into the lions' den. The king said to Daniel, "May your God, whom you continually serve, rescue you!" ¹⁷ A stone was brought and placed over the mouth of the den. The king sealed it with his own signet ring and with the signet rings of his nobles, so that nothing in regard to Daniel could be changed. ¹⁸ Then the king went to his palace and spent the night fasting. No diversions were brought to him, and he could not sleep.

¹⁹ At the first light of dawn the king got up and hurried to the lions' den. ²⁰ When he reached the den, he cried out in anguish to Daniel. "Daniel, servant of the living God," the king said, "has your God, whom you continually serve, been able to rescue you from the lions?"

²¹ Then Daniel spoke with the king: "May the king live forever. ²² My God sent his angel and shut the lions' mouths; and they haven't harmed me, for I was found innocent before him. And also before you, Your Majesty, I have not done harm."

²³ The king was overjoyed and gave orders to take Daniel out of the den. When Daniel was brought up from the den, he was found to be unharmed, for he trusted in his God. ²⁴ The king then gave the command, and those men who had maliciously accused Daniel were brought and thrown into the lions' den — they, their children, and their wives. They had not reached the bottom of the den before the lions overpowered them and crushed all their bones.

²⁵ Then King Darius wrote to those of every people, nation, and language who live on the whole earth: "May your prosperity abound. ²⁶ I issue a decree that in all my royal dominion, people must tremble in fear before the God of Daniel:

> For he is the living God,
> and he endures forever;
> his kingdom will never be destroyed,
> and his dominion has no end.
> ²⁷ He rescues and delivers;
> he performs signs and wonders

in the heavens and on the earth,
for he has rescued Daniel
from the power of the lions."

[28] So Daniel prospered during the reign of Darius and the reign of Cyrus the Persian.

Jonah 1

¹ The word of the LORD came to Jonah son of Amittai: ² "Get up! Go to the great city of Nineveh and preach against it because their evil has come up before me." ³ Jonah got up to flee to Tarshish from the LORD's presence. He went down to Joppa and found a ship going to Tarshish. He paid the fare and went down into it to go with them to Tarshish from the LORD's presence.

⁴ But the LORD threw a great wind onto the sea, and such a great storm arose on the sea that the ship threatened to break apart. ⁵ The sailors were afraid, and each cried out to his god. They threw the ship's cargo into the sea to lighten the load. Meanwhile, Jonah had gone down to the lowest part of the vessel and had stretched out and fallen into a deep sleep.

⁶ The captain approached him and said, "What are you doing sound asleep? Get up! Call to your god. Maybe this god will consider us, and we won't perish."

⁷ "Come on!" the sailors said to each other. "Let's cast lots. Then we'll know who is to blame for this trouble we're in." So they cast lots, and the lot singled out Jonah. ⁸ Then they said to him, "Tell us who is to blame for this trouble we're in. What is your business, and where are you from? What is your country, and what people are you from?"

⁹ He answered them, "I'm a Hebrew. I worship the LORD, the God of the heavens, who made the sea and the dry land."

¹⁰ Then the men were seized by a great fear and said to him, "What is this you've done?" The men knew he was fleeing from the LORD's presence because he had told them. ¹¹ So they said to him, "What should we do to you so that the sea will calm down for us?" For the sea was getting worse and worse.

¹² He answered them, "Pick me up and throw me into the sea so that it will calm down for you, for I know that I'm to blame for this great storm that is against you." ¹³ Nevertheless, the men rowed hard to get back to dry land, but they couldn't because the sea was raging against them more and more.

¹⁴ So they called out to the LORD: "Please, LORD, don't let us perish because of this man's life, and don't charge us with innocent blood! For you, LORD, have done just as you pleased." ¹⁵ Then they picked up Jonah and threw him into the sea, and the sea stopped its raging. ¹⁶ The men

were seized by great fear of the LORD, and they offered a sacrifice to the LORD and made vows.

¹⁷ The LORD appointed a great fish to swallow Jonah, and Jonah was in the belly of the fish three days and three nights.

John 1

[1] In the beginning was the Word, and the Word was with God, and the Word was God. [2] He was with God in the beginning. [3] All things were created through him, and apart from him not one thing was created that has been created. [4] In him was life, and that life was the light of men. [5] That light shines in the darkness, and yet the darkness did not overcome it.

[6] There was a man sent from God whose name was John. [7] He came as a witness to testify about the light, so that all might believe through him. [8] He was not the light, but he came to testify about the light. [9] The true light that gives light to everyone, was coming into the world.

[10] He was in the world, and the world was created through him, and yet the world did not recognize him. [11] He came to his own, and his own people did not receive him. [12] But to all who did receive him, he gave them the right to be children of God, to those who believe in his name, [13] who were born, not of natural descent, or of the will of the flesh, or of the will of man, but of God.

[14] The Word became flesh and dwelt among us. We observed his glory, the glory as the one and only Son from the Father, full of grace and truth. [15] (John testified concerning him and exclaimed, "This was the one of whom I said, 'The one coming after me ranks ahead of me, because he existed before me.'") [16] Indeed, we have all received grace upon grace from his fullness, [17] for the law was given through Moses; grace and truth came through Jesus Christ. [18] No one has ever seen God. The one and only Son, who is himself God and is at the Father's side — he has revealed him.

[19] This was John's testimony when the Jews from Jerusalem sent priests and Levites to ask him, "Who are you?"

[20] He didn't deny it but confessed: "I am not the Messiah."

[21] "What then?" they asked him. "Are you Elijah?"

"I am not," he said.

"Are you the Prophet?"

"No," he answered.

[22] "Who are you, then?" they asked. "We need to give an answer to those who sent us. What can you tell us about yourself?"

[23] He said, "I am a voice of one crying out in the wilderness: Make straight the way of the Lord — just as Isaiah the prophet said."

²⁴ Now they had been sent from the Pharisees. ²⁵ So they asked him, "Why then do you baptize if you aren't the Messiah, or Elijah, or the Prophet?"

²⁶ "I baptize with water," John answered them. "Someone stands among you, but you don't know him. ²⁷ He is the one coming after me, whose sandal strap I'm not worthy to untie." ²⁸ All this happened in Bethany across the Jordan, where John was baptizing.

²⁹ The next day John saw Jesus coming toward him and said, "Here is the Lamb of God, who takes away the sin of the world! ³⁰ This is the one I told you about: 'After me comes a man who ranks ahead of me, because he existed before me.' ³¹ I didn't know him, but I came baptizing with water so he might be revealed to Israel." ³² And John testified, "I saw the Spirit descending from heaven like a dove, and he rested on him. ³³ I didn't know him, but he who sent me to baptize with water told me, 'The one you see the Spirit descending and resting on — he is the one who baptizes with the Holy Spirit.' ³⁴ I have seen and testified that this is the Son of God."

³⁵ The next day, John was standing with two of his disciples. ³⁶ When he saw Jesus passing by, he said, "Look, the Lamb of God!"

³⁷ The two disciples heard him say this and followed Jesus. ³⁸ When Jesus turned and noticed them following him, he asked them, "What are you looking for?"

They said to him, "Rabbi" (which means "Teacher"), "where are you staying?"

³⁹ "Come and you'll see," he replied. So they went and saw where he was staying, and they stayed with him that day. It was about four in the afternoon.

⁴⁰ Andrew, Simon Peter's brother, was one of the two who heard John and followed him. ⁴¹ He first found his own brother Simon and told him, "We have found the Messiah" (which is translated "the Christ"), ⁴² and he brought Simon to Jesus.

When Jesus saw him, he said, "You are Simon, son of John. You will be called Cephas" (which is translated "Peter").

⁴³ The next day Jesus decided to leave for Galilee. He found Philip and told him, "Follow me."

⁴⁴ Now Philip was from Bethsaida, the hometown of Andrew and Peter. ⁴⁵ Philip found Nathanael and told him, "We have found the one

Moses wrote about in the law (and so did the prophets): Jesus the son of Joseph, from Nazareth."

⁴⁶ "Can anything good come out of Nazareth?" Nathanael asked him.

"Come and see," Philip answered.

⁴⁷ Then Jesus saw Nathanael coming toward him and said about him, "Here truly is an Israelite in whom there is no deceit."

⁴⁸ "How do you know me?" Nathanael asked.

"Before Philip called you, when you were under the fig tree, I saw you," Jesus answered.

⁴⁹ "Rabbi," Nathanael replied, "You are the Son of God; you are the King of Israel!"

⁵⁰ Jesus responded to him, "Do you believe because I told you I saw you under the fig tree? You will see greater things than this." ⁵¹ Then he said, "Truly I tell you, you will see heaven opened and the angels of God ascending and descending on the Son of Man."

Luke 2

¹ In those days a decree went out from Caesar Augustus that the whole empire should be registered. ² This first registration took place while Quirinius was governing Syria. ³ So everyone went to be registered, each to his own town.

⁴ Joseph also went up from the town of Nazareth in Galilee, to Judea, to the city of David, which is called Bethlehem, because he was of the house and family line of David, ⁵ to be registered along with Mary, who was engaged to him and was pregnant. ⁶ While they were there, the time came for her to give birth. ⁷ Then she gave birth to her firstborn Son, and she wrapped him tightly in cloth and laid him in a manger, because there was no guest room available for them.

⁸ In the same region, shepherds were staying out in the fields and keeping watch at night over their flock. ⁹ Then an angel of the Lord stood before them, and the glory of the Lord shone around them, and they were terrified. ¹⁰ But the angel said to them, "Don't be afraid, for look, I proclaim to you good news of great joy that will be for all the people: ¹¹ Today in the city of David a Savior was born for you, who is the Messiah, the Lord. ¹² This will be the sign for you: You will find a baby wrapped tightly in cloth and lying in a manger."

¹³ Suddenly there was a multitude of the heavenly host with the angel, praising God and saying:

¹⁴ Glory to God in the highest heaven,
and peace on earth to people he favors!

¹⁵ When the angels had left them and returned to heaven, the shepherds said to one another, "Let's go straight to Bethlehem and see what has happened, which the Lord has made known to us."

¹⁶ They hurried off and found both Mary and Joseph, and the baby who was lying in the manger. ¹⁷ After seeing them, they reported the message they were told about this child, ¹⁸ and all who heard it were amazed at what the shepherds said to them. ¹⁹ But Mary was treasuring up all these things in her heart and meditating on them. ²⁰ The shepherds returned, glorifying and praising God for all the things they had seen and heard, which were just as they had been told.

²¹ When the eight days were completed for his circumcision, he was named Jesus — the name given by the angel before he was conceived. ²² And when the days of their purification according to the law of Moses were finished, they brought him up to Jerusalem to present him to the Lord ²³ (just as it is written in the law of the Lord, Every firstborn male will be dedicated to the Lord) ²⁴ and to offer a sacrifice (according to what is stated in the law of the Lord, a pair of turtledoves or two young pigeons).

²⁵ There was a man in Jerusalem whose name was Simeon. This man was righteous and devout, looking forward to Israel's consolation, and the Holy Spirit was on him. ²⁶ It had been revealed to him by the Holy Spirit that he would not see death before he saw the Lord's Messiah. ²⁷ Guided by the Spirit, he entered the temple. When the parents brought in the child Jesus to perform for him what was customary under the law, ²⁸ Simeon took him up in his arms, praised God, and said,

²⁹ Now, Master,
you can dismiss your servant in peace,
as you promised.
³⁰ For my eyes have seen your salvation.
³¹ You have prepared it
in the presence of all peoples —
³² a light for revelation to the Gentiles
and glory to your people Israel.

³³ His father and mother were amazed at what was being said about him. ³⁴ Then Simeon blessed them and told his mother Mary: "Indeed, this child is destined to cause the fall and rise of many in Israel and to be a sign that will be opposed — ³⁵ and a sword will pierce your own soul — that the thoughts of many hearts may be revealed."

³⁶ There was also a prophetess, Anna, a daughter of Phanuel, of the tribe of Asher. She was well along in years, having lived with her husband seven years after her marriage, ³⁷ and was a widow for eighty-four years. She did not leave the temple, serving God night and day with fasting and prayers. ³⁸ At that very moment, she came up and began to thank God and to speak about him to all who were looking forward to the redemption of Jerusalem.

³⁹ When they had completed everything according to the law of the Lord, they returned to Galilee, to their own town of Nazareth. ⁴⁰ The boy grew up and became strong, filled with wisdom, and God's grace was on him.

⁴¹ Every year his parents traveled to Jerusalem for the Passover Festival. ⁴² When he was twelve years old, they went up according to the custom of the festival. ⁴³ After those days were over, as they were returning, the boy Jesus stayed behind in Jerusalem, but his parents did not know it. ⁴⁴ Assuming he was in the traveling party, they went a day's journey. Then they began looking for him among their relatives and friends. ⁴⁵ When they did not find him, they returned to Jerusalem to search for him. ⁴⁶ After three days, they found him in the temple sitting among the teachers, listening to them and asking them questions. ⁴⁷ And all those who heard him were astounded at his understanding and his answers. ⁴⁸ When his parents saw him, they were astonished, and his mother said to him, "Son, why have you treated us like this? Your father and I have been anxiously searching for you."

⁴⁹ "Why were you searching for me?" he asked them. "Didn't you know that it was necessary for me to be in my Father's house?" ⁵⁰ But they did not understand what he said to them.

⁵¹ Then he went down with them and came to Nazareth and was obedient to them. His mother kept all these things in her heart. ⁵² And Jesus increased in wisdom and stature, and in favor with God and with people.

Matthew 5

¹ When he saw the crowds, he went up on the mountain, and after he sat down, his disciples came to him. ² Then he began to teach them, saying:

³ "Blessed are the poor in spirit,
for the kingdom of heaven is theirs.
⁴ Blessed are those who mourn,
for they will be comforted.
⁵ Blessed are the humble,
for they will inherit the earth.
⁶ Blessed are those who hunger and thirst for righteousness,
for they will be filled.
⁷ Blessed are the merciful,
for they will be shown mercy.
⁸ Blessed are the pure in heart,
for they will see God.
⁹ Blessed are the peacemakers,
for they will be called sons of God.
¹⁰ Blessed are those who are persecuted because of righteousness,
for the kingdom of heaven is theirs.

¹¹ "You are blessed when they insult you and persecute you and falsely say every kind of evil against you because of me. ¹² Be glad and rejoice, because your reward is great in heaven. For that is how they persecuted the prophets who were before you.

¹³ "You are the salt of the earth. But if the salt should lose its taste, how can it be made salty? It's no longer good for anything but to be thrown out and trampled under people's feet.

¹⁴ "You are the light of the world. A city situated on a hill cannot be hidden. ¹⁵ No one lights a lamp and puts it under a basket, but rather on a lampstand, and it gives light for all who are in the house. ¹⁶ In the same way, let your light shine before others, so that they may see your good works and give glory to your Father in heaven.

¹⁷ "Don't think that I came to abolish the Law or the Prophets. I did not come to abolish but to fulfill. ¹⁸ For truly I tell you, until heaven and earth pass away, not the smallest letter or one stroke of a letter will pass away

from the law until all things are accomplished. ¹⁹ Therefore, whoever breaks one of the least of these commands and teaches others to do the same will be called least in the kingdom of heaven. But whoever does and teaches these commands will be called great in the kingdom of heaven. ²⁰ For I tell you, unless your righteousness surpasses that of the scribes and Pharisees, you will never get into the kingdom of heaven.

²¹ "You have heard that it was said to our ancestors, Do not murder, and whoever murders will be subject to judgment. ²² But I tell you, everyone who is angry with his brother or sister will be subject to judgment. Whoever insults his brother or sister, will be subject to the court. Whoever says, 'You fool!' will be subject to hellfire. ²³ So if you are offering your gift on the altar, and there you remember that your brother or sister has something against you, ²⁴ leave your gift there in front of the altar. First go and be reconciled with your brother or sister, and then come and offer your gift. ²⁵ Reach a settlement quickly with your adversary while you're on the way with him to the court, or your adversary will hand you over to the judge, and the judge to the officer, and you will be thrown into prison. ²⁶ Truly I tell you, you will never get out of there until you have paid the last penny.

²⁷ "You have heard that it was said, Do not commit adultery. ²⁸ But I tell you, everyone who looks at a woman lustfully has already committed adultery with her in his heart. ²⁹ If your right eye causes you to sin, gouge it out and throw it away. For it is better that you lose one of the parts of your body than for your whole body to be thrown into hell. ³⁰ And if your right hand causes you to sin, cut it off and throw it away. For it is better that you lose one of the parts of your body than for your whole body to go into hell.

³¹ "It was also said, Whoever divorces his wife must give her a written notice of divorce. ³² But I tell you, everyone who divorces his wife, except in a case of sexual immorality, causes her to commit adultery. And whoever marries a divorced woman commits adultery.

³³ "Again, you have heard that it was said to our ancestors, You must not break your oath, but you must keep your oaths to the Lord. ³⁴ But I tell you, don't take an oath at all: either by heaven, because it is God's throne; ³⁵ or by the earth, because it is his footstool; or by Jerusalem, because it

is the city of the great King. [36] Do not swear by your head, because you cannot make a single hair white or black. [37] But let your 'yes' mean 'yes,' and your 'no' mean 'no.' Anything more than this is from the evil one.

[38] "You have heard that it was said, An eye for an eye and a tooth for a tooth. [39] But I tell you, don't resist an evildoer. On the contrary, if anyone slaps you on your right cheek, turn the other to him also. [40] As for the one who wants to sue you and take away your shirt, let him have your coat as well. [41] And if anyone forces you to go one mile, go with him two. [42] Give to the one who asks you, and don't turn away from the one who wants to borrow from you.

[43] "You have heard that it was said, Love your neighbor and hate your enemy. [44] But I tell you, love your enemies and pray for those who persecute you, [45] so that you may be children of your Father in heaven. For he causes his sun to rise on the evil and the good, and sends rain on the righteous and the unrighteous. [46] For if you love those who love you, what reward will you have? Don't even the tax collectors do the same? [47] And if you greet only your brothers and sisters, what are you doing out of the ordinary? Don't even the Gentiles do the same? [48] Be perfect, therefore, as your heavenly Father is perfect."

Matthew 6

[1] "Be careful not to practice your righteousness in front of others to be seen by them. Otherwise, you have no reward with your Father in heaven. [2] So whenever you give to the poor, don't sound a trumpet before you, as the hypocrites do in the synagogues and on the streets, to be applauded by people. Truly I tell you, they have their reward. [3] But when you give to the poor, don't let your left hand know what your right hand is doing, [4] so that your giving may be in secret. And your Father who sees in secret will reward you.

[5] "Whenever you pray, you must not be like the hypocrites, because they love to pray standing in the synagogues and on the street corners to be seen by people. Truly I tell you, they have their reward. [6] But when you pray, go into your private room, shut your door, and pray to your Father who is in secret. And your Father who sees in secret will reward you. [7] When you pray, don't babble like the Gentiles, since they imagine they'll be heard for their many words. [8] Don't be like them, because your Father knows the things you need before you ask him.

[9] "Therefore, you should pray like this:

> Our Father in heaven,
> your name be honored as holy.
> [10] Your kingdom come.
> Your will be done
> [11] on earth as it is in heaven.
> Give us today our daily bread.
> [12] And forgive us our debts,
> as we also have forgiven our debtors.
> [13] And do not bring us into temptation,
> but deliver us from the evil one.

[14] "For if you forgive others their offenses, your heavenly Father will forgive you as well. [15] But if you don't forgive others, your Father will not forgive your offenses.

[16] "Whenever you fast, don't be gloomy like the hypocrites. For they make their faces unattractive so that their fasting is obvious to people.

Truly I tell you, they have their reward. ¹⁷ But when you fast, put oil on your head and wash your face, ¹⁸ so that your fasting isn't obvious to others but to your Father who is in secret. And your Father who sees in secret will reward you.

¹⁹ "Don't store up for yourselves treasures on earth, where moth and rust destroy and where thieves break in and steal. ²⁰ But store up for yourselves treasures in heaven, where neither moth nor rust destroys, and where thieves don't break in and steal. ²¹ For where your treasure is, there your heart will be also.

²² "The eye is the lamp of the body. If your eye is healthy, your whole body will be full of light. ²³ But if your eye is bad, your whole body will be full of darkness. So if the light within you is darkness, how deep is that darkness!

²⁴ "No one can serve two masters, since either he will hate one and love the other, or he will be devoted to one and despise the other. You cannot serve both God and money.

²⁵ "Therefore I tell you: Don't worry about your life, what you will eat or what you will drink; or about your body, what you will wear. Isn't life more than food and the body more than clothing? ²⁶ Consider the birds of the sky: They don't sow or reap or gather into barns, yet your heavenly Father feeds them. Aren't you worth more than they? ²⁷ Can any of you add one moment to his life-span by worrying? ²⁸ And why do you worry about clothes? Observe how the wildflowers of the field grow: They don't labor or spin thread. ²⁹ Yet I tell you that not even Solomon in all his splendor was adorned like one of these. ³⁰ If that's how God clothes the grass of the field, which is here today and thrown into the furnace tomorrow, won't he do much more for you — you of little faith? ³¹ So don't worry, saying, 'What will we eat?' or 'What will we drink?' or 'What will we wear?' ³² For the Gentiles eagerly seek all these things, and your heavenly Father knows that you need them. ³³ But seek first the kingdom of God and his righteousness, and all these things will be provided for you. ³⁴ Therefore don't worry about tomorrow, because tomorrow will worry about itself. Each day has enough trouble of its own."

Matthew 7

"Do not judge, so that you won't be judged. ² For you will be judged by the same standard with which you judge others, and you will be measured by the same measure you use. ³ Why do you look at the splinter in your brother's eye but don't notice the beam of wood in your own eye? ⁴ Or how can you say to your brother, 'Let me take the splinter out of your eye,' and look, there's a beam of wood in your own eye? ⁵ Hypocrite! First take the beam of wood out of your eye, and then you will see clearly to take the splinter out of your brother's eye. ⁶ Don't give what is holy to dogs or toss your pearls before pigs, or they will trample them under their feet, turn, and tear you to pieces.

⁷ "Ask, and it will be given to you. Seek, and you will find. Knock, and the door will be opened to you. ⁸ For everyone who asks receives, and the one who seeks finds, and to the one who knocks, the door will be opened. ⁹ Who among you, if his son asks him for bread, will give him a stone? ¹⁰ Or if he asks for a fish, will give him a snake? ¹¹ If you then, who are evil, know how to give good gifts to your children, how much more will your Father in heaven give good things to those who ask him. ¹² Therefore, whatever you want others to do for you, do also the same for them, for this is the Law and the Prophets.

¹³ "Enter through the narrow gate. For the gate is wide and the road broad that leads to destruction, and there are many who go through it. ¹⁴ How narrow is the gate and difficult the road that leads to life, and few find it.

¹⁵ "Be on your guard against false prophets who come to you in sheep's clothing but inwardly are ravaging wolves. ¹⁶ You'll recognize them by their fruit. Are grapes gathered from thornbushes or figs from thistles? ¹⁷ In the same way, every good tree produces good fruit, but a bad tree produces bad fruit. ¹⁸ A good tree can't produce bad fruit; neither can a bad tree produce good fruit. ¹⁹ Every tree that doesn't produce good fruit is cut down and thrown into the fire. ²⁰ So you'll recognize them by their fruit.

²¹ "Not everyone who says to me, 'Lord, Lord,' will enter the kingdom of heaven, but only the one who does the will of my Father in heaven. ²² On that day many will say to me, 'Lord, Lord, didn't we prophesy in your name, drive out demons in your name, and do many miracles in

your name?' ²³ Then I will announce to them, 'I never knew you. Depart from me, you lawbreakers!'

²⁴ "Therefore, everyone who hears these words of mine and acts on them will be like a wise man who built his house on the rock. ²⁵ The rain fell, the rivers rose, and the winds blew and pounded that house. Yet it didn't collapse, because its foundation was on the rock. ²⁶ But everyone who hears these words of mine and doesn't act on them will be like a foolish man who built his house on the sand. ²⁷ The rain fell, the rivers rose, the winds blew and pounded that house, and it collapsed. It collapsed with a great crash."

²⁸ When Jesus had finished saying these things, the crowds were astonished at his teaching, ²⁹ because he was teaching them like one who had authority, and not like their scribes.

Luke 8

¹ Afterward he was traveling from one town and village to another, preaching and telling the good news of the kingdom of God. The Twelve were with him, ² and also some women who had been healed of evil spirits and sicknesses: Mary, called Magdalene (seven demons had come out of her); ³ Joanna the wife of Chuza, Herod's steward; Susanna; and many others who were supporting them from their possessions.

⁴ As a large crowd was gathering, and people were coming to Jesus from every town, he said in a parable: ⁵ "A sower went out to sow his seed. As he sowed, some seed fell along the path; it was trampled on, and the birds of the sky devoured it. ⁶ Other seed fell on the rock; when it grew up, it withered away, since it lacked moisture. ⁷ Other seed fell among thorns; the thorns grew up with it and choked it. ⁸ Still other seed fell on good ground; when it grew up, it produced fruit: a hundred times what was sown." As he said this, he called out, "Let anyone who has ears to hear listen."

⁹ Then his disciples asked him, "What does this parable mean?" ¹⁰ So he said, "The secrets of the kingdom of God have been given for you to know, but to the rest it is in parables, so that

Looking they may not see,
and hearing they may not understand.

¹¹ "This is the meaning of the parable: The seed is the word of God. ¹² The seed along the path are those who have heard and then the devil comes and takes away the word from their hearts, so that they may not believe and be saved. ¹³ And the seed on the rock are those who, when they hear, receive the word with joy. Having no root, these believe for a while and fall away in a time of testing. ¹⁴ As for the seed that fell among thorns, these are the ones who, when they have heard, go on their way and are choked with worries, riches, and pleasures of life, and produce no mature fruit. ¹⁵ But the seed in the good ground — these are the ones who, having heard the word with an honest and good heart, hold on to it and by enduring, produce fruit.

¹⁶ "No one, after lighting a lamp, covers it with a basket or puts it under a bed, but puts it on a lampstand so that those who come in may see its

light. ¹⁷ For nothing is concealed that won't be revealed, and nothing hidden that won't be made known and brought to light. ¹⁸ Therefore take care how you listen. For whoever has, more will be given to him; and whoever does not have, even what he thinks he has will be taken away from him."

¹⁹ Then his mother and brothers came to him, but they could not meet with him because of the crowd. ²⁰ He was told, "Your mother and your brothers are standing outside, wanting to see you."

²¹ But he replied to them, "My mother and my brothers are those who hear and do the word of God."

²² One day he and his disciples got into a boat, and he told them, "Let's cross over to the other side of the lake." So they set out, ²³ and as they were sailing he fell asleep. Then a fierce windstorm came down on the lake; they were being swamped and were in danger. ²⁴ They came and woke him up, saying, "Master, Master, we're going to die!"

Then he got up and rebuked the wind and the raging waves. So they ceased, and there was a calm. ²⁵ He said to them, "Where is your faith?"

They were fearful and amazed, asking one another, "Who then is this? He commands even the winds and the waves, and they obey him!"

²⁶ Then they sailed to the region of the Gerasenes, which is opposite Galilee. ²⁷ When he got out on land, a demon-possessed man from the town met him. For a long time he had worn no clothes and did not stay in a house but in the tombs. ²⁸ When he saw Jesus, he cried out, fell down before him, and said in a loud voice, "What do you have to do with me, Jesus, Son of the Most High God? I beg you, don't torment me!" ²⁹ For he had commanded the unclean spirit to come out of the man. Many times it had seized him, and though he was guarded, bound by chains and shackles, he would snap the restraints and be driven by the demon into deserted places.

³⁰ "What is your name?" Jesus asked him.

"Legion," he said, because many demons had entered him. ³¹ And they begged him not to banish them to the abyss.

³² A large herd of pigs was there, feeding on the hillside. The demons begged him to permit them to enter the pigs, and he gave them permission. ³³ The demons came out of the man and entered the pigs, and the herd rushed down the steep bank into the lake and drowned.

³⁴ When the men who tended them saw what had happened, they ran off and reported it in the town and in the countryside. ³⁵ Then people went out to see what had happened. They came to Jesus and found the man the demons had departed from, sitting at Jesus's feet, dressed and in his right mind. And they were afraid. ³⁶ Meanwhile, the eyewitnesses reported to them how the demon-possessed man was delivered. ³⁷ Then all the people of the Gerasene region asked him to leave them, because they were gripped by great fear. So getting into the boat, he returned.

³⁸ The man from whom the demons had departed begged him earnestly to be with him. But he sent him away and said, ³⁹ "Go back to your home, and tell all that God has done for you." And off he went, proclaiming throughout the town how much Jesus had done for him.

⁴⁰ When Jesus returned, the crowd welcomed him, for they were all expecting him. ⁴¹ Just then, a man named Jairus came. He was a leader of the synagogue. He fell down at Jesus's feet and pleaded with him to come to his house, ⁴² because he had an only daughter about twelve years old, and she was dying.

While he was going, the crowds were nearly crushing him. ⁴³ A woman suffering from bleeding for twelve years, who had spent all she had on doctors and yet could not be healed by any, ⁴⁴ approached from behind and touched the end of his robe. Instantly her bleeding stopped.

⁴⁵ "Who touched me?" Jesus asked.

When they all denied it, Peter said, "Master, the crowds are hemming you in and pressing against you."

⁴⁶ "Someone did touch me," said Jesus. "I know that power has gone out from me." ⁴⁷ When the woman saw that she was discovered, she came trembling and fell down before him. In the presence of all the people, she declared the reason she had touched him and how she was instantly healed. ⁴⁸ "Daughter," he said to her, "your faith has saved you. Go in peace."

⁴⁹ While he was still speaking, someone came from the synagogue leader's house and said, "Your daughter is dead. Don't bother the teacher anymore."

⁵⁰ When Jesus heard it, he answered him, "Don't be afraid. Only believe, and she will be saved." ⁵¹ After he came to the house, he let no one enter with him except Peter, John, James, and the child's father and mother. ⁵² Everyone was crying and mourning for her. But he said, "Stop crying, because she is not dead but asleep."

[53] They laughed at him, because they knew she was dead. [54] So he took her by the hand and called out, "Child, get up!" [55] Her spirit returned, and she got up at once. Then he gave orders that she be given something to eat. [56] Her parents were astounded, but he instructed them to tell no one what had happened.

John 3

¹ There was a man from the Pharisees named Nicodemus, a ruler of the Jews. ² This man came to him at night and said, "Rabbi, we know that you are a teacher who has come from God, for no one could perform these signs you do unless God were with him."

³ Jesus replied, "Truly I tell you, unless someone is born again, he cannot see the kingdom of God."

⁴ "How can anyone be born when he is old?" Nicodemus asked him. "Can he enter his mother's womb a second time and be born?"

⁵ Jesus answered, "Truly I tell you, unless someone is born of water and the Spirit, he cannot enter the kingdom of God. ⁶ Whatever is born of the flesh is flesh, and whatever is born of the Spirit is spirit. ⁷ Do not be amazed that I told you that you must be born again. ⁸ The wind blows where it pleases, and you hear its sound, but you don't know where it comes from or where it is going. So it is with everyone born of the Spirit."

⁹ "How can these things be?" asked Nicodemus.

¹⁰ "Are you a teacher of Israel and don't know these things?" Jesus replied. ¹¹ "Truly I tell you, we speak what we know and we testify to what we have seen, but you do not accept our testimony. ¹² If I have told you about earthly things and you don't believe, how will you believe if I tell you about heavenly things? ¹³ No one has ascended into heaven except the one who descended from heaven — the Son of Man.

¹⁴ "Just as Moses lifted up the snake in the wilderness, so the Son of Man must be lifted up, ¹⁵ so that everyone who believes in him may have eternal life. ¹⁶ For God loved the world in this way: He gave his one and only Son, so that everyone who believes in him will not perish but have eternal life. ¹⁷ For God did not send his Son into the world to condemn the world, but to save the world through him. ¹⁸ Anyone who believes in him is not condemned, but anyone who does not believe is already condemned, because he has not believed in the name of the one and only Son of God. ¹⁹ This is the judgment: The light has come into the world, and people loved darkness rather than the light because their deeds were evil. ²⁰ For everyone who does evil hates the light and avoids it, so that his deeds may not be exposed. ²¹ But anyone who lives by the truth comes to the light, so that his works may be shown to be accomplished by God."

²² After this, Jesus and his disciples went to the Judean countryside, where he spent time with them and baptized.

²³ John also was baptizing in Aenon near Salim, because there was plenty of water there. People were coming and being baptized, ²⁴ since John had not yet been thrown into prison.

²⁵ Then a dispute arose between John's disciples and a Jew about purification. ²⁶ So they came to John and told him, "Rabbi, the one you testified about, and who was with you across the Jordan, is baptizing — and everyone is going to him."

²⁷ John responded, "No one can receive anything unless it has been given to him from heaven. ²⁸ You yourselves can testify that I said, 'I am not the Messiah, but I've been sent ahead of him.' ²⁹ He who has the bride is the groom. But the groom's friend, who stands by and listens for him, rejoices greatly at the groom's voice. So this joy of mine is complete. ³⁰ He must increase, but I must decrease."

³¹ The one who comes from above is above all. The one who is from the earth is earthly and speaks in earthly terms. The one who comes from heaven is above all. ³² He testifies to what he has seen and heard, and yet no one accepts his testimony. ³³ The one who has accepted his testimony has affirmed that God is true. ³⁴ For the one whom God sent speaks God's words, since he gives the Spirit without measure. ³⁵ The Father loves the Son and has given all things into his hands. ³⁶ The one who believes in the Son has eternal life, but the one who rejects the Son will not see life; instead, the wrath of God remains on him.

Luke 15

¹ All the tax collectors and sinners were approaching to listen to him. ² And the Pharisees and scribes were complaining, "This man welcomes sinners and eats with them."

³ So he told them this parable: ⁴ "What man among you, who has a hundred sheep and loses one of them, does not leave the ninety-nine in the open field and go after the lost one until he finds it? ⁵ When he has found it, he joyfully puts it on his shoulders, ⁶ and coming home, he calls his friends and neighbors together, saying to them, 'Rejoice with me, because I have found my lost sheep!' ⁷ I tell you, in the same way, there will be more joy in heaven over one sinner who repents than over ninety-nine righteous people who don't need repentance.

⁸ "Or what woman who has ten silver coins, if she loses one coin, does not light a lamp, sweep the house, and search carefully until she finds it? ⁹ When she finds it, she calls her friends and neighbors together, saying, 'Rejoice with me, because I have found the silver coin I lost!' ¹⁰ I tell you, in the same way, there is joy in the presence of God's angels over one sinner who repents."

¹¹ He also said: "A man had two sons. ¹² The younger of them said to his father, 'Father, give me the share of the estate I have coming to me.' So he distributed the assets to them. ¹³ Not many days later, the younger son gathered together all he had and traveled to a distant country, where he squandered his estate in foolish living. ¹⁴ After he had spent everything, a severe famine struck that country, and he had nothing. ¹⁵ Then he went to work for one of the citizens of that country, who sent him into his fields to feed pigs. ¹⁶ He longed to eat his fill from the pods that the pigs were eating, but no one would give him anything. ¹⁷ When he came to his senses, he said, 'How many of my father's hired workers have more than enough food, and here I am dying of hunger! ¹⁸ I'll get up, go to my father, and say to him, "Father, I have sinned against heaven and in your sight. ¹⁹ I'm no longer worthy to be called your son. Make me like one of your hired workers."' ²⁰ So he got up and went to his father. But while the son was still a long way off, his father saw him and was filled with compassion. He ran, threw his arms around his neck, and kissed him. ²¹ The son said to him, 'Father, I have sinned against heaven and in your sight. I'm no longer worthy to be called your son.'

²² "But the father told his servants, 'Quick! Bring out the best robe and put it on him; put a ring on his finger and sandals on his feet. ²³ Then bring the fattened calf and slaughter it, and let's celebrate with a feast, ²⁴ because this son of mine was dead and is alive again; he was lost and is found!' So they began to celebrate.

²⁵ "Now his older son was in the field; as he came near the house, he heard music and dancing. ²⁶ So he summoned one of the servants, questioning what these things meant. ²⁷ 'Your brother is here,' he told him, 'and your father has slaughtered the fattened calf because he has him back safe and sound.'

²⁸ "Then he became angry and didn't want to go in. So his father came out and pleaded with him. ²⁹ But he replied to his father, 'Look, I have been slaving many years for you, and I have never disobeyed your orders, yet you never gave me a goat so that I could celebrate with my friends. ³⁰ But when this son of yours came, who has devoured your assets with prostitutes, you slaughtered the fattened calf for him.'

³¹ "'Son,' he said to him, 'you are always with me, and everything I have is yours. ³² But we had to celebrate and rejoice, because this brother of yours was dead and is alive again; he was lost and is found.'"

Mark 15

¹ As soon as it was morning, having held a meeting with the elders, scribes, and the whole Sanhedrin, the chief priests tied Jesus up, led him away, and handed him over to Pilate.

² So Pilate asked him, "Are you the King of the Jews?"

He answered him, "You say so."

³ And the chief priests accused him of many things. ⁴ Pilate questioned him again, "Aren't you going to answer? Look how many things they are accusing you of!" ⁵ But Jesus still did not answer, and so Pilate was amazed.

⁶ At the festival Pilate used to release for the people a prisoner whom they requested. ⁷ There was one named Barabbas, who was in prison with rebels who had committed murder during the rebellion. ⁸ The crowd came up and began to ask Pilate to do for them as was his custom. ⁹ Pilate answered them, "Do you want me to release the King of the Jews for you?" ¹⁰ For he knew it was because of envy that the chief priests had handed him over. ¹¹ But the chief priests stirred up the crowd so that he would release Barabbas to them instead. ¹² Pilate asked them again, "Then what do you want me to do with the one you call the King of the Jews?"

¹³ Again they shouted, "Crucify him!"

¹⁴ Pilate said to them, "Why? What has he done wrong?"

But they shouted all the more, "Crucify him!"

¹⁵ Wanting to satisfy the crowd, Pilate released Barabbas to them; and after having Jesus flogged, he handed him over to be crucified.

¹⁶ The soldiers led him away into the palace (that is, the governor's residence) and called the whole company together. ¹⁷ They dressed him in a purple robe, twisted together a crown of thorns, and put it on him. ¹⁸ And they began to salute him, "Hail, King of the Jews!" ¹⁹ They were hitting him on the head with a stick and spitting on him. Getting down on their knees, they were paying him homage. ²⁰ After they had mocked him, they stripped him of the purple robe and put his clothes on him.

They led him out to crucify him. ²¹ They forced a man coming in from the country, who was passing by, to carry Jesus's cross. He was Simon of Cyrene, the father of Alexander and Rufus.

²² They brought Jesus to the place called *Golgotha* (which means Place of the Skull). ²³ They tried to give him wine mixed with myrrh, but he did not take it.

²⁴ Then they crucified him and divided his clothes, casting lots for them to decide what each would get. ²⁵ Now it was nine in the morning when they crucified him. ²⁶ The inscription of the charge written against him was: THE KING OF THE JEWS. ²⁷ They crucified two criminals with him, one on his right and one on his left.

²⁹ Those who passed by were yelling insults at him, shaking their heads, and saying, "Ha! The one who would destroy the temple and rebuild it in three days, ³⁰ save yourself by coming down from the cross!" ³¹ In the same way, the chief priests with the scribes were mocking him among themselves and saying, "He saved others, but he cannot save himself! ³² Let the Messiah, the King of Israel, come down now from the cross, so that we may see and believe." Even those who were crucified with him taunted him.

³³ When it was noon, darkness came over the whole land until three in the afternoon. ³⁴ And at three Jesus cried out with a loud voice, "*Eloi, Eloi, lemá sabachtháni?*" which is translated, "My God, my God, why have you abandoned me?"

³⁵ When some of those standing there heard this, they said, "See, he's calling for Elijah."

³⁶ Someone ran and filled a sponge with sour wine, fixed it on a stick, offered him a drink, and said, "Let's see if Elijah comes to take him down."

³⁷ Jesus let out a loud cry and breathed his last. ³⁸ Then the curtain of the temple was torn in two from top to bottom. ³⁹ When the centurion, who was standing opposite him, saw the way he breathed his last, he said, "Truly this man was the Son of God!"

⁴⁰ There were also women watching from a distance. Among them were Mary Magdalene, Mary the mother of James the younger and of Joses, and Salome. ⁴¹ In Galilee these women followed him and took care of him. Many other women had come up with him to Jerusalem.

⁴² When it was already evening, because it was the day of preparation (that is, the day before the Sabbath), ⁴³ Joseph of Arimathea, a prominent member of the Sanhedrin who was himself looking forward to the kingdom of God, came and boldly went to Pilate and asked for Jesus's body. ⁴⁴ Pilate was surprised that he was already dead. Summoning the centurion, he asked him whether he had already died. ⁴⁵ When he found

out from the centurion, he gave the corpse to Joseph. [46] After he bought some linen cloth, Joseph took him down and wrapped him in the linen. Then he laid him in a tomb cut out of the rock and rolled a stone against the entrance to the tomb. [47] Mary Magdalene and Mary the mother of Joses were watching where he was laid.

Matthew 28

¹ After the Sabbath, as the first day of the week was dawning, Mary Magdalene and the other Mary went to view the tomb. ² There was a violent earthquake, because an angel of the Lord descended from heaven and approached the tomb. He rolled back the stone and was sitting on it. ³ His appearance was like lightning, and his clothing was as white as snow. ⁴ The guards were so shaken by fear of him that they became like dead men.

⁵ The angel told the women, "Don't be afraid, because I know you are looking for Jesus who was crucified. ⁶ He is not here. For he has risen, just as he said. Come and see the place where he lay. ⁷ Then go quickly and tell his disciples, 'He has risen from the dead and indeed he is going ahead of you to Galilee; you will see him there.' Listen, I have told you."

⁸ So, departing quickly from the tomb with fear and great joy, they ran to tell his disciples the news. ⁹ Just then Jesus met them and said, "Greetings!" They came up, took hold of his feet, and worshiped him. ¹⁰ Then Jesus told them, "Do not be afraid. Go and tell my brothers to leave for Galilee, and they will see me there."

¹¹ As they were on their way, some of the guards came into the city and reported to the chief priests everything that had happened. ¹² After the priests had assembled with the elders and agreed on a plan, they gave the soldiers a large sum of money ¹³ and told them, "Say this, 'His disciples came during the night and stole him while we were sleeping.' ¹⁴ If this reaches the governor's ears, we will deal with him and keep you out of trouble." ¹⁵ They took the money and did as they were instructed, and this story has been spread among Jewish people to this day.

¹⁶ The eleven disciples traveled to Galilee, to the mountain where Jesus had directed them. ¹⁷ When they saw him, they worshiped, but some doubted. ¹⁸ Jesus came near and said to them, "All authority has been given to me in heaven and on earth. ¹⁹ Go, therefore, and make disciples of all nations, baptizing them in the name of the Father and of the Son and of the Holy Spirit, ²⁰ teaching them to observe everything I have commanded you. And remember, I am with you always, to the end of the age."

Acts 1

¹ I wrote the first narrative, Theophilus, about all that Jesus began to do and teach ² until the day he was taken up, after he had given instructions through the Holy Spirit to the apostles he had chosen. ³ After he had suffered, he also presented himself alive to them by many convincing proofs, appearing to them over a period of forty days and speaking about the kingdom of God.

⁴ While he was with them, he commanded them not to leave Jerusalem, but to wait for the Father's promise. "Which," he said, "you have heard me speak about; ⁵ for John baptized with water, but you will be baptized with the Holy Spirit in a few days."

⁶ So when they had come together, they asked him, "Lord, are you restoring the kingdom to Israel at this time?"

⁷ He said to them, "It is not for you to know times or periods that the Father has set by his own authority. ⁸ But you will receive power when the Holy Spirit has come on you, and you will be my witnesses in Jerusalem, in all Judea and Samaria, and to the end of the earth."

⁹ After he had said this, he was taken up as they were watching, and a cloud took him out of their sight. ¹⁰ While he was going, they were gazing into heaven, and suddenly two men in white clothes stood by them. ¹¹ They said, "Men of Galilee, why do you stand looking up into heaven? This same Jesus, who has been taken from you into heaven, will come in the same way that you have seen him going into heaven."

¹² Then they returned to Jerusalem from the Mount of Olives, which is near Jerusalem — a Sabbath day's journey away. ¹³ When they arrived, they went to the room upstairs where they were staying: Peter, John, James, Andrew, Philip, Thomas, Bartholomew, Matthew, James the son of Alphaeus, Simon the Zealot, and Judas the son of James. ¹⁴ They all were continually united in prayer, along with the women, including Mary the mother of Jesus, and his brothers.

¹⁵ In those days Peter stood up among the brothers and sisters — the number of people who were together was about a hundred and twenty — and said: ¹⁶ "Brothers and sisters, it was necessary that the Scripture be fulfilled that the Holy Spirit through the mouth of David foretold

about Judas, who became a guide to those who arrested Jesus. [17] For he was one of our number and shared in this ministry." [18] Now this man acquired a field with his unrighteous wages. He fell headfirst, his body burst open and his intestines spilled out. [19] This became known to all the residents of Jerusalem, so that in their own language that field is called *Hakeldama* (that is, Field of Blood). [20] "For it is written in the Book of Psalms:

> Let his dwelling become desolate;
> let no one live in it; and
> Let someone else take his position.

[21] "Therefore, from among the men who have accompanied us during the whole time the Lord Jesus went in and out among us — [22] beginning from the baptism of John until the day he was taken up from us — from among these, it is necessary that one become a witness with us of his resurrection."

[23] So they proposed two: Joseph, called Barsabbas, who was also known as Justus, and Matthias. [24] Then they prayed, "You, Lord, know everyone's hearts; show which of these two you have chosen [25] to take the place in this apostolic ministry that Judas left to go where he belongs." [26] Then they cast lots for them, and the lot fell to Matthias and he was added to the eleven apostles.

Acts 2

¹ When the day of Pentecost had arrived, they were all together in one place. ² Suddenly a sound like that of a violent rushing wind came from heaven, and it filled the whole house where they were staying. ³ They saw tongues like flames of fire that separated and rested on each one of them. ⁴ Then they were all filled with the Holy Spirit and began to speak in different tongues, as the Spirit enabled them.

⁵ Now there were Jews staying in Jerusalem, devout people from every nation under heaven. ⁶ When this sound occurred, a crowd came together and was confused because each one heard them speaking in his own language. ⁷ They were astounded and amazed, saying, "Look, aren't all these who are speaking Galileans? ⁸ How is it that each of us can hear them in our own native language? ⁹ Parthians, Medes, Elamites; those who live in Mesopotamia, in Judea and Cappadocia, Pontus and Asia, ¹⁰ Phrygia and Pamphylia, Egypt and the parts of Libya near Cyrene; visitors from Rome (both Jews and converts), ¹¹ Cretans and Arabs—we hear them declaring the magnificent acts of God in our own tongues." ¹² They were all astounded and perplexed, saying to one another, "What does this mean?" ¹³ But some sneered and said, "They're drunk on new wine."

¹⁴ Peter stood up with the Eleven, raised his voice, and proclaimed to them: "Fellow Jews and all you residents of Jerusalem, let me explain this to you and pay attention to my words. ¹⁵ For these people are not drunk, as you suppose, since it's only nine in the morning. ¹⁶ On the contrary, this is what was spoken through the prophet Joel:

¹⁷ And it will be in the last days, says God,
that I will pour out my Spirit on all people;
then your sons and your daughters will prophesy,
your young men will see visions,
and your old men will dream dreams.
¹⁸ I will even pour out my Spirit
on my servants in those days, both men and women
and they will prophesy.
¹⁹ I will display wonders in the heaven above
and signs on the earth below:
blood and fire and a cloud of smoke.

²⁰ The sun will be turned to darkness
and the moon to blood
before the great and glorious day of the Lord comes.
²¹ Then everyone who calls
on the name of the Lord will be saved.

²² "Fellow Israelites, listen to these words: This Jesus of Nazareth was a man attested to you by God with miracles, wonders, and signs that God did among you through him, just as you yourselves know. ²³ Though he was delivered up according to God's determined plan and foreknowledge, you used lawless people to nail him to a cross and kill him. ²⁴ God raised him up, ending the pains of death, because it was not possible for him to be held by death. ²⁵ For David says of him:

I saw the Lord ever before me;
because he is at my right hand,
I will not be shaken.
²⁶ Therefore my heart is glad
and my tongue rejoices.
Moreover, my flesh will rest in hope,
²⁷ because you will not abandon me in Hades
or allow your holy one to see decay.
²⁸ You have revealed the paths of life to me;
you will fill me with gladness
in your presence.

²⁹ "Brothers and sisters, I can confidently speak to you about the patriarch David: He is both dead and buried, and his tomb is with us to this day. ³⁰ Since he was a prophet, he knew that God had sworn an oath to him to seat one of his descendants on his throne. ³¹ Seeing what was to come, he spoke concerning the resurrection of the Messiah: He was not abandoned in Hades, and his flesh did not experience decay.

³² "God has raised this Jesus; we are all witnesses of this. ³³ Therefore, since he has been exalted to the right hand of God and has received from the Father the promised Holy Spirit, he has poured out what you both see and hear. ³⁴ For it was not David who ascended into the heavens, but he himself says:

The Lord declared to my Lord,
'Sit at my right hand

35 until I make your enemies your footstool.'

36 "Therefore let all the house of Israel know with certainty that God has made this Jesus, whom you crucified, both Lord and Messiah."

37 When they heard this, they were pierced to the heart and said to Peter and the rest of the apostles: "Brothers, what should we do?"
38 Peter replied, "Repent and be baptized, each of you, in the name of Jesus Christ for the forgiveness of your sins, and you will receive the gift of the Holy Spirit. 39 For the promise is for you and for your children, and for all who are far off, as many as the Lord our God will call." 40 With many other words he testified and strongly urged them, saying, "Be saved from this corrupt generation!" 41 So those who accepted his message were baptized, and that day about three thousand people were added to them.

42 They devoted themselves to the apostles' teaching, to the fellowship, to the breaking of bread, and to prayer.
43 Everyone was filled with awe, and many wonders and signs were being performed through the apostles. 44 Now all the believers were together and held all things in common. 45 They sold their possessions and property and distributed the proceeds to all, as any had need. 46 Every day they devoted themselves to meeting together in the temple, and broke bread from house to house. They ate their food with joyful and sincere hearts, 47 praising God and enjoying the favor of all the people. Every day the Lord added to their number those who were being saved.

Acts 9

¹ Now Saul was still breathing threats and murder against the disciples of the Lord. He went to the high priest ² and requested letters from him to the synagogues in Damascus, so that if he found any men or women who belonged to the Way, he might bring them as prisoners to Jerusalem. ³ As he traveled and was nearing Damascus, a light from heaven suddenly flashed around him. ⁴ Falling to the ground, he heard a voice saying to him, "Saul, Saul, why are you persecuting me?"

⁵ "Who are you, Lord?" Saul said.

"I am Jesus, the one you are persecuting," he replied. ⁶ "But get up and go into the city, and you will be told what you must do."

⁷ The men who were traveling with him stood speechless, hearing the sound but seeing no one. ⁸ Saul got up from the ground, and though his eyes were open, he could see nothing. So they took him by the hand and led him into Damascus. ⁹ He was unable to see for three days and did not eat or drink.

¹⁰ There was a disciple in Damascus named Ananias, and the Lord said to him in a vision, "Ananias."

"Here I am, Lord," he replied.

¹¹ "Get up and go to the street called Straight," the Lord said to him, "to the house of Judas, and ask for a man from Tarsus named Saul, since he is praying there. ¹² In a vision he has seen a man named Ananias coming in and placing his hands on him so that he may regain his sight."

¹³ "Lord," Ananias answered, "I have heard from many people about this man, how much harm he has done to your saints in Jerusalem. ¹⁴ And he has authority here from the chief priests to arrest all who call on your name."

¹⁵ But the Lord said to him, "Go, for this man is my chosen instrument to take my name to Gentiles, kings, and Israelites. ¹⁶ I will show him how much he must suffer for my name."

¹⁷ Ananias went and entered the house. He placed his hands on him and said, "Brother Saul, the Lord Jesus, who appeared to you on the road you were traveling, has sent me so that you may regain your sight and be filled with the Holy Spirit."

¹⁸ At once something like scales fell from his eyes, and he regained his sight. Then he got up and was baptized. ¹⁹ And after taking some food, he regained his strength.

Saul was with the disciples in Damascus for some time. [20] Immediately he began proclaiming Jesus in the synagogues: "He is the Son of God."

[21] All who heard him were astounded and said, "Isn't this the man in Jerusalem who was causing havoc for those who called on this name and came here for the purpose of taking them as prisoners to the chief priests?"

[22] But Saul grew stronger and kept confounding the Jews who lived in Damascus by proving that Jesus is the Messiah.

[23] After many days had passed, the Jews conspired to kill him, [24] but Saul learned of their plot. So they were watching the gates day and night intending to kill him, [25] but his disciples took him by night and lowered him in a large basket through an opening in the wall.

[26] When he arrived in Jerusalem, he tried to join the disciples, but they were all afraid of him, since they did not believe he was a disciple. [27] Barnabas, however, took him and brought him to the apostles and explained to them how Saul had seen the Lord on the road and that the Lord had talked to him, and how in Damascus he had spoken boldly in the name of Jesus. [28] Saul was coming and going with them in Jerusalem, speaking boldly in the name of the Lord. [29] He conversed and debated with the Hellenistic Jews, but they tried to kill him. [30] When the brothers found out, they took him down to Caesarea and sent him off to Tarsus.

[31] So the church throughout all Judea, Galilee, and Samaria had peace and was strengthened. Living in the fear of the Lord and encouraged by the Holy Spirit, it increased in numbers.

[32] As Peter was traveling from place to place, he also came down to the saints who lived in Lydda. [33] There he found a man named Aeneas, who was paralyzed and had been bedridden for eight years. [34] Peter said to him, "Aeneas, Jesus Christ heals you. Get up and make your bed," and immediately he got up. [35] So all who lived in Lydda and Sharon saw him and turned to the Lord.

[36] In Joppa there was a disciple named Tabitha (which is translated Dorcas). She was always doing good works and acts of charity. [37] About that time she became sick and died. After washing her, they placed her in a room upstairs. [38] Since Lydda was near Joppa, the disciples heard that Peter was there and sent two men to him who urged him, "Don't delay in

coming with us." [39] Peter got up and went with them. When he arrived, they led him to the room upstairs. And all the widows approached him, weeping and showing him the robes and clothes that Dorcas had made while she was with them. [40] Peter sent them all out of the room. He knelt down, prayed, and turning toward the body said, "Tabitha, get up." She opened her eyes, saw Peter, and sat up. [41] He gave her his hand and helped her stand up. He called the saints and widows and presented her alive. [42] This became known throughout Joppa, and many believed in the Lord. [43] Peter stayed for some time in Joppa with Simon, a leather tanner.

Acts 10

¹ There was a man in Caesarea named Cornelius, a centurion of what was called the Italian Regiment. ² He was a devout man and feared God along with his whole household. He did many charitable deeds for the Jewish people and always prayed to God. ³ About three in the afternoon he distinctly saw in a vision an angel of God who came in and said to him, "Cornelius."

⁴ Staring at him in awe, he said, "What is it, Lord?"

The angel told him, "Your prayers and your acts of charity have ascended as a memorial offering before God. ⁵ Now send men to Joppa and call for Simon, who is also named Peter. ⁶ He is lodging with Simon, a tanner, whose house is by the sea."

⁷ When the angel who spoke to him had gone, he called two of his household servants and a devout soldier, who was one of those who attended him. ⁸ After explaining everything to them, he sent them to Joppa.

⁹ The next day, as they were traveling and nearing the city, Peter went up to pray on the roof about noon. ¹⁰ He became hungry and wanted to eat, but while they were preparing something, he fell into a trance. ¹¹ He saw heaven opened and an object that resembled a large sheet coming down, being lowered by its four corners to the earth. ¹² In it were all the four-footed animals and reptiles of the earth, and the birds of the sky. ¹³ A voice said to him, "Get up, Peter; kill and eat."

¹⁴ "No, Lord!" Peter said. "For I have never eaten anything impure and ritually unclean."

¹⁵ Again, a second time, the voice said to him, "What God has made clean, do not call impure." ¹⁶ This happened three times, and suddenly the object was taken up into heaven.

¹⁷ While Peter was deeply perplexed about what the vision he had seen might mean, right away the men who had been sent by Cornelius, having asked directions to Simon's house, stood at the gate. ¹⁸ They called out, asking if Simon, who was also named Peter, was lodging there.

¹⁹ While Peter was thinking about the vision, the Spirit told him, "Three men are here looking for you. ²⁰ Get up, go downstairs, and go with them with no doubts at all, because I have sent them."

²¹ Then Peter went down to the men and said, "Here I am, the one you're looking for. What is the reason you're here?"

²² They said, "Cornelius, a centurion, an upright and God-fearing man, who has a good reputation with the whole Jewish nation, was divinely directed by a holy angel to call you to his house and to hear a message from you." ²³ Peter then invited them in and gave them lodging.

The next day he got up and set out with them, and some of the brothers from Joppa went with him. ²⁴ The following day he entered Caesarea. Now Cornelius was expecting them and had called together his relatives and close friends. ²⁵ When Peter entered, Cornelius met him, fell at his feet, and worshiped him.

²⁶ But Peter lifted him up and said, "Stand up. I myself am also a man." ²⁷ While talking with him, he went in and found a large gathering of people. ²⁸ Peter said to them, "You know it's forbidden for a Jewish man to associate with or visit a foreigner, but God has shown me that I must not call any person impure or unclean. ²⁹ That's why I came without any objection when I was sent for. So may I ask why you sent for me?"

³⁰ Cornelius replied, "Four days ago at this hour, at three in the afternoon, I was praying in my house. Just then a man in dazzling clothing stood before me ³¹ and said, 'Cornelius, your prayer has been heard, and your acts of charity have been remembered in God's sight. ³² Therefore send someone to Joppa and invite Simon here, who is also named Peter. He is lodging in Simon the tanner's house by the sea.' ³³ So I immediately sent for you, and it was good of you to come. So now we are all in the presence of God to hear everything you have been commanded by the Lord."

³⁴ Peter began to speak: "Now I truly understand that God doesn't show favoritism, ³⁵ but in every nation the person who fears him and does what is right is acceptable to him. ³⁶ He sent the message to the Israelites, proclaiming the good news of peace through Jesus Christ — he is Lord of all. ³⁷ You know the events that took place throughout all Judea, beginning from Galilee after the baptism that John preached: ³⁸ how God anointed Jesus of Nazareth with the Holy Spirit and with power, and how he went about doing good and healing all who were under the tyranny of the devil, because God was with him. ³⁹ We ourselves are witnesses of everything he did in both the Judean country and in Jerusalem, and yet they killed him by hanging him on a tree. ⁴⁰ God raised up this man on the third day and caused him to be seen, ⁴¹ not by all the people, but by us whom God appointed as witnesses, who ate and drank with him after he rose from the dead. ⁴² He commanded us to preach to the people and

to testify that he is the one appointed by God to be the judge of the living and the dead. [43] All the prophets testify about him that through his name everyone who believes in him receives forgiveness of sins."

[44] While Peter was still speaking these words, the Holy Spirit came down on all those who heard the message. [45] The circumcised believers who had come with Peter were amazed because the gift of the Holy Spirit had been poured out even on the Gentiles. [46] For they heard them speaking in other tongues and declaring the greatness of God.

Then Peter responded, [47] "Can anyone withhold water and prevent these people from being baptized, who have received the Holy Spirit just as we have?" [48] He commanded them to be baptized in the name of Jesus Christ. Then they asked him to stay for a few days.

Revelation 22

¹ Then he showed me the river of the water of life, clear as crystal, flowing from the throne of God and of the Lamb ² down the middle of the city's main street. The tree of life was on each side of the river, bearing twelve kinds of fruit, producing its fruit every month. The leaves of the tree are for healing the nations, ³ and there will no longer be any curse. The throne of God and of the Lamb will be in the city, and his servants will worship him. ⁴ They will see his face, and his name will be on their foreheads. ⁵ Night will be no more; people will not need the light of a lamp or the light of the sun, because the Lord God will give them light, and they will reign forever and ever.

⁶ Then he said to me, "These words are faithful and true. The Lord, the God of the spirits of the prophets, has sent his angel to show his servants what must soon take place."

⁷ "Look, I am coming soon! Blessed is the one who keeps the words of the prophecy of this book."

⁸ I, John, am the one who heard and saw these things. When I heard and saw them, I fell down to worship at the feet of the angel who had shown them to me. ⁹ But he said to me, "Don't do that! I am a fellow servant with you, your brothers the prophets, and those who keep the words of this book. Worship God!"

¹⁰ Then he said to me, "Don't seal up the words of the prophecy of this book, because the time is near. ¹¹ Let the filthy still be filthy; let the righteous go on in righteousness; let the holy still be holy."

¹² "Look, I am coming soon, and my reward is with me to repay each person according to his work. ¹³ I am the Alpha and the Omega, the first and the last, the beginning and the end.

¹⁴ "Blessed are those who wash their robes, so that they may have the right to the tree of life and may enter the city by the gates. ¹⁵ Outside are the dogs, the sorcerers, the sexually immoral, the murderers, the idolaters, and everyone who loves and practices falsehood.

¹⁶ "I, Jesus, have sent my angel to attest these things to you for the churches. I am the root and descendant of David, the bright morning star."

¹⁷ Both the Spirit and the bride say, "Come!" Let anyone who hears, say, "Come!" Let the one who is thirsty come. Let the one who desires take the water of life freely.

¹⁸ I testify to everyone who hears the words of the prophecy of this book: If anyone adds to them, God will add to him the plagues that are written in this book. ¹⁹ And if anyone takes away from the words of the book of this prophecy, God will take away his share of the tree of life and the holy city, which are written about in this book.

²⁰ He who testifies about these things says, "Yes, I am coming soon." Amen! Come, Lord Jesus!

²¹ The grace of the Lord Jesus be with everyone. Amen.

Romans 8

¹ Therefore, there is now no condemnation for those in Christ Jesus, ² because the law of the Spirit of life in Christ Jesus has set you free from the law of sin and death. ³ What the law could not do since it was weakened by the flesh, God did. He condemned sin in the flesh by sending his own Son in the likeness of sinful flesh as a sin offering, ⁴ in order that the law's requirement would be fulfilled in us who do not walk according to the flesh but according to the Spirit. ⁵ For those who live according to the flesh have their minds set on the things of the flesh, but those who live according to the Spirit have their minds set on the things of the Spirit. ⁶ Now the mind-set of the flesh is death, but the mind-set of the Spirit is life and peace. ⁷ The mind-set of the flesh is hostile to God because it does not submit to God's law. Indeed, it is unable to do so. ⁸ Those who are in the flesh cannot please God. ⁹ You, however, are not in the flesh, but in the Spirit, if indeed the Spirit of God lives in you. If anyone does not have the Spirit of Christ, he does not belong to him. ¹⁰ Now if Christ is in you, the body is dead because of sin, but the Spirit gives life because of righteousness. ¹¹ And if the Spirit of him who raised Jesus from the dead lives in you, then he who raised Christ from the dead will also bring your mortal bodies to life through his Spirit who lives in you.

¹² So then, brothers and sisters, we are not obligated to the flesh to live according to the flesh, ¹³ because if you live according to the flesh, you are going to die. But if by the Spirit you put to death the deeds of the body, you will live. ¹⁴ For all those led by God's Spirit are God's sons. ¹⁵ You did not receive a spirit of slavery to fall back into fear. Instead, you received the Spirit of adoption, by whom we cry out, "*Abba*, Father!" ¹⁶ The Spirit himself testifies together with our spirit that we are God's children, ¹⁷ and if children, also heirs — heirs of God and coheirs with Christ — if indeed we suffer with him so that we may also be glorified with him.

¹⁸ For I consider that the sufferings of this present time are not worth comparing with the glory that is going to be revealed to us. ¹⁹ For the creation eagerly waits with anticipation for God's sons to be revealed. ²⁰ For the creation was subjected to futility — not willingly, but because of him who subjected it — in the hope ²¹ that the creation itself will also be set free from the bondage to decay into the glorious freedom of God's children. ²² For we know that the whole creation has been groaning

together with labor pains until now. ²³ Not only that, but we ourselves who have the Spirit as the firstfruits — we also groan within ourselves, eagerly waiting for adoption, the redemption of our bodies. ²⁴ Now in this hope we were saved, but hope that is seen is not hope, because who hopes for what he sees? ²⁵ Now if we hope for what we do not see, we eagerly wait for it with patience.

²⁶ In the same way the Spirit also helps us in our weakness, because we do not know what to pray for as we should, but the Spirit himself intercedes for us with unspoken groanings. ²⁷ And he who searches our hearts knows the mind of the Spirit, because he intercedes for the saints according to the will of God.

²⁸ We know that all things work together for the good of those who love God, who are called according to his purpose. ²⁹ For those he foreknew he also predestined to be conformed to the image of his Son, so that he would be the firstborn among many brothers and sisters. ³⁰ And those he predestined, he also called; and those he called, he also justified; and those he justified, he also glorified.

³¹ What then are we to say about these things? If God is for us, who is against us? ³² He did not even spare his own Son but offered him up for us all. How will he not also with him grant us everything? ³³ Who can bring an accusation against God's elect? God is the one who justifies. ³⁴ Who is the one who condemns? Christ Jesus is the one who died, but even more, has been raised; he also is at the right hand of God and intercedes for us. ³⁵ Who can separate us from the love of Christ? Can affliction or distress or persecution or famine or nakedness or danger or sword? ³⁶ As it is written:

> Because of you
> we are being put to death all day long;
> we are counted as sheep to be slaughtered.

³⁷ No, in all these things we are more than conquerors through him who loved us. ³⁸ For I am persuaded that neither death nor life, nor angels nor rulers, nor things present nor things to come, nor powers, ³⁹ nor height nor depth, nor any other created thing will be able to separate us from the love of God that is in Christ Jesus our Lord.

1 Corinthians 13

[1] If I speak human or angelic tongues but do not have love, I am a noisy gong or a clanging cymbal. [2] If I have the gift of prophecy and understand all mysteries and all knowledge, and if I have all faith so that I can move mountains but do not have love, I am nothing. [3] And if I give away all my possessions, and if I give over my body in order to boast but do not have love, I gain nothing.

[4] Love is patient, love is kind. Love does not envy, is not boastful, is not arrogant, [5] is not rude, is not self-seeking, is not irritable, and does not keep a record of wrongs. [6] Love finds no joy in unrighteousness but rejoices in the truth. [7] It bears all things, believes all things, hopes all things, endures all things.

[8] Love never ends. But as for prophecies, they will come to an end; as for tongues, they will cease; as for knowledge, it will come to an end. [9] For we know in part, and we prophesy in part, [10] but when the perfect comes, the partial will come to an end. [11] When I was a child, I spoke like a child, I thought like a child, I reasoned like a child. When I became a man, I put aside childish things. [12] For now we see only a reflection as in a mirror, but then face to face. Now I know in part, but then I will know fully, as I am fully known. [13] Now these three remain: faith, hope, and love —but the greatest of these is love.

Galatians 5

¹ For freedom, Christ set us free. Stand firm then and don't submit again to a yoke of slavery. ² Take note! I, Paul, am telling you that if you get yourselves circumcised, Christ will not benefit you at all. ³ Again I testify to every man who gets himself circumcised that he is obligated to do the entire law. ⁴ You who are trying to be justified by the law are alienated from Christ; you have fallen from grace. ⁵ For we eagerly await through the Spirit, by faith, the hope of righteousness. ⁶ For in Christ Jesus neither circumcision nor uncircumcision accomplishes anything; what matters is faith working through love.

⁷ You were running well. Who prevented you from being persuaded regarding the truth? ⁸ This persuasion does not come from the one who calls you. ⁹ A little leaven leavens the whole batch of dough. ¹⁰ I myself am persuaded in the Lord you will not accept any other view. But whoever it is that is confusing you will pay the penalty. ¹¹ Now brothers and sisters, if I still preach circumcision, why am I still persecuted? In that case the offense of the cross has been abolished. ¹² I wish those who are disturbing you might also let themselves be mutilated!

¹³ For you were called to be free, brothers and sisters; only don't use this freedom as an opportunity for the flesh, but serve one another through love. ¹⁴ For the whole law is fulfilled in one statement: Love your neighbor as yourself. ¹⁵ But if you bite and devour one another, watch out, or you will be consumed by one another.

¹⁶ I say then, walk by the Spirit and you will certainly not carry out the desire of the flesh. ¹⁷ For the flesh desires what is against the Spirit, and the Spirit desires what is against the flesh; these are opposed to each other, so that you don't do what you want. ¹⁸ But if you are led by the Spirit, you are not under the law.

¹⁹ Now the works of the flesh are obvious: sexual immorality, moral impurity, promiscuity, ²⁰ idolatry, sorcery, hatreds, strife, jealousy, outbursts of anger, selfish ambitions, dissensions, factions, ²¹ envy, drunkenness, carousing, and anything similar. I am warning you about these things — as I warned you before — that those who practice such things will not inherit the kingdom of God.

²² But the fruit of the Spirit is love, joy, peace, patience, kindness, goodness, faithfulness, ²³ gentleness, and self-control. The law is not

against such things. [24] Now those who belong to Christ Jesus have crucified the flesh with its passions and desires. [25] If we live by the Spirit, let us also keep in step with the Spirit. [26] Let us not become conceited, provoking one another, envying one another.

James 1

¹ James, a servant of God and of the Lord Jesus Christ:
To the twelve tribes dispersed abroad.
Greetings.

² Consider it a great joy, my brothers and sisters, whenever you experience various trials, ³ because you know that the testing of your faith produces endurance. ⁴ And let endurance have its full effect, so that you may be mature and complete, lacking nothing.

⁵ Now if any of you lacks wisdom, he should ask God — who gives to all generously and ungrudgingly — and it will be given to him. ⁶ But let him ask in faith without doubting. For the doubter is like the surging sea, driven and tossed by the wind. ⁷ That person should not expect to receive anything from the Lord, ⁸ being double-minded and unstable in all his ways.

⁹ Let the brother of humble circumstances boast in his exaltation, ¹⁰ but let the rich boast in his humiliation because he will pass away like a flower of the field. ¹¹ For the sun rises and, together with the scorching wind, dries up the grass; its flower falls off, and its beautiful appearance perishes. In the same way, the rich person will wither away while pursuing his activities.

¹² Blessed is the one who endures trials, because when he has stood the test he will receive the crown of life that God has promised to those who love him.

¹³ No one undergoing a trial should say, "I am being tempted by God," since God is not tempted by evil, and he himself doesn't tempt anyone. ¹⁴ But each person is tempted when he is drawn away and enticed by his own evil desire. ¹⁵ Then after desire has conceived, it gives birth to sin, and when sin is fully grown, it gives birth to death.

¹⁶ Don't be deceived, my dear brothers and sisters. ¹⁷ Every good and perfect gift is from above, coming down from the Father of lights, who does not change like shifting shadows. ¹⁸ By his own choice, he gave us birth by the word of truth so that we would be a kind of firstfruits of his creatures.

¹⁹ My dear brothers and sisters, understand this: Everyone should be quick to listen, slow to speak, and slow to anger, ²⁰ for human anger does not accomplish God's righteousness. ²¹ Therefore, ridding yourselves

of all moral filth and the evil that is so prevalent, humbly receive the implanted word, which is able to save your souls.

[22] But be doers of the word and not hearers only, deceiving yourselves. [23] Because if anyone is a hearer of the word and not a doer, he is like someone looking at his own face in a mirror. [24] For he looks at himself, goes away, and immediately forgets what kind of person he was. [25] But the one who looks intently into the perfect law of freedom and perseveres in it, and is not a forgetful hearer but a doer who works — this person will be blessed in what he does.

[26] If anyone thinks he is religious without controlling his tongue, his religion is useless and he deceives himself. [27] Pure and undefiled religion before God the Father is this: to look after orphans and widows in their distress and to keep oneself unstained from the world

1 John 3

¹ See what great love the Father has given us that we should be called God's children — and we are! The reason the world does not know us is that it didn't know him. ² Dear friends, we are God's children now, and what we will be has not yet been revealed. We know that when he appears, we will be like him because we will see him as he is. ³ And everyone who has this hope in him purifies himself just as he is pure.

⁴ Everyone who commits sin practices lawlessness; and sin is lawlessness. ⁵ You know that he was revealed so that he might take away sins, and there is no sin in him. ⁶ Everyone who remains in him does not sin; everyone who sins has not seen him or known him.

⁷ Children, let no one deceive you. The one who does what is right is righteous, just as he is righteous. ⁸ The one who commits sin is of the devil, for the devil has sinned from the beginning. The Son of God was revealed for this purpose: to destroy the devil's works. ⁹ Everyone who has been born of God does not sin, because his seed remains in him; he is not able to sin, because he has been born of God. ¹⁰ This is how God's children and the devil's children become obvious. Whoever does not do what is right is not of God, especially the one who does not love his brother or sister.

¹¹ For this is the message you have heard from the beginning: We should love one another, ¹² unlike Cain, who was of the evil one and murdered his brother. And why did he murder him? Because his deeds were evil, and his brother's were righteous.

¹³ Do not be surprised, brothers and sisters, if the world hates you. ¹⁴ We know that we have passed from death to life because we love our brothers and sisters. The one who does not love remains in death. ¹⁵ Everyone who hates his brother or sister is a murderer, and you know that no murderer has eternal life residing in him. ¹⁶ This is how we have come to know love: He laid down his life for us. We should also lay down our lives for our brothers and sisters. ¹⁷ If anyone has this world's goods and sees a fellow believer in need but withholds compassion from him — how does God's love reside in him? ¹⁸ Little children, let us not love in word or speech, but in action and in truth.

¹⁹ This is how we will know that we belong to the truth and will reassure our hearts before him ²⁰ whenever our hearts condemn us; for God is greater than our hearts, and he knows all things.

[21] Dear friends, if our hearts don't condemn us, we have confidence before God [22] and receive whatever we ask from him because we keep his commands and do what is pleasing in his sight. [23] Now this is his command: that we believe in the name of his Son Jesus Christ, and love one another as he commanded us. [24] The one who keeps his commands remains in him, and he in him. And the way we know that he remains in us is from the Spirit he has given us.